DANGEROUS LEADERS

DANGEROUS LEADERS

HOW AND WHY LAWYERS
MUST BE TAUGHT TO LEAD

Anthony C. Thompson

STANFORD UNIVERSITY PRESS • STANFORD, CALIFORNIA

Stanford University Press
Stanford, California

Printed in the United States of America on acid-free, archival-quality paper

Library of Congress Cataloging-in-Publication Data

Names: Thompson, Anthony C., author.
Title: Dangerous leaders : how and why lawyers must be taught to lead / Anthony C. Thompson.
Description: Stanford, California : Stanford University Press, 2018. | Includes bibliographical references and index.
Identifiers: LCCN 2018007726 (print) | LCCN 2018012111 (ebook) | ISBN 9781503606531 | ISBN 9780804799256 (cloth : alk. paper)
Subjects: LCSH: Lawyers—United States. | Leadership—United States. | Practice of law—United States. | Law—Study and teaching—United States. | Leadership—Study and teaching—United States. | Lawyers—Training of—United States.
Classification: LCC KF298 (ebook) | LCC KF298 .T46 2018 (print) | DDC 340.071/173—dc23
LC record available at https://lccn.loc.gov/2018007726

Cover design: Preston Thomas, Cadence Design Studio

Typeset by Newgen in Baskerville 10.5/15

For Kim
You have been with me from the beginning of this journey
Your love and understanding has taught me
that you always lead with grace. . . .
All my love

Contents

Acknowledgments

I gratefully acknowledge financial support from the Filomen D'Agostino and Max E. Greenberg Research Fund at the New York University School of Law. I would like to thank Dean Trevor Morrison, for recognizing that legal education must include leadership. I would like to thank Diana Limongi and Noelia Rodriquez for their administrative support. I received superb research assistance from Leslie Cahill and Mitchell Brown. I would also like to thank Jane Isay, Jen Gonnerman and Jenna Johnson for comments on an early draft. Special thanks to the "Bonaire Crew"—Jane and Jim Madden; Joe Pilarz; and the Rannou family, Patrice, Kerenza, Dillon, and Megan—for their never-ending support. I especially want to thank my editor, Michelle Lipinski, who saw promise in this project from the outset. And finally I want to thank Kim Taylor-Thompson for her support and substantive assistance in this work.

DANGEROUS LEADERS

A New Vision of Leadership for Lawyers

TAYLOR MATTHIAS WILLIAMS could not breathe at birth. Born three months premature, Taylor depended on a ventilator to keep him breathing and a heart monitor to track his vital signs. This is not unusual for premature babies. But Taylor's situation was particularly precarious. Taylor was born in Flint, Michigan, in 2016. His mother had bathed in Flint's contaminated water throughout her pregnancy; she had contracted listeria, which caused the premature birth. Following the delivery, doctors tested Taylor and detected lead in his bloodstream. Children are especially vulnerable to lead poisoning because it attacks the developing brain and central nervous system. Exposure can cause behavioral disorders, cognitive difficulties, and other developmental problems. Right now, it is still too soon to say whether Taylor will experience these health effects,[1] but he and his family will face, at a minimum, years of worry and possibly a lifetime of suffering. It is a heartbreaking story but one among thousands arising from the water crisis in Flint. And these stories move from heartbreaking to disturbing to infuriating as we realize that they are all rooted in the financial decisions and leadership failures of men and women who not only should have known better but should have done better.

The political choice to prioritize budget cuts over citizens' health returns as a theme throughout the events triggering the water contamination in Flint. In 2011, an audit conducted by the State of Michigan's Department of the Treasury projected a $25 million budget deficit for the city of Flint, inciting the State of Michigan to place Flint's finances under the control of an emergency manager answering to the governor. The emergency manager's mandate was to cut the budget at any cost. Flint's water supply alone accounted for $9 million of the deficit. Officials had been using some of that money to cover shortfalls in the general fund. To reduce the water fund shortfall, the city switched in 2014 from paying Detroit for water supplied from Lake Huron to drawing water from the Flint River. The state treasurer, Andrew Dillon, applauded the decision, saying it would bring "desperately needed" savings.[2] Government officials intended this move as a stopgap measure until a pipeline connecting Flint to water from Lake Huron could be completed.

But the Flint River, running through town, was known to local residents for the filth and waste polluting it. Almost immediately after the changeover occurred, residents noticed a murky color and odor to their water and complained to city officials, who insisted the water was safe. Soon after, the city detected bacteria and other disease-causing organisms contaminating the water and took steps to add chlorine to the system. Five months after the chlorine "fix," experts discovered a buildup of a cancer-causing byproduct of mixing chlorine and organic matter. Then, in June 2015, an Environmental Protection Agency (EPA) report warned of high levels of lead in Flint water, and a study conducted by the Hurley Medical Center revealed that the number of children with elevated lead levels in their blood had nearly doubled after the city altered its water source. In July, a spokesperson for the Michigan Department of Environmental Quality stated in a media interview that "anyone who is concerned about lead in the drinking water in Flint can relax."[3] Later that month, the governor's chief of staff sent an email to the state health department indicating that Flint residents were rightfully concerned about lead in the water and "they are basically getting blown off by us (as a state we're not sympathizing with their plight)."[4] The health department responded that their data showed no increase in lead poisoning.[5]

In October, the local General Motors plant refused to use the river water because it was rusting car parts.[6] So the city arranged for the company to tap into a different water line. Meanwhile, Flint residents still had to drink the river water.[7] In December 2015, the city of Flint and the county of Genesee declared a health emergency.[8] One month later, the governor's office finally issued a statement declaring a state of emergency.[9] Later in January, the state attorney general opened an investigation to uncover whether any Michigan laws had been violated that resulted in the contamination crisis.[10] When details of the inquiry surfaced, the story made national headlines.[11] And the nation demanded answers.

Given the choices made and the stakes involved, everyone was eager to hold someone liable. There is plenty of blame to assign. With the benefit of hindsight and careful investigation, it seems clear that the responsibility for this failure to safeguard the Flint population falls both on technical experts (engineers and environmental officials) who did not sound the alarm or recommend appropriate solutions and on the elected officials in Flint who neglected their duty or failed to respond quickly enough to the crisis. As of August 2016, the attorney general for Michigan charged state and local officials with offenses ranging from neglect of duty to conspiracy to withhold information.[12] Closing out the year, the attorney general charged four more officials—two of Flint's former emergency managers who reported directly to the governor, and two water plant officials—with felonies of false pretenses and conspiracy.[13]

One group of leaders has thus far escaped both criticism and charges: the lawyers who were involved throughout this crisis. Why should we think of lawyers and their responsibilities when this seems to be a matter of failing government? Ask yourself: Where were the lawyers who worked for the water companies paid to advise Flint officials whether the water was safe to drink? Where were the lawyers in the Michigan Department of Environmental Quality who allowed their department spokesperson to assure the general public that there was no reason for concern over water from the Flint River? Where were the lawyers from the city attorney's office who failed to help local officials make the case to state authorities once health professionals began to document the contamination problems? Sitting atop this crisis was Governor Rick Snyder—a lawyer by training. Governor Snyder did, in the end, acknowledge that he was ultimately responsible as governor, but only after he had blamed "career bureaucrats" for the water crisis. He never acknowledged that those same career bureaucrats were serving in his administration and executing what they perceived to be his priorities. The governor as the leader of his administration sets the tone and priorities that will guide the choices of state employees. The tone that Governor Snyder set, at a minimum, enabled the state officials to perceive fiscal controls as the most pressing priority.

Why bother asking where the lawyers were? Certainly, where individual officials broke the law, lawyers had a role to play advising their clients not to take such steps. But the lawyers in both the public and private sectors had *leadership* obligations that they failed to exercise: to step up and raise critical questions about the decisions that state officials were making. Lawyers recognizing and embracing that leadership role might have asked, "What are the risks involved in the options we are considering?" "What do these financial choices say about who we are as a state?" "What are the competing stakes in this decision?" If lawyers had seen themselves as part of a larger ecosystem, situated to see conflicting vantage points and interests—as an engaged leader would—these events would likely not have occurred. This was not a question of professional ethics or a violation of governing rules of professional conduct. This was a question of leadership. Lawyers were intimately aware of the events and decisions that led to a crisis endangering countless lives. That awareness triggered a leadership responsibility beyond asking the technical legal question—"Can we do this?" They had the responsibility to ask, "Should we do this?"

Flint offers one recent example of a catastrophic event where lawyers played a role. But if we were to examine the major events or key decisions made in any industry in the world, we would likely find lawyers involved. Lawyers are often positioned to make or advise others on many of the most critical decisions in today's world. Given that reality, their ability to lead effectively in those positions matters. The world has become infinitely more complex, dangerous, and connected. In our current culture, we face great uncertainty. Surprise and volatility that occur even in remote parts of small regions can produce unexpected outcomes that reverberate around the world.[14] This vast unpredictability has become relentless largely because of global connectedness. Assessing the range of uncertainties happening around us and figuring out the best course of action requires a breadth of perspectives and a quickness in insight that are elusive for any single leader. Indeed, this new normal demands a new kind of leader. But a disjunction exists between the ways that we prepare our best minds to lead and the demands of a volatile world. When we look at the one profession from which we often draw our political, business, and organizational leaders—the legal profession—we find a deep chasm between what law schools teach lawyers to do and what the world expects of these lawyers who so often become leaders. Legal education ignores leadership as a subject of study and as an inevitability and responsibility for many law school graduates. The legal profession is sending the next generation of likely leaders into a dynamic world dangerously unprepared.

Some discernible global trends—a continuing shift in economic power away from the West, greater global connectivity driven by technology, and growing social unrest given a widening gap between the "haves" and "have-nots"—have shifted the expectations and forces at work in the populations that leaders will need to activate and guide. The interdependent nature of these challenges, coupled with the need to develop multidimensional solutions, has proven to be quite disorienting. Unpredictability has become a mainstay, but we expect leaders to foresee and prepare for problems even in this chaotic environment. The next generation of leaders requires new tools and methods to lead effectively. They will need to be adept at leveraging a range of voices and perspectives to generate effective approaches and viable solutions for their ever-changing context. They will need to recognize and read nascent trends. To enable their organizations and institutions to withstand and move through massive challenges, they will need to bring people together at various intersections and manage their understanding of each other as well as what may seem to be competing interests. Effective leadership will require both focused attention and new forms of learning.

Business schools have recognized the need to address questions of leadership as they prepare their graduates for potential positions of authority. But even their efforts have come up short. As the 2008 global financial crisis underscored, an overreliance on static models and Western case studies will not effectively prepare leaders for the world that they will encounter. For too long, leadership training has been preoccupied with—and premised on—dangerously outdated models.[15] The operating assumption has been that businesses (even global companies) are functioning within the context of relatively stable developed economies. But that is not today's reality. New, powerful players are coming from emerging markets rather than solely from developed economies. Markets are changing rapidly and unexpectedly, so experience with turbulence may prove more important than lessons gleaned from historical success in more stable contexts. Of course, with the benefit of hindsight, it is easy to debate and criticize the effectiveness of leadership training that business schools have provided to date. But, at least, business schools have acknowledged that they are in the business of developing and preparing leaders.

Law schools have not yet recognized that they are in a similar business; they have fundamentally misunderstood their task. Law schools are preparing law students to become practitioners of the law in various forms but are not accounting for the leadership positions our culture fills from the pool of legal professionals. A surprising proportion of political leaders, leaders of industry, and global influencers have been legally trained. Given the cultural tendency to place lawyers in these key positions, law schools must acknowledge that likely role and prepare lawyers for it. Effective leadership today means adapting to context. The problem is that legal education looks backward by definition: it is precedent driven. The legal system privileges prior interpretations of the law to create a stable and predictable legal framework for decision making. Those characteristics arguably enable a large legal system to operate effectively. However, a retrospective view as well as an insistence on stability can prove dangerously narrow when contemplating new issues in an otherwise dynamic environment. The world that law graduates are stepping up to lead is not a static scene of precedent and deductive reasoning.

Research in the past few decades has debunked the notion that leadership cannot be learned.[16] But law schools seem to have ignored the discussion as well as the evidence. Despite the danger and full-throated claims to the contrary, legal education does not equip its graduates to lead in today's dynamic environment. They are simply not teaching leadership as a substantive focus. Why? Some law schools actively reject the notion that law schools should teach leadership because they believe the purpose of a legal education is to immerse students in the law. This anachronistic thinking typically characterizes those law schools that maintain that lawyers either will possess innate leadership traits or will somehow develop the necessary skills on the job. Other law schools fail to prepare law students for leadership out of laziness or ineptitude. They see the trend and the need but do not know how to teach the skills necessary for leadership. Others still pay lip service to their preparation of the next generation of leaders but somehow fail to update their approach or pedagogy. The numbers reveal the importance as well as the enormity of the task. There are 205 ABA-approved law schools and about 32 non-ABA-approved law schools. That means there are roughly 237 law schools in the United States.[17] Those law schools have produced over 1.22 million lawyers in the United States.[18]

While the development and honing of leadership skills ought to be part of a continuous process of learning throughout a professional trajectory, the thinking and approaches that one adopts at the launch of a career can help shape habits that will develop into more effective leadership behaviors over time. Student reflection prior to the start of a career—on ways that he or she will engage with colleagues, address professional challenges, and ultimately exercise leadership, even in the absence of an official title or organizational recognition—is a necessary first step toward effective leadership. Still, some law schools attempt to rationalize their failure to teach leadership by arguing insufficient student interest. But the role of legal education is to recognize and then make the case for leadership training for law students who may not yet see its value. Even if law students cannot imagine themselves assuming leadership roles, they likely will at some point over the course of their career. Even those who will not assume formal leadership roles will find that they will become more effective lawyers if they adopt leadership behaviors. But instead of embracing this reality, legal education sidesteps its responsibility to guide and enhance students' learning at this formative stage.

Dangerous Leaders exposes the risks and consequences of these lapses. It also hopes to provide law schools, law students, and the legal profession with tools and models to help build a better foundation for leadership acumen. *Dangerous Leaders* examines real problems that arise in a contemporary context and proposes real solutions. Through the use of case studies, the book explores catastrophic political, business, and legal failures that have occurred precisely because of a lapse in leadership, specifically from those with a background primarily in the legal profession. These failures range from corrupt practices in business and politics to the smaller yet equally toxic failures in judgment that affect countless individuals and communities but escape notice because they occur out of view. To the extent that the public or pundits have addressed such failures, they have misinterpreted them as personal ethical lapses. The premise of this book challenges that view: these failures are the result of chronic practices that not only could have been addressed but also could have been avoided.

Dangerous Leaders proposes a fundamental rethinking of legal education and leadership training aimed specifically at preparing lawyers to assume the types of roles that the emerging world requires. To that end, *Dangerous Leaders* offers a new leadership model that brings divergent sets of experiences and styles together to enable individuals to lead given what the world has become. This new leadership framework—intersectional leadership—challenges leaders to see the world through a different lens and expects a form of inclusion and respect for other perspectives and experiences that will prove critical to maneuvering in an environment that is at once complex and uncertain. This new form of leadership can and must be taught and experienced in law schools to prepare the next generation of leaders. The book also offers tools to lawyers currently in practice, enabling them to fill gaps in learning and perform more effectively as leaders in the current environment.

I come to this work through a cross section of experiences in the law and in executive education focused on leadership and strategy execution. I spent a decade as a public defender in Northern California. I have been a law professor for the past twenty-two years. In that capacity, I have also developed and taught a course specifically focused on leadership. Over the last fifteen years, I have consulted with Fortune 100 and Global 100 companies on a range of issues related to leadership and strategy execution. This work has focused on developing leadership capabilities in those already at the top of the house and in executives exhibiting high potential for greater responsibility. I have worked with countless leaders as they have grappled with the reality that transforming an organization and equipping it for today's challenges involves changing themselves at an individual level, only to then develop and hone skills to energize and inspire the collective actions of their teams. These executive education programs have often included lawyers such as executives in general counsel offices, regulatory offices, or other legal units. More often than not, these lawyer participants have expressed surprise that they too have gleaned critical lessons from these programs, largely because they tend to see their roles as separate and distinct from other executives in the company.

This is a fair assumption on their part; the lawyer's role is usually distinct. In thinking about that distinctive role, I recognized that lawyers often face unique leadership challenges. Whether they work in a legal unit in a global company, as a partner in a law firm, or as an elected or appointed official in government, lawyers have obligations that often create an inherent tension in their role as a leader. In a business, leading as a lawyer means understanding the economic and industry imperatives, not just thinking through the lens of the legal unit. Leading as a lawyer means taking part in collaborative efforts not as the person who says "no" at the end of the process but as the person who helps to guide the process of innovation and collaboration by saying, "Here's how we can do this and not run afoul of any regulatory constraints or legal barriers." Lawyers need to become arbitrators rather than the arbiters they were taught to be in law school. And, in government, lawyers as leaders are not just advocates, as their leader-peers from other backgrounds might be able to be; they have greater responsibilities to issues of justice and fairness. Far too frequently, we see lawyers as leaders making poor decisions because they have failed to appreciate and navigate the pervasive, specific tensions in their roles. This book seeks to highlight the fact that lawyers who lead without significant and focused exposure to leadership lessons often make the sort of judgments that can derail organizations or pervert entire systems, which makes them dangerous. Many of the leadership issues that *Dangerous Leaders* examines are ones that all leaders face. But the book uses case studies that feature lawyers, and will work through them with lawyers in mind, to help lawyers begin to see how leadership challenges affect them.

Many talk about the need for leadership, but these discussions too often suffer from narrow definitions of the term. First, some authors frame leadership in terms of the position or title an individual assumes. If your position authorizes you to make certain decisions and to have individuals reporting to you, then, functionally, you are a leader. Or so the argument goes. But leadership is not role-specific. Today's leaders must learn to lead with—and *without*—formal authority. Second, others suggest that a leader is someone who possesses the skills necessary to run a meeting, to set expectations for subordinates, and to define and delineate outcomes for the enterprise that he or she leads. These skills, while operationally important, conflate leadership with management and fundamentally misunderstand the concept and goals of leadership—developing a shared vision and engaging others in the achievement of a shared goal. Third, some authors contend that leadership involves the ability to align a group's thinking to whatever the leader considers important. This definition proceeds from a flawed premise: the presumption that the leader is somehow all-knowing and simply needs to articulate and impose his or her view.

My definition of leadership takes issue with these conventional views. Simply put, exercising effective leadership does not depend on hierarchy or position. The best leadership involves engaging others in a collaborative process of imagining, defining, and working toward a common cause or greater mission that is meaningful for the enterprise and for its stakeholders. To lead effectively, the individual does not have to be omniscient or heroic. Quite frankly, no single individual can have all of the answers to the range of problems leaders will likely encounter in our complex environment. The most influential leader may not even sit at the top of the organization. Instead, such leaders will place themselves in the middle of intersecting and often competing attitudes, listening to and learning from them. Through the creative tension that emerges when cultures and experiences collide, effective leaders begin to see problems differently and engage in a process of addressing them that is inclusive, collaborative, and, ultimately, more effective.

This is intersectional leadership.

My vision of intersectional leadership has five key components. The first involves developing—and relying on—a team that brings traits, styles, and experiences dissimilar to the leader. The complexity of the world and the leadership challenges it poses places the leader in unexpected and unfamiliar settings. To thrive in that environment, the lawyer as leader needs to engage with individuals whose perspectives have been born from a different set of experiences and life lessons. The leader's role does not involve promoting harmony above all else in the team. Instead, the leader must help teams live and thrive in the dilemma of collective action and robust debate.

The second component is related but distinct. The intersectional leader must recognize that learning often comes from unlikely sources. Seeking out viewpoints from the least experienced individuals in an organization or from people outside the expected set of experts can create a learning juncture that expands the thinking of all involved. Embracing diversity in all of its dimensions and actively looking to derive insights from individuals whose interests, needs, and expectations diverge from those of the lawyer-leader distinguishes the intersectional leader.

The third component expects leaders to engage in genuine collaboration where they expect to subordinate their own interests in the service of a greater goal. Collaboration is to be distinguished from teaming, where groups function as a team operating collectively because they have shared goals and incentives. Collaboration hurts—in a good way—when it is done right. It often involves working across units and functions to achieve a goal that may not be immediately apparent to all members of the group. It also means giving up something meaningful to the lawyer-leader—such as credit, time, and talent—to help advance a larger objective. The leader must subordinate his or her agenda and power for the greater good.

Fourth, the intersectional leader adopts a mind-set that insists on being suspicious of agreement. Some roles create both the opportunity and necessity for dichotomous thinking. But even when the lawyer-leader's role does not demand it, he or she needs to question, seek out alternate views as a way to challenge assumptions, and push his or her thinking.

Finally, the intersectional lawyer-leader must act with moral courage, even behind closed doors. The global financial crisis offered glaring examples of the corrosive effect of elevating personal ambition and gain above all else, and how much easier it may be to let this happen when one's choices are hidden from scrutiny. Lawyer-leaders must develop processes and disciplines that force them to question their own judgment rigorously and to put checks in place to elevate the good of the enterprise over personal ambition.

The lawyer-leader will operate in environments that are far less homogenous than those met by leaders in the past. Intersectional leadership can be learned, practiced, and developed. Indeed, teaching leadership early in a career can better position individuals to exercise leadership as they move through their career trajectory. Education in leadership is particularly important for lawyers because conventional legal training may interfere with their ability to lead well in business, political, and legal settings. Legal education emphasizes cognitive skills almost to the exclusion of emotional skills that will be critical to a leader's effectiveness and influence. Law students learn that they can rely on the rigor of their training to reach a conclusion, then trust in their own judgment. This singular focus on an individualized rather than a collaborative approach to issue identification and problem solving sits at the core of what is distorting and dangerous about legal education. The operative premise is that the critical and analytical skills that law students acquire and develop will prepare them better than their non-legally-trained counterparts to detect and resolve a wide range of legal, social, and political challenges. Law school then teaches law students to develop and assert a point of view with a degree of confidence that brooks no objection. What too often flows from this confidence is a degree of arrogance about one's personal expertise that can lead lawyers to underestimate and misread the value and contributions of others who may not be legally trained. Such lawyers afford greater weight to their personal abilities and judgment and, in the process, often distance themselves from nonlawyers. This insularity blinds the lawyer-leader to the need to collaborate, to listen, and to make room for competing views and ideas.

Dangerous Leaders starts with the challenge that law schools are failing to prepare lawyers to assume leadership roles in the dynamic world unfolding around us. This failure can be traced to basic structural problems with legal education. Law schools have misunderstood that their central task—preparing law students for the practice of law—also involves training lawyers to lead. Many critics of the legal profession have sounded the alarm that legal education needs to identify and demonstrate its relevance in the world, yet far too many law schools are ignoring that call. Second, the pedagogical methods law schools typically employ reinforce outdated and limited approaches to problem solving that reinforce the mistaken view that change is principally incremental. Recent world events continue to expose the limitations of this perspective. What we have come to see through experience and have been reminded of, particularly lately, is that change is constant and involves periods of incremental adjustments punctuated by quite disruptive transformation. Leaders need to be ready for both. Third, the experiences and missteps of lawyers in leadership positions offer law schools an opportunity to examine their mistakes, to learn from them, and to pivot. To make the case for change, I analyze a series of case studies that highlight the types of skills contemporary lawyers need and the leadership pitfalls these skills will help to avoid. These case studies alternate between large and small failures. The examples of dangerous behaviors and choices by lawyer-leaders offer not only cautionary tales but concrete lessons that the reader can learn to avoid similar missteps. These case studies also lead to specific suggestions to educators regarding ways that leadership training can address and prevent such failures. In the final chapters, the book lays out the ways that law schools and lawyers in practice can implement the intersectional model of leadership as a new framework in the emergent world. This chapter will emphasize the need to engage adult learners differently so they enhance learning this form of leadership. It will examine various approaches to engage individuals in the experience of leadership as a way of helping them practice, reflect on, and adopt the behaviors of the intersectional model.

The bottom line is simple: lawyers routinely hold key decision-making positions and unless they understand the leadership components of those roles, they will continue to be dangerously ill-prepared for the world in which they are expected to perform. The examples offered in *Dangerous Leaders* are tailored to lawyers to highlight the varied challenges and tensions that arise both for leaders generally and specifically for lawyers as leaders. This book examines not just the failings of law schools but how things can be set right. We have reached a point in the maturation of the discipline and the profession where it is high time for legal educators to develop and teach leadership frameworks to prepare lawyer-leaders for their likely roles in order to reduce the danger they currently pose.

CHAPTER ONE

Piloting the Boat by Looking at the Wake

Leadership Challenges for the Legal Profession

LAWYERS ARE LIKELY TO BE LEADERS. Of the forty-five American presidents, twenty-four have been lawyers.[1] In the 114th Congress, members with law degrees held 53 of the Senate's 100 seats and 160 of the 435 seats in the House of Representatives.[2] The list of Fortune 500 companies in 2012 boasted forty-six lawyers serving as CEOs.[3] If we add to that inventory state legislators, cabinet members on the state and local level, city council members, and mayors, the total number of lawyer-leaders skyrockets. Lawyers also occupy key leadership roles in industries that perhaps are somewhat less expected: technology,[4] media,[5] pharmaceutical,[6] and toys,[7] to name just a few. They run nonprofit organizations and philanthropic foundations. Lawyer-leaders are tapped to play key roles in virtually every industry and sector. While all law schools pay lip service to their commitment to preparing law students to become the next generation of leaders, the disturbing reality is that law schools more often than not fail even to offer courses on leadership or to surface leadership concepts and dilemmas in the standard curriculum. Given their likely positions, lawyer-leaders will need to develop and exercise the skills and behaviors that will enable them to perform successfully in a leadership role. In addition to understanding the law, they will need to be more self-aware, more comfortable with ambiguity, and more globally fluent than any who have preceded them. The good news is that these skills will not only make them better leaders but will also make them better lawyers.

LEAVING THE DOCK

More must be done even before the lawyer-leader enters practice. When I first proposed specifically teaching leadership skills to law students, my colleagues in the academy were quick to raise objections. Some of the responses were rather predictable: "Won't the students be too immature to internalize these types of lessons?" "Will they have been exposed to enough practical considerations to make sense of leadership lessons?" "They probably won't hold leadership roles for a long time, so how will this be helpful early in their careers?" I pointed out that leadership skills were like any other skill set—if practiced, they improve. Taking the conversation further, I mentioned the difference between leadership and authority; many colleagues responded with blank stares. I drew quizzical looks when I insisted that law students could—and should—begin to exercise leadership before leaving law school since, soon after graduation, many law students will begin making significant decisions affecting clients' lives and businesses. One colleague quipped, "Leadership? I thought that people joined the military to learn leadership."

For the most part, law professor colleagues were unclear what leadership was, why it made any sense for law students to study it, and why anyone would want to teach such a subject. The questions were part of the overall rigidity of the structure of legal education. American legal education has remained remarkably unchanged since it first took modern form in the 1870s.[8] It has carried with it a correspondingly stable body of critiques,[9] centering on the need to prepare law students better for legal practice and the need to introduce perspectives in the study of law that might shape the law but were too often ignored by the law. For example, scholars criticized the legal academy for failing to expose law students to the critical intersection of race, gender, power, and the law as a means of understanding how the law is developed and applied.

The debate over what to teach in law school has been transpiring for at least a century.[10] Critics have centered on the structure and content of the legal curriculum, looking to determine ways to ensure the best use of the three years of law school. These assessments, ranging from historical critiques to the more recent warnings of a crisis in legal education, share a consistent theme and diagnosis: law schools fail to prepare their graduates adequately for legal practice. No one questions that law schools teach their students to tackle and grapple with legal theory. But the worry is that a legal education focuses almost exclusively on the law's theoretical underpinnings and possibilities and ignores the practical realities that lawyers and their clients face. In essence, law schools fail to impart the precise skills that lawyers will need to meet the demands of both their employers and their clients. For example, most law students graduate without knowing how to read or write a contract, interview a client, or conduct a deposition. Law schools uniformly offer courses in legal writing to provide some basic training in legal research and writing. But to move beyond the basics and to develop practice-ready skills, law students often need to take clinical courses or experiential classes. Only a small percentage of law students elect to take such courses. The net result is that law students do not learn these skills before entering practice. If their first employer does not adequately train them to practice well, these new lawyers may learn at the expense of the client.

As importantly, legal education does not prepare students for the world in which they will practice because the traditional curriculum ignores critical issues of race, culture, and professional values. The core legal curriculum does not acknowledge or address the salience of race in the law. Much of what occurs in the U.S. legal system implicates race, but law schools typically pretend that race does not affect legal analyses or that the decisions that actors in the legal system make somehow occur in a race-neutral vacuum. Law schools rarely examine the intersection of race, law, and power as part of their core training and instead relegate questions of race to the margins. Because they are not trained to examine questions in the law using a lens that focuses on race, class, gender, or difference, law students can easily miss or misunderstand their significance in understanding the law, its application, and its implications. Similarly, law schools do not address the ways that culture can influence our understanding of the law and legal institutions. U.S. law schools typically operate from the assumption that there is a single dominant culture and, in that mistaken approach, fail to help law students develop the tools to see and appreciate cultural signals and differences. Law schools simply squander the opportunity to teach law students ways that they might begin to integrate cultural awareness and competency into their professional experience. Finally, to the extent that legal education addresses professional values at all, it does so in a limited context: ethics classes. But decisions and questions that implicate a lawyer's values abound, and by insisting that such questions arise only in the context of ethical rules or guidelines fundamentally weakens law students' ability to recognize that their choices, behaviors, and perspectives reflect and convey values. At the start of students' careers, law schools should help them begin to think about who they will be as lawyers and how they can begin to develop a purpose-driven trajectory for their careers. However, law schools do not provide this in-depth career planning.

In recent years, questions about the efficacy and value of a legal education have entered the public dialogue. The general public has begun to question the worth of a legal education given its expense. Governing bodies such as the American Bar Association (ABA) and the Association of American Law Schools (AALS) have received a share of the criticism for their lack of oversight and standardization of law schools. The positions the ABA takes in the next few years may be key in determining the general future of law schools, deciding whether they will be more practical or will remain more theoretical and doctrinally focused. But even without the mandate from these bodies, law schools need to reimagine what they are doing to prepare lawyers for their roles in the workforce or they will continue to put clients at risk.

When people ask about the purpose of a legal education, the standard response is that a legal education prepares students to "think like a lawyer."[11] The meaning of this well-worn phrase has long been the subject of considerable debate in the legal community. On one hand, thinking like a lawyer means being exposed to legal doctrine, understanding the methods of analytical thinking, and learning to raise critical questions in the law. The proponents of this perspective emphasize that law school is not in the business of training students for the workforce but is designed to introduce students to larger theoretical questions about the law and how it should operate. Thinking like a lawyer thus means that students are able to pose and examine the sorts of questions that will enhance understanding of the law's potential, intersections, and limitations. In effect, this casts law school as a doctoral program in the law.

On the other hand, thinking like a lawyer involves exposing students to the practice of law, often through clinical education or experiential learning.

The intent is to bridge the gap between theory and practice. Proponents of this position argue that a legal education must teach practical skills to prepare students for the demands of the profession. Students should learn basic skills such as client interviewing, negotiating, legal research, and writing. Skills such as working with statutes, administrative rules, complex factual records, and treaties are also integral to a comprehensive legal education.[12] Students often get the opportunity to practice these skills as part of the law school's social justice mission. Many schools breathe life into that mission by finding ways to serve the communities located around the law school and offering the services of students to help traditionally underrepresented segments of those communities. The practical skills theory also contends that teaching students how legal institutions actually operate is key to preparing them for practice.[13] In essence, proponents of the practical emphasis in legal education stress that law school ought to prepare students not just to think like lawyers but to *be* lawyers.[14]

What does the standard debate miss? A legal education has the obligation to do more. It must prepare students to lead. Given that large numbers of lawyers become leaders, law schools must openly acknowledge and embrace their role in helping their students understand the dynamics of leadership. It is not enough for law schools simply to claim that they mold future leaders and policy makers. They must consider the skills such leaders will need and give students opportunities to learn and practice them.

CHARTING THE WAY FORWARD— INTERSECTIONAL LEADERSHIP

In order to prepare lawyers for leadership, both legal education and practical training must break from the habit of looking backward for guidance. Preparing lawyers to be leaders means paying closer attention to the world that exists and unfolds around them and then teaching lawyers the skills and attributes needed to be successful leaders given that context. The dangers and lessons examined in the next chapters flow from my observations of lawyers in practice and the challenges they experience because of a failed understanding of their leadership roles. The principal way that lawyers can escape the backward-glancing methods that typify legal interactions is to use and develop an "intersectional leadership" framework, which expects the leader to sit at the cross-section of formal and informal networks and to leverage that nodal position to see further, perceive events more fully, and anticipate issues better.

Before delving into the dimensions of intersectional leadership, it is essential to examine the theoretical background against which it sits and from which it departs. Over the past forty years, a host of leadership models have emerged in an effort to improve our understanding of effective leadership. Two principal leadership theories have gained popularity and traction over time—transactional leadership[15] and transformational leadership.[16] Interestingly, many consider them to present somewhat opposing views of leadership. Transactional leadership views the leader as having the upper hand in what is essentially an exchange relationship with his or her followers. Transactional leaders make their expectations clear to their followers and then leverage organizational incentives and rewards to guide subordinates' behavior and to measure their success. By appealing to employees' self-interest, the leader can motivate compliance with his or her directives, and the follower can then expect some measure of personal gain: promotion, salary increase, or greater recognition. Transformational leadership, on the other hand, focuses on motivating others to higher performance using teams, motivation, and collaboration. Transformational leaders offer their subordinates a greater purpose beyond the day-to-day work by creating and articulating a vision of change that transcends short-term goals and focuses on a higher set of needs or principles. What moves followers to align their behavior to the leader's vision is the leader's inspiration and charisma. As importantly, the transformational leader provides followers with individualized focus and attention as a commitment to the followers' professional development. The transformation model views the leader/follower association as less of an exchange relationship and more of a relationship built on commitment to overriding values and aspirations.

Intersectional leadership certainly finds value in some parts of each of these leadership theories, but it also takes issue with the foundational premise of both. Let's start with the similarities. As in transactional leadership, intersectional leadership recognizes that the leader and his or her teams have distinct and sometimes mutual interests that the leader can leverage to move issues forward. Similarly, the intersectional leadership model shares the transformational leadership theory's insistence on the leader's need to motivate his or her teams by appealing to greater goals than just day-to-day efficiencies. But intersectional leadership diverges from both models because they anchor their understanding of leadership in a hierarchical framework. They assume that a leader sits atop a structure and the "followers" respond to the leader because of their own ambition or because they derive a sense of purpose from the leader's vision. In these models, the leader is the most powerful player who dispenses rewards and punishments, and who singularly frames the problem and then enthusiastically drives followers to achieve the goal he or she has set. Traditional leadership models envision the leader's role as emanating from positional authority—at the top of an organization, as the head of a unit, as the focal point of a team. But positional leadership constitutes only one possible avenue of leadership. And exploring leadership as only manifesting at the apex of an organizational structure fundamentally misunderstands the ways that leaders can and must exercise influence at every level.

With that in mind, intersectional leadership does not single out the leader in this way. Intersectional leaders exercise leadership by virtue of the juncture where they sit—they are situated at the intersection of formal and informal networks; they have access to different stakeholders and viewpoints; they wear multiple hats and can step outside a single role to consider and pursue different ideas and approaches. To do this, intersectional leaders must have a broad view of what it means to lead that extends beyond the leader's individual expertise and experience. They must then erect a broad tent that invites different and even opposing views. Leading at the intersections of people and perspectives demands that leaders treat others as equals from whom they can learn. They collaborate with others as they grapple to articulate a vision for the team, to detect and identify issues and opportunities, and to develop a range of options to achieve their goals and to address obstacles. And finally, intersectional leaders look to build connections that enable them and their teams to identify and move toward a shared greater purpose or common good.

This sounds good on paper, but what does it really look like? At its most basic level, intersectional leadership involves a fundamental reorientation away from an individualized, discrete focus toward a broader, enterprise view of the work that the organization undertakes and the leader affects. Conventional legal education focuses primarily on the development of narrow, technical skills to the detriment of broader skills that will prove necessary to lawyer-leaders in their careers. Wherever they sit, leaders must remain alert to the needs of and outcomes for the entire organization, not just the part over which they have direct control. Leadership, in its most basic form, can be described as falling on two axes. The vertical I axis involves the development of deep, technical, subject-matter expertise. Lawyer-leaders often define themselves and their contributions along this axis. Legal education provides them with the foundations for this expertise, and then practice exposes them to the particularized information that enables them to be experts in a given field or specialty. Technical expertise becomes the basis for promotions and distinguishing oneself as a lawyer. But a horizontal axis that cuts across the I also exists, forming a T.[17] This axis involves broader thinking across the enterprise in which the lawyer operates. As lawyers rise in a field, their leadership roles have to expand. They need to move beyond the individual contributor role and assume more of an enterprise function, thinking vertically and horizontally. In the end, lawyer-leaders must engage and maintain deep expertise and strategic interest.

Building on that foundation, let's take an even closer look at the five central dimensions of intersectional leadership. First, to develop and maintain a wide view, the intersectional leader needs to build and nurture a broad team. A lawyer-leader must form a team composed of members who bring traits and views that are dissimilar to those of the leader. This means including and engaging a range of perspectives—not just those of other lawyers—to be able to see issues from multiple vantage points. The problem is that lawyers, all too often, believe that they do not need to consult others but simply can rely on their technical expertise to identify and solve problems. Far too frequently, that view leads them to isolate themselves from others. But intersectional leaders see their technical expertise as a lens, not as the definitive answer, and they value thinking and working with others who bring experience from outside their specialty, unit, and field.

Like other professionals, lawyers belong to both formal and informal networks inside and outside their organizations. Inside their companies, they may function within a legal unit, but they serve clients and stakeholders who can have interests and concerns that align or diverge on any given issue. The lawyer's job routinely involves understanding the nature of those views as well as the conflicts they produce and then helping clients chart a course of action that accomplishes the clients' goals within the bounds of a legal or regulatory framework. In advising on the best course of action, the lawyer-leader needs to understand more than what technically conforms to the law; the lawyer-leader needs to be able to understand and appreciate the context in which the action will be taken and the likely reactions and repercussions of a choice both within a legal framework and in the court of public opinion. Outside work, lawyers belong to a variety of networks that inform their thinking and expose them to different perspectives—they participate in bar associations or community organizations or serve on boards; they are members of parent-teacher associations or coach sports teams, to name a few examples. These broader networks of associations benefit intersectional leaders because those external relationships expose them to vantage points that can help to broaden their thinking even about issues at work. Putting together teams of advisors, inside and outside the work environment, enables intersectional leaders to gain insights from them in a variety of ways: they can serve as sounding boards, as early-warning systems for issues that might affect the organization, or as supporting constituencies for novel or controversial moves the leader may want to make or advise others to take.

Second, intersectional leaders not only assemble a diverse team but recognize that they can and will learn from often unexpected sources. This means that intersectional leaders need to surround themselves with dissimilar teams that may well create a degree of discomfort but will also enable the leader to see issues from different angles. Soliciting views of individuals who fall outside the conventional reporting structure may expose the leader to information that is less filtered. As leaders assume more senior roles, they are often removed from issues on the ground that could inform the leader's strategic judgment if known. Leaders who receive their information only through the formal chain of command can miss signals and sentiments that are critical to the success of the organization. Similarly, intersectional leaders will want to include on the team members who are new to the organization or unit because they have not yet learned the organization's orthodoxies and are not saddled by the conventions of the organization's past. In other words, the newcomer does not yet have a sense of what the organization can and cannot do. Freed to imagine possibilities, the newcomer or outsider may identify issues or avenues of approach that the more seasoned members of the team would overlook or simply not consider. A mix of perspectives and experiences can lead to healthy discussion and debate about options.

The problem is that our work environments increasingly lack genuine diversity of perspectives and have failed to move the needle sufficiently on racial, ethnic, and gender diversity and inclusion. Leaders continue to hire in their own image, believing strongly that their path is the best route to leadership. The net result is homogenous leadership teams that share similar biases and perspectives. Diversity matters in decision making across the board in all industries. In its groundbreaking 2015 study *Diversity Matters*,[18] McKinsey & Co. examined proprietary data sets for 366 public companies across a range of industries in Canada, Latin America, the United Kingdom, and the United States.[19] The researchers concluded that companies in the top quartile for gender or racial and ethnic diversity were more successful financially. They found that those companies were more likely to have financial returns above national industry medians.[20] They further discovered that companies in the bottom quartile in these dimensions were statistically less likely to achieve above-average returns.[21] While correlation does not equal causation, the study found that

[the] correlation does indicate that when companies commit themselves to diverse leadership, they are more successful. More diverse companies, we believe, are better able to win top talent and improve their customer orientation, employee satisfaction, and decision making, and all that leads to a virtuous cycle of increasing returns. More diverse companies, we believe, are better able to win top talent and improve their customer orientation, employee satisfaction, and decision making, and all that leads to a virtuous cycle of increasing returns. This in turn suggests that other kinds of diversity—for example, in age, sexual orientation, and experience (such as a global mind-set and cultural fluency)—are also likely to bring some level of competitive advantage for companies that can attract and retain such diverse talent.[22]

The study also concluded that in the United States, "there is a linear relationship between racial and ethnic diversity and better financial performance:

for every 10 percent increase in racial and ethnic diversity on the senior-executive team, earnings before interest and taxes (EBIT) rise."[23] While the data on the positive effects of diversity on a business's bottom line presents a compelling business case, companies' leadership teams still overwhelmingly lack diversity.

Law schools contribute to the lack of diversity in the legal profession and bear some responsibility for the lack of diversity in leadership ranks. The legal profession is one of the least racially diverse professions in the country. Students of color are underrepresented in law schools, and people of color are underrepresented on law faculties. The net result is that law schools are not adding large numbers of lawyers to the profession and are not exposing White lawyers to the racial and ethnic diversity that they will encounter as they operate around the globe. As we release these lawyers into the market, they are inadequately prepared to engage in diverse teams let alone lead them. African Americans, Latinos, Asian Americans and Native Americans now constitute about a third of the population but only a fifth of law school graduates. They make up fewer than 7 percent of law firm partners and 9 percent of general counsels of large corporations.[24] Law schools funnel high numbers of White men into the workplace and leadership roles in the profession without helping them develop an appreciation for and understanding of the value of difference.

Being able to lead teams whose members come from different backgrounds and cultures is especially important given the global character of today's work environment. The interconnectedness of our markets in an increasingly globalized world has led to the need for leaders to have global fluency. Failure to understand the globalizing nature of organizations as well as the flattening of the world[25] is causing problems in political, commercial, and environmental leadership. A lack of global fluency results in large part from a failure to create learning opportunities to better understand different cultures. If a lack of diversity means leading with similar racial or gender norms, a lack of global fluency means assuming that one's cultural norms apply everywhere. Being serious about developing global leaders means making a concentrated pivot from focusing on management skills to increasing self-awareness, emotional intelligence, and resilience so students become effective across cultures.[26] Many years ago, law schools began a competitive push to become more globally focused. This meant that a number of schools established campuses in other countries. Despite their ambitions, these global experiences turned out merely to be American experiences transplanted to a different setting. Too often, law schools placed U.S. law students in enclaves of other U.S. students in other countries. These "study abroad" opportunities did precious little to integrate students into other cultures or to expose students to political, economic, or market structures in these locations. Given often limited interaction with foreign nationals or foreign cultures, U.S. law students rarely returned home with any unique insights about the culture of the country in which they studied.

The third dimension of intersectional leadership requires that the leader engage in genuine collaboration with others who have different sorts of expertise, interests, and experience that they can bring to the table in identifying and solving problems. Knowing not only the value of collaboration but ways to engage in collaboration are critical skills for lawyer-leaders. Law schools have acknowledged the importance of this skill and often claim to teach collaboration.[27] However, what they really teach is teaming. Faculty will place students together in a group to work on a class project or, in a clinical setting, to work on a case together. The faculty member gives overall directions for the task and is the ultimate decision maker regarding the success of the team. While teamwork of this sort is an important lesson for students—and does begin to move law students away from the traditional perception that working in the law is a solitary venture—this is not collaboration.

Understanding the difference between teaming and collaboration is critical. Teaming involves coming together generally in the context of a hierarchical structure. There are clear leaders and a shared goal. Collaboration, on the other hand, rarely has a single leader or decision maker. Instead, collaborators are equal partners and need to develop rules of engagement to make decisions and to move the group forward. The goals of collaborators may be different, even competing, so it is quite common for collaborators to feel that collaboration "hurts."[28] Collaboration means that you are giving up something—such as revenue, recognition, or resources—for a greater good. Lawyer-leaders need to develop more collaborative approaches as they look to lead with influence.

The fourth component of intersectional leadership involves adopting a mind-set that is wary of easy agreement. Given the tensions and volatility in the environment in which leaders operate, it is understandable that leaders may want to ensure that the workplace is harmonious. But problems develop when an insistence on harmony or consensus stifles inquiry or dissent. Leaders need to remain open to questioning their own judgment by reaching beyond the familiar circle and soliciting dissenting views. When leaders assemble a team that operates as little more than an echo chamber, they miss concerns that a particular approach might raise; they miss the sharpened thinking that can come as a result of conflict and having to defend a position. The intersectional leader cannot use an insular type of leadership. Quite often, the lawyer-leader's role demands dichotomous thinking. For example, how can the lawyer-leader be an advocate and a minister of justice? How can the lawyer-leader protect a business and its shareholders? By reaching broadly and deeply to get divergent views, the intersectional leader can raise questions and develop alternate ways of examining an issue. Achieving agreement too quickly should raise flags for the intersectional leader. For the sake of argument and to encourage broader thinking, the intersectional leader can play devil's advocate when his or her team quickly reaches consensus. This sort of constructive challenge engages the team in a process of optionality, asking "what if" and "how could we look at this differently?" By leveraging his or her position as a player at the juncture of networks, people, and ideas, the intersectional leader is more likely to develop the sort of agility in thinking that helps teams better define and clarify both issues and potential solutions.

Some conventional leadership theories—such as affiliative leadership[29]— suggest that the leader's job is to build teams and promote harmony among his or her followers. Affiliate leadership pushes leaders to heal rifts within teams and to focus their leadership energy on consensus building. Intersectional leadership similarly sees the value in team building but cautions that an emphasis on consensus can dangerously narrow the leader's vision. Respectful disagreement and challenging the notion of harmony and consensus does not mean stoking chaos or aggressive disagreement. The leader's role does not involve reifying harmony and insisting on agreement; it instead entails seeking out dissent and inviting challenge to hone the thinking of both the leader and the team. Of course, the team will ultimately need to align once a decision has been made. But until that point, divergent views and competing perspectives are critical tools in helping the leader and team identify and assess issues more comprehensively and identify the most beneficial solutions. The intersectional leader needs to be strong enough to let the debate occur and to encourage team members to challenge the leader's thinking. But the conflict that the intersectional leader needs to encourage is the type that is built on trust and respect and emerges from a desire to think broadly rather than myopically about an issue. By having open, honest conversations, intersectional leaders recognize that they may learn something valuable from someone who sees the world and the issues differently. The leader who wants agreement at all costs is a dictator, not an intersectional leader.

The final component of intersectional leadership insists that the leader act with integrity and moral courage even when his or her decisions occur outside public view. Much of the work of lawyers occurs behind closed doors, given the protections of attorney-client confidentiality. In those instances, the only check on the lawyer's decisions may be his or her own ethics and integrity. For the intersectional leader, integrity is a key behavioral attribute. Intersectional leaders recognize that their words, actions, and attitudes help to build an organizational culture. Leaders who model integrity and hold themselves accountable for acting with integrity signal their expectations for others working with them. Leaders who fail to act with integrity set a tone at the intersections of the networks and teams where they sit that behavior that lacks integrity is acceptable. Their conduct and lack of integrity can have a corrosive effect on the ecosystems in which they lead. So intersectional leaders need to create processes and disciplines that serve as checks on their decisions. They must find ways to hold themselves accountable by empowering their teams to question their choices and judgment.

To ensure that intersectional leaders act with integrity, they must work collectively with others to identify a greater purpose that drives their and their team's work. Recent years have offered countless examples of leaders elevating personal ambition or gain above all else. When a leader's choices or decisions are shielded from public scrutiny, it becomes easier to engage in such conduct. But by setting a higher goal for their own work and the work of the team, intersectional leaders can embrace the practice of doing the right thing for the right reason no matter the consequence. And by envisioning and articulating a greater purpose or bold ambition for the work, intersectional leaders can help the disparate members of their teams and networks engage their hearts and minds in the service of that goal.

The intersectional leadership framework's focus on integrity can be seen as drawing on a leadership model called *servant leadership*.[30] Although the model originated in the 1970s, it has gained renewed popularity in the twenty-first century. Servant leadership defines the job of the leader as one of service—service to a greater goal, service to his or her subordinates. The primary role of the servant leader is to delegate responsibilities and then to provide direct support to his or her subordinates to enable their individual growth. What is different, though, is that intersectional leadership does not expect leader to be devoid of self-interest or to be wholly altruistic in setting a purpose for themselves and their people. It does expect the leader to set a tone, and not to wait for his or her followers to do that. But in setting that tone or in establishing that goal, the intersectional leader should invite the views of others in his or her networks and teams to help identify a broad goal that is not simply limited to the leader's personal interest or gain.

ADAPTING TO CURRENT NAVIGATIONAL CONDITIONS

Learning to operate as an intersectional leader takes on even greater urgency as we prepare lawyers to lead in the volatility of today's environment.

The 2008 global financial crisis served as an unambiguous wake-up call and an unmistakable dividing line in history. The precrisis world functioned quite differently from the postcrisis world. Before the financial crisis, the world followed familiar rules: It was relatively stable and it operated in fairly predictable ways. Disruptive change certainly occurred, but with much less frequency than would become the norm after the crisis. In those conditions, preparing individuals for leadership work generally meant exposing them to existing models that had proven successful in the past and then helping them to apply relevant lessons. Leaders needed to recognize the historical patterns, and with that in mind, guide with a steady hand, making incremental changes that kept the organization or office afloat and moving forward. When the organization encountered problems, leaders looked to similar occurrences within their own company, industry, or field for the navigational chart to get them through rough waters. More often than not, leaders simply piloted the boat by looking at the wake.

This leadership expectation played well to lawyers' strengths and technical legal training. Law school, without any specialized effort, prepared lawyers to excel in a predictable, stable environment. Legal training underscored the importance of adhering to precedent and the value of preserving the status quo. Lawyers learn from day one in law school the need to be critical, analytical, and alert to detail—all of which remain vital skills for the practice of law. But that training also leads lawyers to be somewhat slow, restrained, and inclined to urge caution. It is no surprise that lawyers have a reputation for being naysayers or harbingers of doom because they routinely say no when others are anxious to make novel moves. Lawyers look to minimize change by making—and urging others to make—gradual adjustments rather than radical moves. Legal training is precisely geared toward a process that encourages lawyers to control, or at least slow, the rate of change to levels that an organization can absorb with the least disruption. Lawyers were ideally suited to the precrisis world.

When the financial crisis hit with the force of a tidal wave, it swept away what we knew about the ways the world operated. The repercussions of the crisis shook our confidence in stability. Indeed, when the crisis waters receded, the world that was revealed was far less certain. The old models seemed out of phase. Navigating this new normal demanded radically different leadership skills. Postcrisis, we find ourselves living and working in a *VUCA* world, an acronym aptly developed by the military in the 1990s to capture the dynamics of this global environment—one characterized by volatility, uncertainty, complexity, and ambiguity.[31] Given those characteristics, the slow, cautious, backward-glancing leadership techniques that once prevailed have proven inadequate to today's leadership tasks. That does not mean that lawyer-leaders should now become reckless and cast off all the strategies they have used for generations. But it does suggest that to remain relevant and to assume a functioning leadership role, lawyer-leaders need to rethink many of their operating assumptions and methods.

So, what exactly is this VUCA world? The V in VUCA stands for volatility. The first two decades of the twenty-first century have provided ample evidence of the wide range of volatility that leaders will likely encounter as the world adjusts to its new normal. Technological advances and market disruption, increased global competition and heightened protectionism, and terrorism and cyberattacks are just a few of the issues that leaders will have to face domestically and globally. Today's leaders will need to develop the agility to juggle multiple, even competing issues simultaneously. Where we once comfortably assumed that leaders could simply prioritize the issues they would address—picking one issue over another as an area of focus—we now see that such "either/or" thinking has become dangerously outdated. The world that has emerged is a "both/and" environment. Today's leaders need to accept volatility as a given. This means that adherence to static models will be less helpful, so leaders need to develop the skills to build optionality into their decision making. Leaders likely need to make decisions with imperfect information at hand. Asking "what if?" and formulating scenarios and simulations will help leaders better anticipate risks and keep up with shifting dynamics in their operating environments.

The U in VUCA reminds us that this environment is uncertain. Today's environment lacks predictability, which means that leaders will encounter disruptions and surprises with increasing frequency. Some of that uncertainty arises from the global interconnectedness of today's environment, where an issue occurring in one corner of the world can have an unexpected but real impact in another. The lines between cause and effect are less clear, and it has become more difficult for leaders to use past experience as predictors of the future. As answers will not be easily known or discovered, leaders need to become accustomed to a degree of discomfort, to not being reasonably positive of an outcome before taking action. This presents special challenges for lawyer-leaders. Law schools have trained lawyers to rely on their technical legal expertise to solve problems. While that technical expertise continues to be relevant, it is not enough on its own. Uncertainty forces leaders to move beyond their technical comfort zone and pushes them to develop nontraditional responses to problems. Leaders must develop and consult networks beyond their own teams, divisions, or areas of expertise. They need to leverage diversity to draw on multiple points of view. Developing broad information sources—both internal and external—helps provide an early warning system for changes on the horizon.

The C in VUCA stands for the complexity that has become a defining feature of today's increasingly global, technological, and interconnected world. Keeping up with changes in the legal and regulatory framework governing choices—particularly in a global economy—is more than any single individual can master. And understanding the shifting social, political, and economic contexts that can influence the law and its boundaries will place new demands on lawyers as leaders because they may change from moment to moment. Being clear about your own skills as well as the skills that are missing in your immediate leadership team is critical. Emotional intelligence and the ability to see and understand the myriad dimensions of problems will emerge as critical capabilities for leaders. To navigate complexity successfully, a leader needs to recognize the impermanence of solutions and the need to stay attuned to change so that decisions can be refined, reshaped, and adjusted based on new information.

The A in VUCA reflects the ambiguity of most situations. What distinguished decision making for leaders precrisis, in part, was the confidence that in any given scenario, relevant issues were knowable. Postcrisis, there is a considerable lack of clarity about both the full meaning and impact of events and the ways to respond to situations. Today's leaders must be comfortable with a high degree of ambiguity. In the precrisis environment, lawyer-leaders carved out a space as technical experts who could give clear direction or at least clear warnings against certain paths. That advice was premised on the fact that history pointed the way toward desired outcomes if the same steps were taken. For example, financial investments in emerging markets rife with corruption were once considered no-go investments. Today, prestigious publications such as the *Harvard Business Review* point to these same environments as important opportunities in many instances.[32] Making strategic calls with certainty now is nearly impossible. Given the many and constantly shifting variables that must be analyzed, there are fewer prescriptive or algorithmic decisions that leaders can make today. Instead, leaders must be more agile in their preparation, and they must learn to experiment, test, and rethink approaches to problems in real time. Interestingly, with just a bit of reorientation, lawyer-leaders could be well suited to this environment. The law often raises questions that have no clear answer—there is a split of opinion on the law in different jurisdictions, or a regulation is open to interpretation, for example. The lawyer's task is to assess the best option given a set of knowns and unknowns. Lawyer-leaders may simply need to regain their own comfort with ambiguity and may need to reorient those with whom they work to the fact that they may not always be able to identify clear direction but may be able to be alert to possible degrees of danger given different strategic choices.

Former president Barack Obama, a lawyer-leader, encountered a rather dramatic VUCA challenge that tested his ability in the first few weeks of his presidency. Obama had to decide whether to assist General Motors (GM) and Chrysler as they teetered on the verge of bankruptcy. At the end of 2008, President George W. Bush agreed that the federal government would provide a temporary bailout for these two companies but left the details to his successor. GM and Chrysler were hemorrhaging billions of dollars monthly. Both companies lacked sufficient cash to pay their bills. At stake were not only the jobs of all of GM and Chrysler's employees but the jobs of people who worked for hundreds of suppliers—such as stereo manufacturers and steel and rubber producers. Estimates of potential job losses topped one million.[33] With the nation's economy reeling from the worst downturn since the Great Depression, Obama understood that despite the lack of an obvious answer, he had to take action.

The newly elected president had no exact template from which to draw. Virtually no one believed that GM and Chrysler deserved to be protected from failure. But no bank or consortium of banks stepped up in 2009 to provide financing for a GM or Chrysler bankruptcy. Even partisan politics did not make the decision clearer. Liberal think tanks, such as the Brookings Institution, recommended that the federal government allow these companies to fail and recommended that the government sell off their factories and machinery to recoup whatever they could.[34] Republican leaders said much the same thing. Mitt Romney wrote an op-ed in the *New York Times* titled "Let Detroit Go Bankrupt," decrying an auto industry bailout.[35] But far-reaching ramifications could flow from any decision that the president made. Obama created a task force to investigate and uncover the issues. He asked the task force to make recommendations regarding the fate of GM and Chrysler. The companies themselves offered their own solutions. They offered to downsize, but the task force wanted deeper changes. In March 2009, Obama rejected the companies' proposal and adhered to the views of his task force. He made clear that if the firms wanted federal money, they had to go through bankruptcy. The car companies quickly filed for bankruptcy in June and emerged in July.[36]

Almost immediately, partisan politics returned to more familiar terrain. Conservatives criticized the president's decision as an unprecedented government power grab. Liberals were not fond of his decision but defended it as necessary to save one of America's anchor industries. With the benefit of hindsight, most view his decision not only to have saved a vital U.S. industry but to have salvaged at least some of the economic fortunes of the Midwest.[37] But at the time, Obama had no hindsight; he had to venture where no recent leaders had gone and make sense of complex issues and volatile conditions that the country had never experienced—the essence of decision making in a VUCA world.

A fundamental reorientation toward more complex and adaptive thinking is critical to success in a VUCA world for all who look to lead effectively. Preparing today's leaders, including lawyer-leaders, to succeed will involve helping them not to aim for the "correct" answers but rather to aim to identify the pivotal questions in play. Right now, our conventional methods of leadership development do a poor job of this. Lawyers can develop technical legal skills through on-the-job experience. For example, new lawyers learn how to conduct depositions by watching more senior lawyers prepare and depose witnesses. Through an apprentice model, where the firm gives the new lawyer increasing responsibilities under the supervision of a more seasoned lawyer, the new lawyer can learn the techniques involved in taking a deposition. Technical proficiency comes from observation and repetition. The problem is that this model does not work for less technical tasks such as strategy development, which demands the use of adaptive skills necessary to survive and thrive in a volatile environment. We need to rethink the assumptions about what it means to lead.

CHALLENGING ASSUMPTIONS
ABOUT LEADERSHIP

Leadership in business, law, and even politics was once synonymous with formal authority. Holding a position as CEO, executive director, president, or attorney-in-charge designated you as the leader with ultimate authority in a given sphere. Implied in that title was a belief that, as the person in charge, you held all of the answers. That implication is no longer the expectation or the reality. The dynamics of the current environment mean that leaders cannot be all-knowing, if they ever were. As a result, leaders must be more collaborative and broadly engaged in order to see the full range of questions and develop working answers to the problems they detect. Perhaps as significantly, leadership can and must be exercised at all levels of an organization because leadership is not tied to a formal title.

Today's effective leader builds and participates in extended networks inside and outside the organization. Networks should have connections that cross boundaries of all kinds: geographic, practice areas, staff/attorney, customers, contacts outside one's business, and advisors and consultants. They help leaders by exposing them to different streams of information and varying perspectives and insights. Quite often, the leader will occupy the position as a *nodal player* in the various networks of which he or she is a part—the person who sits at the intersection of networks and whom other members tend to include or confide in when there are matters of importance. A leader who is not the nodal player in a given network will need to develop strong relationships with the nodal players. Obviously, discussion of networks, teams, and nodal positions suggests that today's leader is not operating in a hierarchical, command-and-control environment. Indeed, today's leaders will not necessarily lead from the front or from the top. Instead, they will lead with influence through their relationships wherever they sit within an organization.[38] Leaders must build and influence collectives to move an organization forward. This means that leaders may need at times to step up and lead the group or step out of the way to enable a team member's experience and expertise to guide the group. Today's leaders must focus on harnessing the power of their teams, helping them understand not only what they are doing but why it matters. This purpose-driven leadership is of particular importance to the rising generation of millennial employees who expect to find meaning in their work. They are prioritizing their personal values and want to learn alongside leaders who help them see and understand the greater purpose of their jobs.

Finding ways to understand and appreciate the unique dynamics and characteristics in a given operating environment is a skill that leaders need to develop and hone. The unpredictability and complexity that have become mainstays of today's environment place greater demands on today's leader. Today's leaders must engage in decision making while being attuned to multiple constituencies. They must equip themselves to read weak signals in the environment that hint at threats or opportunities, and they must be able to anticipate change that could affect their decisions. Leaders must be willing to question their own judgment about events and to allow others to question that judgment or propose alternative assessments.

Leading well also entails gaining greater access to information. In embracing more collaborative approaches to leading, leaders cannot simply build echo chambers of like-minded people and still expect to understand the dynamics of—and competing interests involved in—a given decision. Leaders must encourage and deeply value debate and discussion. The process of engaging a topic or decision critically enables better thinking and improved insights. In developing teams around them, leaders will need to bring together diverse perspectives and multiple views to enable the leader and the group to gain a clearer understanding of the issues that the group or organization will likely encounter. For the first time in the modern era, emerging and developing countries now account for about half the total world output.[39] Emerging and developing economies are home to 85 percent of the world's population—roughly six billion people. These markets have reached a size where the effects of choices they make and actions they take will be noticed everywhere. Previously, Western nations could treat the economic or security issues experienced in emerging nations as largely irrelevant. Today a drought in the heart of Africa can directly influence markets around the world. Syria or Qatar's internal civil strife has triggered refugee and security issues for Western Europe and the United States. In today's interconnected world, not only do nations depend on each other, but so do organizations and their leaders, often in ways that are not anticipated or easily interpreted. Some of our basic rules of order have changed, and many of the assumptions we made successfully in the past are often no longer valid.[40]

What follows in the next five chapters is a series of case studies that help explore more fully the dimensions of intersectional leadership for today and tomorrow's lawyer-leaders. These cases expose the dangers of our failure to prepare lawyer-leaders for their leadership roles and offer insights into the leadership lessons that can and should be taught.

CHAPTER TWO

Is There an Echo in Here?

Diversity, Tension, and Accountability in the Leadership Team

WHEN A LAWYER IN A POSITION of influence engages in misconduct on a grand scale, the public is often quick to attribute the behavior to a personal lapse in ethics or judgment. Of course, unethical choices and conduct should make us examine the perpetrator closely. But focusing exclusively on that single individual may cause us to miss the leadership failures of those around the actor and skew our understanding of the full situation. Most organizations operate as ecosystems, where individual and group behaviors combine to create either a healthy or toxic environment. Where catastrophic system failures occur, it is most often because of a lack of leadership on the part of *many* participants and not simply an ethical or moral failure of one person or even one office. Similarly, when we see success in an organization—a healthy ecosystem—it is often a result of effective leadership on many levels, not just one. But setting a tone of integrity and an expectation for self-criticism are steps that any leader—at any level—can and must take to enable a healthy ecosystem.

Setting a tone of integrity starts with selecting a diverse leadership team. Wide-ranging and sometimes competing experiences, viewpoints, and approaches enhance a leader's ability to recognize and understand differences at work in the world better. Everyone experiences difficulty stepping outside of his or her own personal world view or cultural tradition. Our background and experience combine to create familiar frames of reference about issues, implications, and solutions. But those frames of reference can limit our thinking and make it more difficult to perceive options that fall outside those experiences. The inability to see beyond personal limitations blurs our vision and can lead to blind spots in our judgment and approaches. Intersectional leadership expects a leader to take steps to guard against such insularity by choosing team members whose views and experiences may at times collide with those of the leader. In the creative friction that inevitably emerges, the leader will learn to consider and navigate differing perspectives and, in the end, may be better able to anticipate problems and steer the organization toward health.

Too often, though, leaders opt for what feels more like smooth sailing. They surround themselves with people whom they like—a coterie of friends or people whom they have trusted in past situations. Their teams include people with whom they socialized in college, professional school, or social organizations, or who have been individuals on whom they could rely throughout their careers. Trust, of course, should not be taken lightly. But being preoccupied with picking members of your team who will watch your back in a complex organization has often led to the selection of team members who mirror the leader's views and fail to question or push back when they should. The intersectional leader may still want to include some friends on the team, but he or she should look to identify individuals who will contest and question the leader's thinking in ways that friends with similar experiences typically cannot. Genuine conflict is often a necessary prerequisite to the exercise of good judgment and good leadership.

What happens when leaders misunderstand or ignore this lesson? Two examples provide insights into the consequences. The first case study—the bridge scandal involving New Jersey governor Chris Christie and his administration—explores the leadership lapses that occur when political leaders surround themselves with a team that is little more than an echo chamber for their politics and policies. The second example, although less known, is no less insidious. This case study involves a federal prosecution team in New Orleans, under the direction of Assistant U.S. Attorney Jim Letten. This team undertook an important effort to root out corruption in the New Orleans criminal justice system but ended up engaging in its own brand of corrupt practices. In both cases, the central leaders insulated themselves from dissenting views and created a culture that failed to question their assumptions or challenge their thinking. In the environment that they shaped, the principal leaders, as well as the circle of leaders around them, cavalierly and callously engaged in harmful conduct that fundamentally breached the trust of the people whom they had been elected to lead and protect.

"TIME FOR SOME TRAFFIC PROBLEMS IN FORT LEE"

In the fall of 2013, Governor Chris Christie's administration and an official at the Port Authority of New York and New Jersey conspired to execute a politically motivated traffic lane realignment on the George Washington Bridge. This resulted in four days of significant traffic problems in Fort Lee, New Jersey. The bridge lane closures appeared to be political payback for the choice of the mayor of Fort Lee not to endorse Governor Christie for reelection. Once the bridge scheme surfaced, it gripped headlines and fueled a steady stream of one-liners for late-night television monologues throughout January 2014. But putting jokes and headlines aside, the story serves as a recent and all-too-familiar tale about insulation, arrogance, and leadership failures. This failure led to the conviction of some of Governor Christie's leadership team.

The trail leading to the bridge scandal did not start with the governor's reelection. A brief examination of Governor Christie's history reveals a pattern of appointing senior staff with whom he shared a professional history.[1] Before his campaign for governor, Christie served as the U.S. Attorney for the District of New Jersey from 2002 to 2008.[2] During his first term, the governor appointed over two dozen former prosecutors either to jobs within his administration or to the Superior Court.[3] Fifteen top officials in his administration formerly served as prosecutors at the U.S. Attorney's Office of New Jersey.[4] At the time of the George Washington Bridge incident, the only staff members with direct access to him were his chief of staff, Kevin O'Dowd, and his former chief counsel, Charles McKenna.[5] Both of these men were former Assistant U.S. Attorneys for the District of New Jersey. McKenna was the Executive Assistant U.S. Attorney under Christie from 2002 to 2008 before leaving the office in 2009 to join the administration.[6]

Governor Christie, like most elected officials, felt comfortable with familiar teams around him. In addition to appointing former prosecutors who served with him, Governor Christie also tended to appoint individuals involved in his two campaigns for Governor. Bridget Anne Kelly, the governor's former deputy chief of staff for legislative and intergovernmental affairs, volunteered during Christie's 2009 campaign, and she was eventually selected to serve as director of legislative relations in the first administration.[7] By April 2013, Kelly was promoted to deputy chief of staff.[8] Kelly was fired in January 2014 for her involvement in the traffic lane scandal.[9] The other member of Christie's leadership team embroiled in the George Washington Bridge political scandal was Bill Stepien, Christie's two-time campaign manager and close advisor.[10] Stepien also served as Christie's deputy chief of staff for legislative and intergovernmental affairs during the first administration.[11] Christie had nominated Stepien to lead the New Jersey Republican Party and sit on the Republican National Committee shortly before the scandal broke, but Stepien was then forced to submit his resignation because of his involvement in the scandal.[12]

Sometime in August 2013, David Wildstein, then director of interstate capital projects for the Port Authority, began pursuing an idea for a traffic study that would close toll lane access to the George Washington Bridge in Fort Lee, New Jersey.[13] Wildstein began pushing the idea for the study to both Port Authority engineers and political contacts.[14] On the political side, Wildstein approached Stepien about the idea to realign the toll lanes.[15] Stepien, who at that point had left Governor Christie's administration to run his reelection campaign, was no help and directed Wildstein to "Trenton" presumably to seek input from the Governor's staff.[16] Wildstein then contacted Kelly, then one of Christie's deputy chiefs of staff, about his plan to realign the Fort Lee toll lanes.[17] Wildstein and Kelly began discussing the topic through their personal email accounts.[18]

On August 12, 2013, Kelly confirmed to her bosses that the mayor of Fort Lee, Mark Sokolich, would not be endorsing Governor Christie for reelection.[19] On August 13, she sent an email to Wildstein that read, "Time for some traffic problems in Fort Lee."[20] At Wildstein's direction, the Port Authority implemented the traffic lane study during morning rush hour on Monday, September 9, 2013.[21] Fort Lee officials, including the mayor, had no prior notice of the study.[22] The realignment reduced toll lane access in Fort Lee from three lanes to one, causing massive traffic problems.[23] The lanes remained closed until the morning of Friday, September 13, when

Patrick Foye, executive director of the Port Authority, learned of the study and ordered its termination.[24]

During the four days of lane closures, Wildstein, Kelly, and former Port Authority deputy executive director Bill Baroni exchanged emails and text messages regarding the Fort Lee traffic problems. On September 9, Baroni forwarded a message from Mayor Sokolich about an "urgent matter of public safety" to Wildstein, who responded: "radio silence."[25] The following morning, Kelly texted Wildstein, "Is it wrong that I am smiling?" to which he responded, "No," and referenced those affected by the lane closures as (Democratic candidate Barbara) "Buono voters."[26] On September 12, Baroni sent another letter from Mayor Sokolich to Wildstein, who then forwarded it to Kelly and Stepien.[27]

In mid-September, the scheme began to come to light. On September 17, 2013, the *Wall Street Journal* ran a story speculating that the traffic lane re-alignment study had been retribution for Mayor Sokolich's decision not to endorse Christie's reelection campaign.[28] Two weeks later, New Jersey assemblyman John Wisniewski announced that the New Jersey Assembly Transportation, Public Works, and Independent Authorities Committee would convene a hearing to investigate the motivations of the lane realignment.[29] Media inquiries continued up until the hearings on November 25 and December 9, 2013.[30] After the hearings, the committee subpoenaed seven Port Authority employees for documents related to the Fort Lee lane realignment.[31] On January 8, 2014, many of the committee's subpoenaed documents became publicly available through the news media.[32] Governor Christie fired Kelly and asked Stepien to resign on January 9,[33] and the governor's office retained the law firm Gibson, Dunn & Crutcher LLP to conduct an internal investigation of the incident on January 16.[34] The firm made the report of their investigation public on March 27, 2014;[35] meanwhile, investigations by the New Jersey legislature and the U.S. Attorney's Office remained ongoing.[36]

Christie's campaign for reelection had all of the hubris of a popular incumbent focused on higher office. Rather than surrounding himself with a team that would push his thinking and serve as intellectual foils for the thought processes in the administration—a team of rivals[37]—the governor surrounded himself with friends and zealots. Not only did he fail to develop a leadership style that encouraged debate and critical thinking, but that lapse encouraged a view that differences of opinion should be targeted and destroyed. The leaders around the governor took their cues from him and, given the way that he led, the result was unsurprising.

Christie's response was unsurprising too: he asserted he was caught unaware. On January 31, 2014, Wildstein's counsel sent a letter to the Port Authority alleging that "evidence exists . . . tying Mr. Christie to having knowledge of the lane closures, during the period when the lanes were closed."[38] The Gibson report responds directly to this allegation. It determines that Wildstein "must have been referring" to a conversation between himself and Governor Christie at the 9/11 memorial event on September 11, 2013.[39] The report questions whether any substantive discussion of the George Washington Bridge study took place at the event, and it argues that there is no reason for the governor to recall such a conversation, if it did occur, considering the circumstances.[40] The governor claims to have no recollection of any conversation regarding Fort Lee at the event.[41] Christie also claimed he had no indication that the lane closings were anything other than a traffic study until January 8, 2014.[42] Wildstein resigned his position at the Port Authority amid the political uproar in September 2013 and admitted in federal court in Newark that he and two other former Christie aides engaged in a politically motivated plot to cause the traffic jam, and that the traffic study they initially said prompted the closures was meant to cover up the conspiracy.[43] Wildstein later entered a guilty plea and ultimately testified against Baroni and Kelly, who were found guilty on all counts in November 2016.[44] Port Authority chair David Samson pleaded guilty to one felony count of conspiracy in July 2016 for acts unrelated to the lane closures but unearthed by the federal "Bridgegate" investigation.[45]

Whether we believe Christie's assertions or not, it is clear that he created a context where his leaders believed that payback was not only within their power but within the realm of right behavior. In selecting individuals who would make high-level decisions for the office of the governor, Christie opted for people whom he personally knew and liked. No one seemed to be keeping Christie's feet to the fire by questioning his choices or judgment. And Christie was not questioning theirs. No elected official can control every action of his or her subordinates. But, at its core, leadership is about the values that the leadership embraces and demonstrates through its actions and decisions. Those behaviors trickle down through role modeling. Christie's personal leadership allowed his team to believe that they could bully their way through the state in seeking complete support for their candidate. He failed to set the right tone inside his leadership team, and we witnessed a resulting failure of others around him to step up to lead.

After months of silence about the incident during the internal investigation, Governor Christie held a press conference on March 28 to address the release of the Gibson report and announce Samson's resignation.[46] After a question about how he had changed his governance since the incident, the governor responded, "I've done a lot of soul searching in this over the last ten or eleven weeks . . . for me, it's going to be about making even clearer to people what is acceptable conduct and what isn't."[47] Notwithstanding, all of the questions about his choices for leadership appointments and his decision to surround himself with friends in a virtual echo chamber for his policies and practices, Christie has said little about changing his leadership selection style. Christie's legal education likely exposed him to ethics classes, but his conduct did not necessarily violate any rules of professional conduct. His law school training should have taught him the value of diverse viewpoints and the danger of only seeking views that blindly supported his own. But instead he reveled in ignoring the naysayers and instead set a tone in his administration that his views were to be followed without question, regardless of the implications of that choice.

THE DANZIGER BRIDGE CASE— RAMPANT ABUSES OF AUTHORITY

An even more disturbing example of what can happen when a leader chooses to surround himself or herself with friends alone occurred in New Orleans. By the turn of the twenty-first century, the criminal justice system in New Orleans had been failing for generations. When federal prosecutors under the direction of Assistant U.S. Attorney Jim Letten began tackling corruption at the state level, they made significant changes, and they made a name for themselves in the process. Along the way, Letten's prosecutors lost sight of their ethical obligations as officers of the court and, instead, began to see themselves as above the law. They flouted ethical rules, leaked information to inflame public opinion, and covered up their own misconduct. Even when questions were raised about the conduct of prosecutors in his office, Letten did little to investigate or question their conduct. He had surrounded himself with people whom he knew and liked, and he "only thought the best of people." In the aftermath of investigations, allegations, and revelations surrounding the prosecution of one instructive case, the Danziger Bridge murder trial, Letten's team—once praised as heroes—would end their careers in disgrace.

Around 9:00 a.m. on September 4, 2005, six days after Hurricane Katrina, police officers shot at eight people on the Danziger Bridge.[48] All of the victims were camping out at the Family Inn on the highway and were crossing the bridge to get to the Winn-Dixie grocery store when police opened fire.[49] The Bartholomew family was the first group shot by the police. Thirty-eight-year-old Susan Bartholomew had gunshot wounds to her thigh, buttock, calf, and heel and ultimately had her right arm amputated.[50] Seventeen-year-old Leonard Bartholomew had gunshot wounds to his right knee and upper back and sustained shotgun pellets to his head.[51] Lesha Bartholomew, age seventeen, had gunshot wounds to the abdomen, thigh, and leg.[52] Leonard Bartholomew escaped harm by diving under the bridge.[53] Nineteen-year-old Jose Holmes, Susan's nephew, sustained gunshot wounds to the abdomen and shotgun blasts to his arm, hand, and jaw.[54] His friend, seventeen-year-old James Brissette, died from gunshot and shotgun wounds to the neck, shoulder, upper arm, forearm, spine, pelvis, buttock, leg, elbow, and heel.[55] On the other side of the bridge, Lance Madison, age forty-nine, escaped harm by staying ahead of the gunfire, only to be charged with attempted murder of the police officers.[56] His intellectually disabled brother, forty-year-old Ronald Madison, died from shotgun wounds to the back and shoulder.[57] All victims on the bridge vehemently denied that they were armed or shooting at police. They insisted police ambushed them and never identified themselves.[58]

The police told a different story. Police officers claimed they received a radio broadcast distress call from Officer Jennifer Dupree shortly before 9:00 a.m. Dupree was one of a number of officers escorting a convoy of rescue workers who had reported that a number of people had shot at them, and she claimed she saw people shooting from the ground at the bridge high-rise.[59] She then reported seeing four people running toward the highway, east from the Danziger Bridge. Officer Dupree later identified the four people only by their clothing.[60]

A number of officers heard the call and concluded that fellow officers where "down" (injured or dead) near the bridge.[61] Dupree continued to track the shooters over the radio while two other officers, Patrick Conaghan and David Ryder, ran to try to catch them.[62] Although there was no physical evidence to support their story, the officers all stated that they started taking fire as soon as they left their truck on the east side of the bridge.[63] One of the officers, Anthony Villavaso, further claimed he heard fellow officers shout, "Police, police, show me your hands!" followed by continuing gunfire in response. Officer Michael Hunter claimed he heard someone say over the police radio, "That's them. That's them."[64] At that point, one of the officers yelled at the group of people running to stop, but one group, the Bartholomew family, dove behind a barrier while the others ran toward the other end of the bridge.[65] Around 9:00 a.m. police officers shot at eight people on the Danziger Bridge.[66] When the dust settled, two people were dead, four people were seriously injured, and another was arrested on eight counts of attempted murder.[67]

The New Orleans Police Department conducted an investigation that cleared the officers of the charges[68] and proclaimed their innocence. But the report contained serious flaws. It was based solely on the officers' accounts, lacked any evidence of interviews with civilian witnesses aside from what was recorded on that day, referenced only one weapon being found, and did not tie that weapon to any of the victims. The report also made no mention of Ronald Madison, the individual who died from police gunshots.[69] Court documents and testimony from officers cooperating with the investigation later revealed that police did not stop firing once they realized the civilians were unarmed and that Madison was shot, as were the others, for no apparent reason.[70] What kept this from coming to light was a brazen police cover-up orchestrated by lieutenants who later arrived on the scene.[71]

Perhaps inevitably, the corruption that riddled the police investigation infected the state prosecution that followed. The local district attorney's office had been plagued with allegations of racism, corruption, and complicity with bad police conduct. This case offered more of the same. Among a host of improprieties in the prosecution, one stood out: Louisiana assistant district attorney Dustin Davis showed clips of the grand jury testimony to the supervisor of several accused officers, which violated state grand jury secrecy laws. The presiding judge then tossed out these charges because of prosecutorial misconduct.[72]

So the New Orleans community turned to the federal government to help them receive justice. Shortly after the dismissal of the state-court prosecution, the Federal Bureau of Investigation (FBI), the Civil Rights Division of the Department of Justice (DOJ), and Jim Letten's office began investigating the incident.[73] The case got its first break in February 2010 when police lieutenant Michael Lohmann pleaded guilty to one count of conspiring to obstruct justice by engaging in a cover-up of the events that happened on the bridge.[74] He acknowledged that he arrived on the scene and discovered that there had been a "bad shoot," so he coached officers to make exculpatory statements and assisted with planting evidence at the scene.[75] In March, a second police officer, Jeffrey Lehrmann, pleaded guilty to a charge related to concealing evidence of a federal crime.[76] Lehrmann and Lohmann agreed to cooperate with federal prosecutors. Michael Hunter, Robert Barrios, and Ignatius Hills, all officers arriving at the scene on the bridge, later pleaded guilty to charges of failure to report a crime and to obstruction of justice, again in cooperation with prosecutors.[77] David Ryder, a key witness to the shootings and later found out to be a felon impersonating a police officer, pleaded guilty to charges of lying to the FBI, obstructing justice, and being a felon in possession of a firearm.[78] Each plea detailed the disturbing facts of the cover-up, prompting Judge Sarah Vance to state at one point, "I don't think you can listen to that account without being sickened by the raw brutality of the shooting and the craven lawlessness of the cover-up."[79] Lehrmann received a three-year jail sentence,[80] Hunter eight years,[81] Hills six and a half years,[82] Barrios five years,[83] and Lohmann five years.[84]

Finally, on July 12, 2010, a federal grand jury indicted six officers—Kenneth Bowen, Robert Gisevius, Robert Faulcon, Anthony Villavaso, Arthur Kaufman, and Gerard Dugue—on numerous civil rights violations, usage of firearms, conspiracy to obstruct justice, falsification of statements and witnesses, and conspiracy to commit civil rights violations.[85] The defendants faced the death penalty for some of their crimes.[86] The jury found all defendants guilty on many counts.[87] Little did anyone expect then that these five convictions would be overturned because of misconduct by prosecutors in Letten's office.

OVER-THE-TOP CONDUCT
BECAME THE CURRENCY OF LETTEN'S OFFICE

To understand Letten's team, we must start with the reason that they gained fame. They were seen as the "good guys" tasked with cleaning up the New Orleans criminal justice system. That system was "plagued with inefficiencies and structural barriers that interfered with the fair administration of justice."[88] The structural problems in New Orleans prior to Hurricane Katrina were legendary. As one report concluded:

Before Katrina, almost all criminal justice system agencies in New Orleans faced substantial funding problems and had been repeatedly criticized for weak management. Under the administration of an often poorly functioning criminal justice system, New Orleans was considered one of the most violent cities in the country.[89]

The New Orleans Police Department, jail, and district attorney's office were all criticized by the U.S. Department of Justice.[90] After Hurricane Katrina, all eyes turned to federal law enforcement to step in to support and save a failing criminal justice system. Federal prosecutors criticized the local district attorney's office[91] and entered into consent decrees with the police department[92] and the jail[93] to force changes and to create oversight into practices and procedures they routinely used. In particular, the U.S. Attorney for New Orleans, Jim Letten, was singled out as a great leader.[94]

Letten was a popular crusader against the crooked traditions of Louisiana's public servants.[95] His team was once referred to as "the untouchables,"[96] in honor of the legendary team that took down Al Capone. By 2010, his office had prosecuted more than 230 individuals for public corruption, charged nearly 150 more with Katrina fraud, and pursued hundreds of other felony cases ranging from child pornography to robbery.[97] Letten became a household name. His reputation led to his reappointment by a Democrat even though he was a Republican originally appointed by President Bush. But the Danziger Bridge case tested his leadership team in ways that reveal how important it is to be reflective and critical within the team, particularly in a culture already susceptible to corruption.

Jim Letten's office had earned a reputation for tackling corruption head-on. They had raked in a massive number of convictions, and they began to believe they could do no wrong—a bravado that would ultimately prove the office's undoing. Starting at the top, Letten chose to surround himself with hard-charging prosecutors. Jan Mann, First Assistant U.S. Attorney and chief of the office's Criminal Division, served as Letten's second-in-command. Sal Perricone served as the office's chief litigation counsel, responsible for training lawyers in the office. Rounding out the leadership triumvirate under Letten was Jim Mann, the head of the Financial Crimes Unit and Jan's husband. Prosecutors in Letten's office saw themselves as crusaders on the side of right. A culture of arrogance ensued, pervading the office and driving behavior. With over-the-top attitudes becoming the currency of the office, it is little wonder that leaders in the office began to act as though they were accountable to no one.

In 2012, the extent of Sal Perricone's and Jan Mann's arrogance came to light. It became public that Perricone and Jan Mann had anonymously posted inappropriate and, at times, derogatory comments on NOLA.com about probes the Justice Department was conducting, targets of those probes, actions taken by their colleagues, and conduct of sitting judges. Their comments not only raised questions about the tone Letten had set in the office and the culture of arrogance that had taken hold, but they also upended the convictions of police officers who had killed unarmed civilians on the Danziger Bridge.

The misconduct began to surface in March 2012, during the course of the trial of the five Danziger Bridge defendants. Sal Perricone admitted to making anonymous online posts on NOLA.com, an affiliate of the *Times-Picayune*, under the alias Mencken1951.[98] Defense lawyers in the Danziger Bridge case filed a motion to delay sentencing to await the results of the investigation into Perricone's actions.[99] There were derogatory comments posted under the Mencken1951 alias relating to the Danziger shootings, NOPD, Kaufman, and Kaufman's attorney.[100] Under at least three other monikers, Perricone excoriated local leaders, national politicians, and per-haps most importantly some individuals under DOJ investigation.[101] He also stated that a U.S. district judge "loves killers" and even attacked his friend and boss Letten for "taking credit for other people's work."[102] He wrote 595 comments under the Mencken1951 moniker.[103] Perricone resigned from office on March 20, 2012.[104] In granting a new trial for the five convicted officers, U.S. District Court Judge Kurt Engelhardt denounced the comments and actions of Letten's office as representing "grotesque prosecutorial misconduct." On April 4, 2012, Judge Engelhardt sentenced the four officers involved in the shooting to up to thirty-eight years in prison and the lead investigator involved in the cover-up to up to six years, but not without first commenting on the flaws in the government's case.[105]

Those flaws would ultimately come back to haunt Letten's office. In May, attorneys for Kaufman filed a motion for a new trial or a hearing on the government's misconduct for waging a "secret public relations campaign" depriving Kaufman of a fair trial.[106] Kaufman claimed that prosecutors sought to inflame public opinion against the defendants and failed to investigate possible leaks to the media.[107] One such leak occurred when newspapers announced, at a time when his records were sealed, that Lohmann would plead guilty.[108] Kaufman also pointed to a series of articles about the federal probe, which he believed were meant to inflame the public against the defendants.[109] The motion questioned the frequency of unnamed law enforcement sources in news reports, noting that the prosecutor's "theories of the defendants' guilt, the activities of the grand jury, the identities of targets, and the status of plea negotiations" were all released to the media.[110]

Judge Engelhardt wanted to get to the bottom of these allegations. He ordered the prosecutors to turn over any documents related to whether there was a leak in the office and scheduled a hearing on the motion in June.[111] At the hearing, Jim Letten infamously stated:

I've said this publicly before: Neither I, nor Jan Mann, nor people in positions in authority in our office, to my knowledge (had) any knowledge of, nor did we authorize, nor did we procure or have any knowledge of Sal Perricone anonymously posting comments about cases or anything like that whatsoever until we learned about it in the filing. That is gospel truth.[112]

Apparently, Letten was trying to choose his words carefully. What later came to light was that Jan Mann had admitted to Letten that she, too, had been posting comments online anonymously. She later indicated that Letten desperately wanted to portray Perricone as a lone wolf, but she kept telling him that he could not say that. Interestingly, as Letten asserted "the gospel truth" before Judge Engelhardt, Jan Mann sat in the courtroom and failed to correct his statements or to own up to her own conduct.

In fact, Jan Mann became the point person for defending the government's integrity. At the judge's request, she investigated whether her office could have been the source of any leaks. Judge Engelhardt simply wanted the prosecutors to investigate whether the leak came from their office and to try to identify the source. Letten allowed this to occur. He did not object or suggest that Jan Mann was compromised. On June 27, 2012, Jan Mann submitted a report denying that anyone associated with her office had leaked information, noting that Perricone was never a part of the Danziger Bridge team and did not have information about the plea bargains from her office.[113] The only person reviewing Perricone's conduct was Jan Mann, and she conducted a one-on-one interview with him, not under oath. On July 9, 2012, dissatisfied with this report, Judge Engelhardt ordered production of more documents from the government. He again ordered more production of related emails on August 13, 2012.[114]

By October, Judge Engelhardt decided to take an even more active role. The judge called Perricone into court to testify at a status hearing under oath.[115] Perricone testified to using the pseudonyms HenryLMencken1951, dramatis personae, and legacyusa to make critical comments online. But he denied using or knowing who used a fourth pseudonym: eweman.[116] Mann, who was present at the hearing, never commented about who had actually made comments under that pseudonym.

Then, in November, the bombshell dropped. Jan Mann had been the prosecutor who had used the moniker eweman to post scathing comments on NOLA.com. This information came to light only after a civil lawsuit was filed alleging that Jan Mann was the person behind the eweman alias.[117] The majority of eweman's posts were made alongside Perricone's.[118] On November 6, 2012, Letten told Judge Engelhardt that Mann had admitted to posting comments on NOLA.com but had not admitted to using that name.[119]

Judge Engelhardt held a status conference the next morning at which only Letten appeared.[120] At that conference, former Assistant U.S. Attorney

Michael Magner told the court that he suspected as early as December 2010 that Perricone might be one of the NOLA.com commenters making incendiary attacks on his skills as an attorney.[121] He told a handful of superiors about his concerns, all of whom expressed that they did not want to take the risk that he was wrong and pursue the rumor.[122] He stated that Jan Mann would have known about Perricone as her husband, Jim Mann, a U.S. Attorney serving as a supervisor of the financial crimes unit, was close friends with him.[123] He believed Letten would not have known because he only thought the best of people.[124] A day after the conference, Letten demoted Jan Mann.[125]

On November 26, 2012, Judge Engelhardt issued a scathing order[126] requesting that the Justice Department restart Jan Mann's now-compromised investigation and declaring that the defendant's motion for a new trial could no longer be considered "frivolous."[127] His language was clear, strong, demanding, and incredulous about the U.S. Attorney's office, stopping just short of deeming the prosecutors completely incompetent.[128] He noted that Perricone almost certainly lied when he testified to the court, insulating another Assistant U.S. Attorney "and perhaps other AUSAs" and that Mann had let Letten unknowingly spread falsehoods to the court, an act he called one of "perfidy."[129]

Jim Letten had taken a see-no-evil/hear-no-evil approach. Federal rules bar prosecutors from making extrajudicial comments that could lead to public condemnation of the accused, and that is precisely what members of Letten's team did. Even when it became clear that his leadership team had engaged in this improper conduct, Letten did not make the hard calls or act to root out the wrongdoing in his ranks. Letten resigned in December 2012 after eleven years in his position. He had been the longest-serving U.S. Attorney in the country.[130] Both of the Manns retired in December.[131] By 2012, just two years after his reappointment, Letten's office was in ruins. Letten survived two presidential administrations of different parties but could not survive the misconduct of his own senior lawyers.[132]

The conduct of Jan Mann and Sal Perricone raises critical questions about prosecutorial misconduct, oversight, and behavior. Their belief that they could—and ultimately should—engage in conduct that undermined the integrity of the justice system that they had sworn to uphold suggests that they insulated themselves and failed to challenge each other's thinking and practices. But, as importantly, Jim Letten's leadership style was at fault. He thought the best of his people—which can be laudable—but when external sources raised serious concerns about the conduct of his lawyers, he asked a friend, rather than an outsider, to investigate. When that friend admitted that she too had been engaged in what was clearly unethical conduct herself, he did not act concerned or change his plans. Armed with the information that at least two of his top lawyers had engaged in questionable conduct, he used the power of his office and position to say that no leader had authorized such conduct. Even when forced to act against his friend, Letten merely "demoted" Jan Mann. She was not the subject of an immediate termination order.

LEADERSHIP LESSONS

Both the Christie and Letten scandals teach important leadership lessons that lawyers too often miss or misunderstand.

Insularity leads to insufficient debate and self-criticism.

The sort of insularity that results from leaders who surround themselves with friends and like-minded individuals can lead to a cascading series of leadership failures. Intersectional leaders envision their role as engaging in robust debate about actions they are taking individually and as a team. Without that debate and the self-criticism that flows from holding a mirror up to oneself and analyzing the appropriateness of choices, we may end up with the scandalous consequences that occurred in both New Jersey and New Orleans.

Precisely when things seem easy or there is complete agreement, the leader ought to ask questions about what he or she might be missing.

When an entire team seems to be in complete agreement is the right moment for a leader to question what outcomes the team might be missing. One of the dangers of a leader surrounding himself or herself with like-minded individuals is the inability to spot issues that are more evident from a different life experience or perspective. Had Christie's or Letten's team been required to talk more openly about the choices they were making—checking their own sense that their actions were appropriate—they likely would not have engaged in the conduct in the first place. The tension from healthy disagreement leads to better outcomes.

*Lack of diversity in the team leads to comfort and misplaced confidence
that what you are doing is right.*

Intersectional leadership reminds us that diverse perspectives enhance the
leadership team. When the team must explain or defend choices—and ultimately convince naysayers or be convinced by them—the results tend to
be more thoughtful and defensible. Lack of diversity in a team often creates
unwarranted comfort in the decision-making process and misplaced confidence that decisions have been sufficiently vetted. Look around the room.
If the people in the room look exactly—or even mostly—like you and share
similar credentials and experiences, your team is too narrow. A diverse team
provides the opportunity for robust dialogue prior to the implementation
of a practice or policy. Equally important, it telegraphs the need for candid
review of each of the decisions under review.

*An intersectional leader creates a healthy operating tension that encourages
the team to ask the tough questions.*

A strong and effective leader must set the tone that tough questions will be
asked at every stage. By modeling a process that expects and encourages
challenges, critical analyses, and rigorous review, the leader can build that
process into the fabric of his or her team. Such rigor becomes the currency
in a strong leadership team and ultimately sets the expectation that the entire team will hold each other accountable as they lead.

WHAT EDUCATORS CAN DO

Law schools and educators in practice can better prepare lawyers to address
these issues in the following ways.

*1) Law schools can underscore the value of working with diverse groups
in the first-year curriculum.*

Law professors often advise law students to organize informal groups to help
them study and examine the legal concepts that they are taught in their core
classes. The basic premise is that a study group offers law students a chance
to talk through legal concepts and issues and to gain a level of comfort with
them. The value of the group is that it teaches law students to see issues
from a variety of vantage points and helps them recognize blind spots in
their analyses. If law schools made a point to recommend that law students

actively seek out fellow students from different backgrounds and experiences in forming the group, law students would take a first step toward understanding the learning that can come from diverse points of view.

2) Law schools should ensure faculty diversity, particularly in the first-year required courses.

Faculty in the first-year curriculum powerfully shape law students' impressions of the law and their role in it. Law schools can signal an important message of diversity of thought and experience by intentionally assigning a diverse group of law faculty to each section of the class. That choice conveys to law students that the law school considers their professor to have the substantive knowledge and skill to teach these subjects that are core to a legal curriculum.

3) In practice, coaches or educators can teach lawyers how to assemble diverse teams.

Lawyer-leaders often operate individually. But teaching lawyers the value of working through legal problems as part of a team can help the lawyer see the value of multiple eyes on a particular issue. In creating that team, the lawyer-leader should be encouraged to include lawyers who may have different sets of expertise and different backgrounds and who are willing to challenge the initial instincts of the leader.

4) Coaches or educators in practice should encourage lawyer-leaders to use autobiographical maps in building their teams.

One method for learning the backgrounds of potential team members is to have individuals within the unit develop autobiographical maps of their experiences. Individuals can share traits and experiences that may not seem directly relevant to their role but may ultimately prove helpful in rounding out a team. An autobiographical map is an outline of an individual's experiences, cultural background, professional training, and skill set. The lawyer-leader should look to create a team with a broad set of perspectives and skills gleaned from those maps. The maps allow the leader to track what may be missing from the team's experiences and to add members who bring a different perspective gained from their particular background.

CHAPTER THREE

"A Fish Rots from the Head Down"

Leadership Failures Behind Closed Doors

GREAT LEADERSHIP INCORPORATES OPERATIONAL and inspirational elements. Operational excellence often represents the minimum table stakes for entry into the ranks of leadership. Leaders, including lawyer-leaders, need to possess and demonstrate deep expertise in the substantive work of the office or unit. So it follows that lawyers who exhibit exceptional ability in conducting the organization's legal work can typically expect to be tapped for promotion. Of course, legal expertise does not fully prepare the lawyer for leadership, nor does technical proficiency comprise the entire mandate for the lawyer's leadership function. The lawyer-leader needs to take seriously the inspirational dimension of the role. One way that the lawyer-leader can fulfill that aspect of the role is by establishing a climate in the workplace that reflects and conveys the leader's values and expectations. That inspirational atmosphere can prove valuable in getting the best out of one's people.

Setting the wrong tone can produce the opposite effect. The most dangerous leaders create a toxic environment by condoning or ignoring ethical and operational lapses. How many times have companies celebrated and promoted financially successful leaders while ignoring the fact that they mistreat and belittle their internal teams? More often than not, such leaders not only escape sanction and reprimand for their abusive conduct but actually enjoy organizational recognition. By permitting such leaders to engage in conduct that at once undercuts and devalues the contributions of the teams of people critical both to the organization and to the leader's own success, the organization sends a message too: it values results at any cost. This single message can undermine the culture and conduct of an entire organization or unit. As the old proverb makes plain, the fish rots from the head down. And a rotten head is a rotten body.

Too often, a troubling gap exists between a leader's public image and the person that his or her people routinely encounter. Outward indications of success—meeting business goals or exceeding client expectations, for example—serve as protective cover for bad leadership behavior where it counts: behind closed doors. During the 2008 global financial crisis, the national media featured countless headlines and stories that revealed leaders choosing short-term, flashy outcomes over steady, ethically sound conduct because the potential rewards were so high and the likelihood of being caught was so low. Leaders and the organizations that promoted them had somehow signaled that behaving with integrity was the enemy of success. When these examples of dishonesty and misconduct came to light, everyone rushed to issue vocal and intense condemnations. With the clarity of hindsight, it was plain to see that individual conduct and decision making that occurred out of public view could still have a significant—and sometimes devastating—public effect. And lest we allow ourselves to enjoy the fiction that such conduct is only episodic, we must look at the sorts of individual choices and actions that occur far too frequently with little regard for the broader impacts.

What happens when leaders distort the inspirational aspect of their roles by tapping into their own and their people's baser instincts? When an office engages in misconduct, how should a leader respond to help the office learn from its mistakes? The following examples expose the leadership dilemmas and costs that inevitably occur when a leader distorts his or her inspirational role by appealing to baseness. Each case study explores leadership lapses that occurred when lawyers failed to recognize that leadership involves raising the game of others and encouraging others to be their best and bring their best. The prosecutors in these examples, although mandated to serve as ministers of justice, permit their own biases to pollute the environment in which they lead. They do not see their role as appealing to a higher purpose but instead engage in the sort of low behavior that poisons the climate. Each example reveals that the leader casts a wide shadow. Others within an organization look to the leader for guidance on behavior and values, and if ugly behavior occurs at the top, it will likely spread across the ranks. Indeed, when the lawyer-leader sinks to base behavior, that choice may not only drag others in the team down to that level, but may actually threaten the integrity of a system the leader is expected to serve.

As key actors in the criminal justice system, prosecutors have authority over a rather extensive domain. The success and integrity of the American criminal justice system relies on the prosecutor's ability to assume and balance a dual role: advocate for the state and minister of justice. The advocacy role expects prosecutors to try the government's case against individuals who have violated the law and to be zealous and passionate in that effort. The minister-of-justice role involves seeking justice, which can mean declining to prosecute or dismissing a case where evidence has been seized in violation of the Constitution, for example. How the prosecutor squares these sometimes-competing roles is critical to the proper functioning of the system. But because much of the discretionary activity of prosecutors happens behind closed doors, their conduct too often goes unnoticed and unchecked by the courts or by the public. Wide latitude and very little judicial intervention has allowed prosecutors, individually and collectively, to avoid direct accountability for incidents of prosecutorial misconduct. Ensuring that the behavior of prosecutors adheres to a higher purpose—dispensing justice fairly—requires some degree of attention to the expectations and incentives set by the leaders within the office.

BOTTOM-FEEDING

In 2003, the Harris County (Houston), Texas, district attorney's office hit upon a problem that dirtied the organization from the top down. Some might be inclined to label the problem an ethical lapse, but at its core, the disturbing behavior that spread through the office stemmed from a fundamental leadership failure: The leadership failure in Harris County was the district attorney's decision to lead without integrity and to tolerate and model the basest of behavior. Individual ethical lapses may at times occur during the heated battle of trials and under the pressure to win. But what distinguishes these moral lapses from leadership failures is the extent to which they are encouraged, tolerated, or modeled by leadership. If such behavior occurs, a leader's failure to confront and condemn the conduct sends an implicit message of approval. Policies that leaders explicitly model or implicitly accept make such moral lapses more likely and more pronounced.

The systemic problem is perhaps best exemplified by an officewide email in which prosecutor Mike Trent congratulated his colleagues on winning a case despite the presence of several "Canadians" on the jury.[1] Prosecutors often used the term "Canadian" as a slur for African Americans. Or it could be best demonstrated by the emails that the elected district attorney for Harris County, Chuck Rosenthal, sent out that included a cartoon depicting an African American suffering from a "fatal overdose" of watermelon and fried chicken.[2] But a lack of diversity in the leadership of the office during Rosenthal's tenure as district attorney had set a tone and culture that pervaded and polluted the operations of the office. The depth of the problem became apparent when a civil rights attorney filed a lawsuit on behalf of two brothers, Sean and Erik Ibarra, alleging that police falsely arrested and abused them after they photographed sheriff's deputies searching a neighbor's home.[3] As part of discovery, their lawyer subpoenaed and received several incriminating emails from Rosenthal[4] that contained racist and sexist comments.[5] Perhaps as telling, Rosenthal chose to destroy thousands of other emails rather than allowing their content to become public.[6]

These racist practices occurred in one of the most diverse counties in Texas. But the Harris County district attorney's office neither reflected nor connected with the county it purported to represent. The office did not employ a large proportion of people of color; the few lawyers of color in its ranks spoke of the toxic environment, given the racist tone set by leadership. Black lawyers in the office met with each other during the Rosenthal administration just to discuss and share their experiences in the office. One felony attorney in the office summed up the feelings of being a Black prosecutor amid the culture and atmosphere in the office:

"I was angry, I was depressed, I was sad," said a felony prosecutor.[7] "For us to walk around the office knowing that he (Rosenthal) has pictures of a man laid up with a watermelon and fried chicken saying 'it's an overdose,' I mean, it's like, the morale is almost like, 'Damn, where's my place here?' I mean, I got to go to the barber shop and they look at me like, 'Are you still working at the DA's office?'[8] "At no point in time has he ever sent an e-mail that says, 'You know what, for those of you who work here who are women, who are minorities, who are Black, I apologize.'"[9]

The lawyers of color expressed concern about the White prosecutors who casually made racist jokes.[10] One young prosecutor recounted an offensive encounter with a senior prosecutor in the office. She explained that while sitting in a dimly lit room, she said "hello" to a senior colleague. The young prosecutor had a dark complexion and the senior colleague quipped, "All I see is eyes and teeth. You need to turn the light on, girl."[11]

The lack of diversity in the leadership and the casual disdain leadership expressed toward people of color affected more than internal team dynamics. It affected the nature of the justice the office sought to dispense. One study by University of Maryland criminology professor Raymond Paternoster found that from 1992 to 1999, Harris County prosecutors sought the death penalty for African Americans more than three times as often as they did for Whites with similar cases. Latinos fared even worse—the DAs pushed for capital punishment four times as often for Latinos as they did for Whites.[12] Harris County has executed more people than any other county in the United States. Blacks have accounted for 56 percent of its executions since 1984, though just 19 percent of the county's population is African American.[13]

The Harris County district attorney's office has long been accused of engaging in racist behavior. Indeed, the Reverend William A. Lawson of Wheeler Avenue Baptist Church said, "The overpopulation of our jails and prisons is in some cases due to the way they were prosecuted and he [Rosenthal] has a negative attitude toward minorities, which makes it easier to prosecute Blacks and Latinos."[14] In the context of a discussion about jury selection, city councilwoman Jolanda Jones noted "a pattern of bias against minorities and the poor."[15] Her statement was also alluding to the fact that there is inequality in punishment doled out by the DA's office.[16] Given the correlation between race and capital punishment in Harris County and the revelation of the racist emails sent by Rosenthal, many wondered if the State of Texas should be allowed to execute inmates sentenced to death in Harris County during the Rosenthal administration.[17]

Black lawyers in the office at that time complained of the "subtle pressures to keep minorities off juries as well as a higher level of scrutiny and second-guessing for Blacks than Whites at the same experience level."[18] One Black prosecutor in the office recalled that a supervisor once criticized her during an in-office evaluation for allowing too many people of color on her juries.[19] The written evaluation that followed was a bit more careful, saying she needed to work on the "makeup" of her juries.[20] White lawyers in the office referred to Hurricane Katrina evacuees as "Katrinians" or "NFLs," which reportedly stands for "[N-word] from Louisiana."[21] It was a matter of routine for White prosecutors to speak in condescending tones to Black defendants or to make jokes about them.[22]

This brazen behavior occurred largely out of public view, but its effect was just as pernicious as if it had been performed overtly. Harris County prosecutors engaged in such conduct because they could do so without consequence, knowing it was condoned and engaged in by the top leadership and that they were safe behind the closed doors of their office—doors that were closed and locked by their like-minded supervisor. The toxic tone was set, and this behavior had become part of the culture of the office. A comfort with this sort of behavior also implicated who would be recruited, hired, and promoted in the office. This misconduct not only easily escaped notice or reprimand because it occurred in secrecy with no outside check, but it also became accepted behavior for lawyers within the office. Prosecutors were not disciplined or punished for this behavior.

LEADERSHIP WHEN NO ONE IS WATCHING

As the preceding case makes clear, a core element of upstanding leaders is that they operate with integrity even when they are *not* in the public eye. Behavior that occurs within the confines of an individual office or team, or takes place solely when an individual chooses to engage in conduct that he or she is under no obligation to explain, is hard to uncover and can enable people to behave differently than they would in full view. Internal mechanisms must be developed and maintained as part of office cultures, particularly where the behaviors of public officials happen without external oversight. Leaders within these offices must hold themselves to a higher standard of conduct because that leadership behavior sends an important message—internally and externally. But if inappropriate conduct occurs, the lawyer-leader still has a key role to play. He or she must acknowledge the misconduct and make clear that such conduct will not be tolerated. The action—or lack of action—sends a strong message to the rest of the organization about the types of behaviors that will and will not be tolerated. This lesson becomes part of the organizational culture.

In any discussion of leadership, such scrutiny is key. And, in the context of lawyers' behavior, one example offers us a vehicle to conduct such an investigation into a leader's individual integrity and leadership values: jury selection.

The general public often pays little attention to the selection of the individuals who will decide the fate of someone accused of a crime. In high-profile criminal cases, the media and, consequently, the general public may take notice of the racial and gender makeup of the jury once convened. Largely, though, what draws and holds the public's attention is the trial, not the preliminaries. Meanwhile, any trial lawyer worth his or her salt will tell you that the preliminary stages, such as jury selection, are critical because this is where the lawyer really wins or loses a case. The stakes could not be higher.

When lawyers select juries for trials in the United States, two types of challenges excuse a potential juror from service: challenges for cause and peremptory challenges. Challenging for cause requires the lawyer to ask the presiding judge to dismiss a particular juror based on some evidence that the person cannot be "fair and impartial" in a particular case.[23] The lawyer makes specific arguments, on the record, either referring to the potential juror's answers during voir dire, or to other evidence, provided to both sides, about the background of the juror that arguably disqualifies him or her. The judge then considers these arguments and makes a factual determination, either allowing the juror to continue or disqualifying him or her from the trial.[24] Lawyers typically have an unlimited number of challenges for cause.

With the second type, the peremptory challenge, the lawyer can simply strike a juror from the panel without any explicit reference to the reason for dismissal. Lawyers typically can use only a limited number of peremptory challenges. The peremptory challenge is an example of the discretionary calls a lawyer can make without public scrutiny; trial procedure permits a lawyer to remove a potential juror without explanation, and the public doesn't usually pay attention to this part of the trial anyway. As you might imagine, given the potential for abuse, concerns have surfaced about the impact of such decisions on the fairness of a trial. So courts carefully watch the use

of peremptory strikes by prosecutors in criminal trials, keeping in mind the
equal protection clause of the U.S. Constitution, which holds that individuals are entitled to equal protection under the law.[25] Individuals accused of
a crime may lack the affirmative right to a trial decided only by members
of their own race,[26] but the prosecution cannot exclude members from the
jury on the basis of race.[27]

The seminal case guiding the use of peremptory challenges in the United
States is *Batson v. Kentucky*, decided in 1986.[28] The *Batson* Court took on the
issue of the relationship between the prosecution's peremptory removal of
Black jurors and the equal protection clause.[29] The case involved James
Batson, an African American man accused of burglary and receiving stolen
goods.[30] The lawyer for the government used his peremptory challenges to
strike six jurors, including all four Black members of the jury panel (venire).
Mr. Batson ended up with a jury that consisted of only White jurors.[31] Once
the jury was empaneled and before the trial commenced, Batson's counsel
asked the court to discharge the jury, claiming that the removal of the Black
jurors had violated Mr. Batson's Sixth Amendment right "to a jury drawn
from a cross section of the community" and his Fourteenth Amendment
right "to equal protection of the laws."[32]

The Supreme Court found for Batson. It held that "a state denies a Black
defendant equal protection . . . when it puts him on trial before a jury from
which members of his race have been purposely excluded."[33] The Court recognized the individual impact of the discriminatory exclusion of jurors, noting
that race-based strikes violated a defendant's right to the law's equal protection in "den[ying] him the protection that a . . . jury is intended to secure."[34]
Further, the discriminatory use of peremptory challenges by the prosecutor
deprives an accused of judgment by his peers, a vital safeguard "against the
arbitrary exercise of power by prosecutor or judge."[35] The Court also noted
a broader public impact that implicated the entire justice system. The government's discriminatory use of peremptory challenges acted as a way for officials
to oppress racial minorities and denied defendants their right to protection
against racial prejudice.[36] Indeed, the Court determined that the racially discriminatory use of the peremptory challenge harmed "the entire community"
by "undermin[ing] public confidence in the fairness of our system of justice."[37]

One might be tempted to believe that the *Batson* decision ended this racially discriminatory practice. But it did not. In 2009, the State of North Carolina decided to take further action by passing the Racial Justice Act (RJA).[38] The act provides that "no person shall be subject to or given a sentence of death or shall be executed pursuant to any judgment that was sought or obtained on the basis of race."[39] A key component of the act's provision enabled individuals to challenge a capital prosecution or death sentence if "race was a significant factor in decisions to exercise peremptory challenges during jury selection."[40] Until the passage of the act, much of this improper conduct escaped notice because it remained hidden from view.

The RJA focused attention on two primary decisions within a capital prosecution: the decision to seek the death penalty made by the prosecutor and the decision to impose the death penalty made by the jury.[41] Proof that race improperly influenced these decisions could include statistical evidence, direct testimony, or other evidence. Perhaps most notably, the act made clear that statistical evidence on its own is sufficient to establish that race played a significant factor in the decision. A controversial U.S. Supreme Court decision, *McCleskey v. Kemp*, severely limited the use of general statistical evidence to prove racial bias in an individual capital case; *McCleskey* indicated that it was insufficient to prove that the prosecutor acted with discriminatory purpose. The defendant would need to produce evidence showing that the prosecutor in this case had a discriminatory intent toward this defendant. So the RJA offered individuals facing a death sentence in North Carolina greater protection. The RJA provides for the introduction of evidence that "death sentences were sought or imposed significantly more frequently upon persons of one race," that it was imposed "more frequently as punishment for capital offenses against persons of one race than as capital offenses against persons of another race," or that "race was a significant factor in decisions to exercise peremptory challenges during jury selection."[42] In each of these categories, the RJA makes central the race of the defendant, the race of the victim, or the race of excused jurors.[43]

The chorus of opposition to the RJA was predictable. The North Carolina Republican Party, prosecutors, law enforcement, and victims' advocate groups expressed vocal opposition to the act and periodically seek to repeal or amend it. The principal argument in opposition seems to be that the act increases the difficulty of sustaining a death penalty conviction. In support of their argument, opponents noted that 152 of the 157 people on death row filed claims under the RJA.[44] In 2011, forty-three of forty-four elected North Carolina district attorneys wrote a letter to state senators urging a repeal of the law and claiming that it threatened public safety. The letter cited four reasons to repeal the act. First, prosecutors expressed concern that White inmates were taking advantage of the law. This was an attack on the legislative history suggesting that only inmates of color should be able to invoke the RJA, a curious argument if the signatories were concerned about justice for all inmates. Second, they cited the significant cost of the law. The DAs elevated financial considerations over the alleged racist and illegal conduct that might have led to a conviction. Third, they expressed concern about the legal quagmire the RJA created in the courts. They insisted that certainty of convictions was more important. And fourth, the DAs attacked the RJA because some inmates sentenced to life without parole rather than death might take advantage of its provisions. Here the DAs were arguing that the RJA's provisions could apply to cases beyond death-sentenced inmates who might want the courts to examine whether race had improperly influenced their convictions.[45] Prosecutors never addressed *Batson* or other procedural questions raised by the RJA. What is perhaps telling is that if they had no fear that the lawyers had engaged in race-based practices, there would have been no reason to object to the RJA.

Advocates of the RJA pointed out that opponents of the act greatly exaggerated their claims. Despite the vehemence, the General Assembly actually repealed the law in 2011, but the governor exercised her veto power to keep the law in place.[46] The new law opened a window to the behavior of individual prosecutors because inmates challenging their convictions were entitled to receive information through discovery and to call witnesses at their RJA hearings. More importantly, it illuminated the leadership practices of prosecutor's offices throughout North Carolina. Because of this act, we have evidence through firsthand accounts of the ways that law enforcement leaders addressed issues of race and jury selection, something that rarely if ever had been previously exposed to public scrutiny.

IMPROPER BEHAVIOR BEHIND CLOSED DOORS:
CUMBERLAND COUNTY'S PATTERNS
AND PRACTICES

One case that offers key insights into why lawyer-leaders must develop practices that reinforce integrity checks beyond the public view and emphasize transparency involved a prisoner named Marcus Robinson. Robinson filed a claim under the RJA, and on January 30, 2012, the Superior Court in the County of Cumberland held an evidentiary hearing on the matter.[47] Up to that date, Robinson had pursued an appeal through the conventional appellate process without any substantive change in his status. In 1991, Robinson, an African American, was indicted for the murder of Erik Tornblom. Four years later, a jury returned a verdict of guilty of first-degree murder and, a year later, the court sentenced Robinson to death.[48] On appeal, the Supreme Court of North Carolina found no prejudicial error in the trial or sentencing hearing,[49] and the U.S. Supreme Court denied review. Ordinarily, this would have ended the legal reviews for Robinson, but he had filed a timely motion under the RJA.[50] On April 20, 2012, four months after the evidentiary hearing, the Cumberland Superior Court found that Robinson met his burden under the RJA, proving by a preponderance of evidence that race operated as a "significant factor" in capital cases across the state of North Carolina. Based on a Michigan State University (MSU) study by Professors Barbara O'Brien and George Woodworth, the court found that the average rate per case at which prosecutors in North Carolina struck eligible Black venire members was significantly higher than the rate at which they struck other eligible venire members.[51] Of the 166 statewide cases from 1990 to 2010 with at least one Black venire member, prosecutors struck an average of 56 percent of eligible Black venire members, compared to 24.8 percent of all other eligible venire members.[52]

After giving a background of the case and evidentiary rulings, the court began a statutory interpretation of the RJA, defining key terms and discussing its provisions as a matter of first impression. In determining whether race was a "significant factor," the court examined whether race "had or likely had an influence or effect on decisions to exercise peremptory strikes during jury selection in capital proceedings."[53] The court held that to establish a prima facie case, a defendant "may introduce statistical proof of unadjusted data demonstrating significant racial disparities in prosecutors' peremptory strikes," and once the defendant establishes this, the state must meet its burden of production actually to rebut the defendant's case, "not merely advance a non-discriminatory explanation."[54]

In Robinson's case, the court found that the prosecutor had used nine peremptory challenges: four to excuse White venire members and five to excuse Black venire members. Fifty percent of the Black venire members were peremptorily excused compared to just 14.4 percent of the other eligible venire members. The court reviewed notes and testimony from the RJA hearing process and found that the probability of this occurring in a race-neutral jury selection process was 3.6 in 100. The court found that the prosecutor's disparate strikes against Black venire members affected the final composition of Robinson's jury by reducing the number of Black venire members from three to two. The court held that race "was a materially, practically, and statistically significant factor in decisions to exercise peremptory challenges during jury selection by prosecutors when seeking to impose death sentences in capital cases" at various points in time, including the time of Robinson's trial in 1994 and in Cumberland County between 1994 and 2007.[55] The court also found that "prosecutors have intentionally discriminated against Black venire members during jury selection" when seeking to impose death sentences in capital cases.

In attempting to rebut Robinson's evidence, the state tried to justify its decision to strike African American venire members based on the assertion that the history of discrimination against African Americans as a whole might affect their individual ability to be fair in death penalty cases. This argument "especially troubled" the court.[56] The state supported its decision to strike one African American juror because of her death penalty beliefs. But the court found that the transcript clearly demonstrated that she was laboring under a misunderstanding of the law that had led to her initial views and once the prosecutor clarified the law, the juror indicated that she no longer held any reservations about the punishment.[57] So, the "belief" did not justify the strike. In the hearing, the prosecutor for the state also supported the choice to strike another African American juror because the juror mistakenly believed an eyewitness was necessary to sustain a conviction. The prosecutor failed to probe further or to correct the juror's misunderstanding.

The court found this to be in stark contrast to the trial prosecutor's practices when engaging non-Black members of the panel. When one White member expressed reservations about the death penalty, the prosecutor appropriately followed up on the reservations, made clarifications, and kept the juror. The court found that many of the explanations provided by prosecutors that appeared neutral on their face were actually pretextual or substantively invalid and evinced an intent to discriminate.[58]

In the end, the court rejected the state's arguments, crediting the defendant's presentation of historical, experimental, and case evidence that race was a significant factor in the State's exercise of its peremptory strikes in his case. The court also concluded that Robinson established race as a significant factor in prosecutorial peremptory strikes in Cumberland County, the former Second Judicial Division, and the State of North Carolina, from 1990 to 1995, from 1990 to 1999, and from 1990 to 2010 respectively.[59] Robinson met his initial burden of production through his use of statistical data. He further satisfied this burden of production with anecdotal, experimental, historical, and statistical evidence.[60] The state's rebuttal evidence was insufficient.

A CLOSER LOOK AT THE CULTURE
OF DISCRIMINATION IN THE
NORTH CAROLINA PROSECUTOR'S OFFICE

The Robinson case magnified the light that the RJA had shined on the otherwise hidden practices of the Cumberland County district attorney's office. The RJA continued to provide leverage to individuals to pry open closed doors in their individual cases. Three individuals facing death sentences, Tilmon Golphin, Christina Walters, and Quintel Augustine, filed a motion for appropriate relief and discovery under the RJA in 2010 and received an evidentiary hearing two years later. Golphin and Augustine are African American and Walters is Lumbee Indian.[61] This hearing revealed practices that took root because leaders within the office failed to set the right tone for office conduct and failed to learn from their mistakes.

Each of the petitioners' individual cases raised a claim of race-based decision making in Cumberland County; together they alleged a pattern of race-based jury selection that had come to define death penalty prosecutions in North Carolina. Each petitioner had been convicted of murder and

sentenced to die in the state. Tilmon Golphin, indicted for the murders of
Edward Lowry and David Hitchcock, filed for a change of venue. A jury
was chosen from Johnston County and bused to the trial in Cumberland
County. On April 29, 1998, he was convicted of two counts of first-degree
murder and, less than a month later, the court sentenced him to death. The
North Carolina Supreme Court affirmed his convictions and sentence. The
U.S. Supreme Court denied review. He unsuccessfully challenged his convic-
tions and death sentences in postconviction proceedings in state and federal
court. Christina Walters, indicted for the August 17, 1998, murders of Susan
Moore and Tracy Lambert, faced prosecution in Cumberland County.[62] On
June 30, 2000, a jury convicted her of two counts of first-degree murder
and, days later, the court sentenced her to death for both murders. Finally,
Quintel Augustine, indicted for the murder of Roy Gene Turner Jr. on February 25, 2002, also applied for a change of venue. His case was transferred
to Brunswick County for the trial. On October 15, 2002, a jury convicted
him of first-degree murder, and he, too, received a death sentence.[63] The
North Carolina Supreme Court affirmed his conviction and sentence.[64] Once
again, the U.S. Supreme Court denied review.[65] Although Augustine's case
had been tried in a neighboring county, he used evidence from Cumberland
County to build a case suggesting that an inappropriate reliance on race was
a common practice in North Carolina.

In their request for relief, the petitioners presented comprehensive evidence from experts and introduced scores of exhibits, transcripts, and affidavits of prosecutors.[66] To establish their case, the petitioners offered testimony
by and evidence of individual prosecutors in the petitioners' trials as well as
evidence presented previously in the Robinson case. The court found that
the petitioners, Walters, Golphin, and Augustine, demonstrated that race
constituted a significant factor in decisions to exercise peremptory challenges
in their individual cases and, more generally, in Cumberland County at the
time each of the sentences were sought or imposed. In each of the cases,
the court deemed that the state failed to rebut the petitioners' prima facie
showing and, even if such evidence were sufficient to do so, the defendants
ultimately carried their burdens of persuasion. The court went on to make
additional conclusions of law, including that the state's use of race in peremptory strike decisions in each of the defendants' cases was intentional.

The court vacated the defendants' sentences and resentenced them to life in prison without the possibility of parole.

Let's take a closer look at what led to this important decision. The petitioners' evidence and arguments focused primarily on the conduct of the trial prosecutors: Margaret B. Russ, who prosecuted all three defendants, and Calvin W. Colyer, who prosecuted Augustine and Golphin. The state called John W. Dickson, a former Cumberland County prosecutor, who had tried the Marcus Robinson case.[67] Russ had exercised ten peremptory challenges against Black venire members in the Walters case.[68] Colyer had used his strikes against four Black venire members in the Golphin case and five Black people in the Augustine case.[69] The testimony that was elicited as part of the RJA hearing revealed that Dickson had struck a number of Black jurors in many of the cases that led to the Robinson decision under the RJA. Despite their claims to the contrary, it became clear that race did play a significant role in their decisions to remove jurors from the trial jury.

The state attempted to offer justifications for the strikes of the Black venire members, including affidavits from prosecutors across North Carolina containing supposedly race-neutral explanations for their peremptory challenges. The reasons they offered simply could not withstand scrutiny. In some of these cases, prosecutors' justifications were explicitly based on race, stating that jurors were struck because they were part of the National Association for the Advancement of Colored People (NAACP) or attended historically Black universities, but they rationalized these decisions by claiming that those experiences meant that the juror would have been biased toward the accused. In others, prosecutors singled out Black members for racially charged questioning. Finally, prosecutors attempted to sustain their strikes based on a characteristic clearly inserted as a proxy for race, such as demeanor, lack of intelligence, or lack of community connection. The court ultimately found that the case examples showed that race was "both a significant factor and intentionally employed factor" in the state's use of peremptory strikes in North Carolina, in Cumberland County, and in the defendants' own individual cases.[70]

Perhaps what proved most telling were the trial preparation notes compiled by assistant district attorney Calvin W. Colyer titled "Jury Strikes." Prior to Augustine's trial, Colyer investigated potential jurors, taking six

pages of notes to guide his jury selection in the case. The notes revealed ir-
refutable evidence that race and racial stereotypes played a role in the jury
selection. He made at least three references to jurors by race, describing one
as "blk. wino—drugs," another as "blk/high drug," referring to the juror's
neighborhood, and another as "respectable blk family."[71] He never made
note of the race of any White juror or mentioned anything about a White
juror's residence. While it is customary for prosecutors to keep notes of the
reasons for their strikes, the State offered no explanation about why he only
recorded the race of Black jurors.[72]

Colyer's description of these jurors and others directly contrasted with
his description of White jurors with similar characteristics.[73] For example, he
described one juror as "blk. wino—drugs" when there was no indication in
the juror's background that he had used drugs or had a record of arrests or
convictions for drug-related activity, but described a White potential juror as
"drinks—country boy—ok" when there was information that the juror drank
alcohol. He described another Black juror as a "thug" based on his criminal record, but a White potential juror with a similar criminal record was
described as "n[e'er] do well" in his notes.[74] Dickson claimed that the Black
venire members whom he had struck had certain disqualifying characteristics.
The problem, though, was that he found the same characteristics acceptable
in non-Black venire members. For example, in the Marcus Robinson case,
Dickson exercised a strike against a Black member, in part, he claimed, because the man had been charged with public drunkenness; he had accepted
two non-Black venire members with "driving while intoxicated" convictions.[75]

Colyer's notes concerned a disproportionate number of African Americans, who at the time of Augustine's trial made up just 14 percent of the
county population.[76] Of the fifty-five potential jurors in Colyer's notes for
whom the petitioners could identify a race, more than 40 percent were
African American and nine of the ten neighborhoods he noted were predominantly African American.[77] Colyer recorded these negative comments
about a disproportionately Black group of potential jurors on every page.
The court found the notes to be powerful evidence that these jurors had a
strike against them even before entering the courtroom.[78]

Margaret Russ's testimony in the hearing revealed similar conduct. The
court found that Russ treated venire members differently based on their race.

She struck a Black juror in one theft trial because he had been a victim of a CD player theft, despite the fact that he never reported the crime. But she was willing to empanel non-Black venire members who had been victims of minor property crimes.[79] Russ struck another Black venire member because of his involvement in a church and his personal connection to police officers. But again, she did not find similar connections troubling when it involved White venire members. She did not move to strike non-Black venire members involved in churches and never asked White members about connections to police officers.[80] Russ would not even acknowledge that racial bias was a historic antecedent or an ongoing challenge in North Carolina. She maintained that race was not a significant factor in her juror selection decisions.[81]

In addition to her questionable conduct in trial, Russ also tended to be evasive in response to probes about the reasons for her behavior. Russ claimed to have exercised her peremptory challenges against ten Black venire members because of the "totality of the circumstances" or because of some unspecified nonverbal communication the potential juror made. Russ freely admitted that there was not a higher incidence of objectionable demeanor among African Americans as compared to Whites, but the frequency with which she claimed that objectionable demeanor accounted for her strikes led the court to discredit such demeanor as a valid explanation. The court found Margaret Russ to be utterly incompetent as a witness[82] because she gave misleading testimony, claimed a lack of any independent or helpful recollection of her own strikes, and made misrepresentations about her own actions. The court actually found "her testimony unpersuasive and unhelpful to the fact-finding process" because of her complete failure to remember the case.[83]

Russ had already been reprimanded by trial and appellate state courts for her actions as a prosecutor. In one case, she made a false comment to the jury. The trial judge sustained an objection to her conduct and an appellate court found that her comment was "calculated to mislead or prejudice the jury."[84] In another case, *State v. Parker*, there was a judicial finding that Russ violated *Batson*.[85] She attempted to strike a Black venire member and offered pretextual reasons for the strike, including that the potential juror was close in age to the defendant. But the court pointed out that she had already approved and seated a non-Black juror with the same birthday as the defendant.[86]

When questioned about both cases by the defense in this RJA action, Russ vehemently denied any wrongdoing in both cases despite these rulings.

The failure by the leadership in the county district attorney's office to monitor or discipline those individual lawyers against whom courts had made findings of intentional discrimination in violation of *Batson* enabled and encouraged the behavior of prosecutors like Russ, Colyer, and Dickson. The court found it significant that the Cumberland County DA's office never undertook any post-*Batson* training to examine prejudices but did have seminars for prosecutors focused on "evading *Batson*." Although Russ denied ever attending a course that taught prosecutors how to withstand *Batson* challenges, North Carolina Bar records reflected that she had attended the seminar and received continuing legal education credit for it.[87] Moreover, Russ's proffered explanations for striking juror members closely tracked a handout given at that training session. She claimed that the strikes she made were based on age, attitude, body language, or juror responses.[88] Her testimony even reflected the language of the handout when she argued these were "*Batson* justifications and articulable reasons."[89]

The behavior and evasions by the prosecutors in the Cumberland County office reveal the consequences of leadership that neither sets a good example nor learns from the mistakes it makes. The office developed a "culture of indifference to the discrimination against African American citizens in jury selection" that affected and infected its decisions. In the RJA hearings, the court found that "the resistance to Batson on the part of Cumberland County prosecutors is a monumental stumbling block to progress and change. Only by acknowledging discrimination against African Americans can we expect to create a justice system where all citizens are truly equal under the law."

LEADERSHIP LESSONS

Both the Harris County and Cumberland County district attorney examples offer important lessons for lawyer-leaders that apply not only to government lawyers but to lawyer-leaders in all contexts. Intersectional leadership teaches that much of what occurred could have been avoided had the district attorneys in each county understood that their leadership role involved conducting themselves with integrity—doing the right thing for the right reasons—even when they were acting behind closed doors. The lawyers in these counties thought no one was watching, so they could easily get away with improper behavior. Leaders adhering to an intersectional leadership framework would have put in place systems of checks and balances that created an expectation that the behavior of these leaders would be discussed, questioned, and debated. If these leaders, for example, had assembled diverse leadership teams with the directive to raise question about policy choices, these leaders would have had to explain and justify their conduct in the face of likely tough questions and criticism.

Of course, the extreme behavior in Harris and Cumberland counties raises the question of whether these particular leaders would have been open to an intersectional leadership framework. Perhaps not, once they had experienced the power that often attends a leadership position and had found ways to insulate themselves and their choices from scrutiny. But had the work of teaching these lawyers what it means to lead effectively begun in law school, they might have learned earlier the role and responsibility of a true leader.

Still, there are leadership lessons that we can glean from these examples.

At its core, leadership involves deliberately cultivating the strengths and capabilities of their team members to enable them to show up as the best versions of themselves.

Lawyers should understand that they operate within ethical boundaries that exhort them to behave morally, with respect for individuals, and with an awareness of the situations that skew judgment. Lawyer-leaders may not always be in situations that fall directly within the literal boundaries of ethics codes and rules of professional responsibility, but they have an obligation to adhere to a set of values that invites and encourages others to bring and be their best. This means recognizing and rewarding the sort of behavior that raises the level of conduct within the team rather than lowers it to its base. By cultivating strengths and demonstrating that base behavior will not be rewarded or tolerated, the intersectional leader can shape the conduct of his or her team and the values of the organization. As importantly, the leader's behavior serves as a model for others to follow. Were the lawyers in these counties following the mandates of intersectional leadership, they would have recognized that a leader's personal behavior—bad or good—is amplified within the organization he or she leads. Everything a leader says, does, or fails to do underscores those sorts of behaviors that he or she believes are appropriate. So working consistently to be his or her best so that others bring their best sits at the core of effective leadership. The goal is to act with integrity, to articulate a higher purpose, and to demand that the organization strive to meet the highest standards of behavior by giving a clear message of repercussions when they do not.

Lawyer-leaders must develop practices that serve as an integrity check on acts carried out beyond public view.

Lawyers often make decisions in roles that are veiled by secrecy. The prosecutor's role is perhaps one of the more obvious examples of this because much of their work occurs behind closed doors. If a prosecutor fails to disclose exculpatory evidence to the defense, that misconduct may never surface. Or if a prosecutor delays disclosure of such information, it may take luck to discover that. But this ability to engage in unscrupulous conduct that may escape notice or sanction is not limited to prosecutors. Lawyers routinely operate in the background of key decision making affecting a broad set of interests. Because there is often little oversight of such decisions or actions, the lawyer, as an intersectional leader, must establish a set of routines and practices that help him or her guard against base behavior and lead to principled behavior. This obligation is amplified because a failure to set such guidelines for oneself as a leader can trickle down to others within an organization and encourage them to engage in questionable conduct because of the belief that no one will know.

Leaders cast a broad shadow that sets a tone and shapes a culture.

The values, shared assumptions, and beliefs within an organization contribute to that organization's unique environment and govern how people within it behave. Had the leaders in these two counties been alert to their roles as intersectional leaders, they would have recognized that their behavior cast a shadow across the unit. Others within the office watch the leader and take cues about their behavior from his or her conduct. The leader's people understand what the leader values often by observing how the leader spends his or her time, what he or she rewards, and what he or she questions. The team discerns priorities and principles of conduct from the leader's behavior. Consequently, patterns of misbehavior can often be traced to the top.

Learning from mistakes must be a guiding principle.
Today's leaders cannot be all-knowing, but they can and must demonstrate the value of taking responsibility for mistakes and then learning from them. When lawyer-leaders admit that they have made errors and surface those mistakes, it creates an environment where others are less likely to hide the errors they have made. The lawyer-leader can use these teachable moments as opportunities to set a new direction if it becomes apparent that many have been making the same or similar mistakes. Learning as a group and committing to a different set of behaviors can be powerful tools of change. As a corollary, the lawyer-leader should adopt the practice of sharing credit when things go well and shouldering the blame when things do not.

WHAT EDUCATORS CAN DO

Law schools and educators in practice can better prepare lawyers to address these issues in the following ways.

1) Lawyering courses should teach integrity as a core value of the profession.
Lawyering courses, which are part of the core curriculum, typically focus on teaching the basic capabilities lawyers will need in practice—skills of legal research, legal writing, advocacy, and negotiation. But lawyering courses have a greater opportunity that is often missed: helping to shape the law student's understanding of his or her identity as a lawyer. By adding a component that underscores the importance of acting with consistency in the public and private aspects of a lawyer's role, lawyering courses could begin to set this expectation for practice.

2) Educators and coaches in practice must underscore the value of transparency.
Too often, we think of transparency as an uneasy by-product of greater access to information: technology enables us to discover and learn information that might once have escaped notice. Emails, internal conversations, and offhand remarks can be captured and revealed through hacking, recordings, and photographs of conduct that might otherwise have been kept secret. But rather than thinking solely of the dangers of transparency, educators and coaches could use it to underscore the value of being the type of leader whose positions would not be undermined by such a release of information because his or her behavior is consistent and value-driven.

CHAPTER FOUR

Getting the Balance Right

Personal Ambition vs. the Greater Good

LAWYER-LEADERS FACE A RANGE of leadership challenges that flow from an obligation to balance competing interests. Sometimes these conflicts are inherent in the role. As the previous chapter observed, the public prosecutor must find ways to balance his or her role as an advocate for the state with the greater role as a minister of justice. Those dual obligations create opposing pulls that demand some effort to be held in balance. The friction intrinsic to the roles lawyer-leaders undertake will be explored further in Chapter Six, as we examine the general counsel's role. But this chapter focuses on a variation of this balancing problem that quite often goes unnoticed. It explores the tensions and challenges a lawyer-leader faces when he or she has skin in the game. Specifically, the choices a leader makes when his or her actions have the potential to impede a personal, professional, or political goal reveal much about the leader's judgment, commitment and *values*. In essence, this chapter asks, "How can a leader create guideposts or structures to help him or her when personal interests and greater goals collide?"

Law schools rarely pose or answer this question. Lawyers receive little, if any, training or preparation for this eventuality. Conventional legal pedagogy does not spend much time exposing students to professional ethics and virtually no time examining questions of morals. This dilemma would tend to be viewed as falling well outside the realm of training in professional responsibility. But it is a key part of leadership training that law schools ought to address. Two important reports on legal education, the MacCrate report and the Carnegie report, strongly urged law schools to undertake the task of teaching specific professional and fundamental values.[1] However, neither report addressed how to convince law school faculties to overcome their deep objections to teaching values. While some law schools have taken the suggestions to teach values seriously in recent years,[2] most have avoided addressing the issue altogether. In reality, the avoidance of any meaningful discussion of adding values to a legal education has led to what some describe as the "moral neutering" of students.[3] Training students to think like lawyers has come to mean only that students learn to develop and defend arguments in support of any position, regardless of the student's values or personal beliefs. There is no space devoted to a discussion or analysis of the ways values can affect your decision making and positions.

The legal academy has advanced four principal reasons for its refusal to change the curriculum on this specific issue. First, law schools espouse the view that a legal education does not need to teach values because values are simply *not a necessary component of legal education*. The rationale here is that legal pedagogy and the case method help develop students' character and "moral imagination" by making them focus on the greater good.[4] Second, opponents of teaching the values of promoting justice argue that because lawyers work for the public good, teaching morals in general is unnecessary. They contrast lawyers with businesspeople, suggesting, somewhat disingenuously, that lawyers do not work in their own self-interest.[5] Third, opponents argue that values quite simply cannot be taught. The focus on facts and shifting circumstances are meant to teach students to become proficient at examining and analyzing facts, statutes, and judicial opinions. And finally, a fourth argument emanates from a critical perspective and worries about which values will be taught.

Let's explore each in turn. The first perspective claims that teaching values is unnecessary to the study, understanding, and practice of law. The process of analyzing cases and examining legal issues from a variety of vantage points helps law students discern the underlying values. Or so the argument goes. But this claim flies in the face of lived experience for so many law students. Supreme Court Justice Ruth Bader Ginsburg captures quite eloquently the prevailing experience in this story from her experience as a first-year student at Harvard Law School. In one of the core first-year courses, a case discussed a particular tactic used by one of the lawyers. This tactic left one law student somewhat "bothered and bewildered."[6] The student asked the professor, "But what about ethics?" and the professor responded, "Ethics is taught in the second year."[7] The unintended result of such an exchange may be that law students see little harm in putting off even thinking about the tough ethical decisions.[8] Most law school professors view legal questions and ethical questions not only as distinct but severable. Rounding out this perspective is the contention that the focus of a legal education ought to be on legal doctrine, and any requirement that professors include other matters—such as material on ethics—means the loss of time for and attention to the *necessary* parts of the curriculum.[9]

These arguments miss the point. Discussions of values are not a distraction but are foundational to the actual understanding of legal doctrine. Legal doctrine is not neutral or objective. It reflects and imposes a set of norms embraced by the electoral majority and imposed on the rest. Recognizing the interplay between values and the law is a key component of understanding the reach and implications of the doctrines law schools teach. Justice Ginsburg's story points out that law professors can be flippant about ethics. But it also suggests that issues of morals and competing values can help students understand not only the behavioral choices facing the lawyer but the doctrine itself. Doctrine will always be important, but as law schools continue to claim that they are preparing law students for the profession, it is important to consider what public and private employers seek in candidates. Prospective employers certainly expect that students will have a working knowledge of doctrine and a genuine understanding of the tools to access, use, develop, and comprehend the law.[10] But they also expect law graduates to come with competency in skills and other professional qualities enabling them to exercise the judgment that legal practice demands.[11]

The second position against teaching values in law school contends that because law schools prepare graduates to work for the public good—no matter what area of practice they choose—there is little need to address the sort of self-interested concerns that might arise if legal education sought to prepare students for business careers. This supposed business/profession dichotomy reflects an outdated view of the practice of law: legal work involves both. The practice of law includes components that carry standards and expectations undergirding the professional obligations. Law practice is also

very much a business with the financial considerations and personal challenges inherent in any business context. The business of lawyering occurs
not only in the private sector but also in the public sector. Lawyers in the
public interest, government, business, and private practice must understand
the business they are in—the mandate, the needs and expectations of clients,
the various indicia of success—if they intend to thrive in that practice. The
notion that lawyers are somehow professionally exempt from the tensions
and personal interests of business seems, at best, fanciful.

Third, opponents to values teaching insist that values simply cannot be
taught. They maintain that "legal ethics, like politeness on subways . . . or
fidelity in marriage" cannot be engendered through classroom moralizing
because ethical conduct springs from a more deeply rooted value system.[12]
There is a corollary to this argument, suggesting that postgraduate ethics
instruction promises too little, too late.[13] By the time students attend law
school, they are older and more mature, and life experiences have already
shaped their worldviews. In other words, they are fully formed beings with
relatively coherent and stable sets of values. Trying to teach values at this
point seems to be at once useless and a waste of a professor's precious time.[14]
But, as Professor Deborah Rhode, a leading scholar in the area of legal
ethics, makes clear, research on ethics education finds that moral views and
strategies continue to change through early adulthood and that education
can enhance moral judgment in specific situations.[15]

Others suggest that even if professors can have an impact in teaching
values, such instruction cannot adequately prepare law graduates for real-
world moral quandaries given that conduct is highly situational.[16] But values
discussions are not intended to mandate a particular answer to a dilemma.
These discussions should model a process of airing issues and sorting through
tensions in order to consider what course of action is most in keeping with
a lawyer's moral mandate. If law schools do not prepare their students to
practice considering and addressing the ethical and moral dilemmas that can
arise, the first time those students face these challenges will be in practice,
when the stakes are quite high and they may have an acutely vested interest
in the outcome. To develop an understanding of the issues, law students need
to be exposed, well before such a moment, to the crucial issues of profes-

sional responsibilities and the complex trade-offs between competing values and professional standards.[17]

Which leads us to the final objection: Whose values will we teach? Even professors who support teaching ethics and values worry about unintentionally instilling their own personal beliefs in students. Opponents use that concern as a justification for refusing to teach values at all.[18] But teaching students to identify when values are competing and the various frameworks they might employ to exercise judgment when the decisions are value-laden is not a question of one set of ethics versus another. Ultimately, to prepare lawyers to assume leadership roles, law schools need to teach that leadership is value-laden and value-driven. When lawyer-leaders make decisions, they must take steps to understand the positions of all stakeholders their decision will affect. They must consider the short-term objectives and the long-term implications. They must be comfortable that they have surfaced and explored the range of reactions, harms, and benefits. Teaching values is not about dictating a single answer. It is about helping students gain comfort with a process that *exposes* the dilemmas and does not ignore them.

The fact that so many lawyers seek elected office makes this aspect of a legal education all the more important. Most lawyers seek elective office out of a higher sense of duty and a commitment to public service. With the increasing politicization of elective office, an increasing number of decisions taken in office not only affect the larger public but also can enhance or derail the elected official's career trajectory. How lawyers lead at that intersection tells us much about the leader's character, commitment, and values.

This chapter includes two such crossroads, where momentous public decisions collided with the lawyer-leader's personal ambition. The first examines sentencing decisions by a judge seeking reelection. It explores the leadership challenges and lapses when the leader's continued political career hangs in the balance. The second examines a famous clemency decision by then-governor Bill Clinton, whose decision making in the case was undoubtedly influenced by his ambition to be president. In both the sentencing and clemency decisions, the lawyer-leader must exercise careful judgment, weighing a host of factors. Because these are such weighty decisions, it is not at all surprising that they test the decision maker's values. But we rarely, if ever, discuss the influence and power of the lawyer-leader's personal stake in the outcome. The failure to prepare the lawyer-leader for this sort of decision making is surely at least partly responsible for the problems that ensue.

THE ELECTION EFFECT

Countless studies have made the case that judges seeking reelection tend to impose longer and harsher sentences. The correlation is particularly glaring in the context of capital cases where the judge must make the choice between life and death. Research reveals that proximity to reelection makes judges more likely to affirm death sentences and even to override jury recommendations for life imprisonment in order to impose the death penalty. According to one study, the election effect is a stronger variable in determining outcomes in a death penalty case than state politics or the race of the accused.[19] Findings indicate that "justices behave much more strategically than originally believed" and that "basic self-interest" may be "an important consideration to the state supreme court justice when rendering decisions."[20] As Supreme Court Justice John Paul Stevens remarked in a dissent for a capital case, "Judges who covet higher office—or who merely wish to remain judges—must constantly profess their fealty to the death penalty."[21] The issue, here, is not whether a judge should impose a death sentence. The leadership issue in play involves the need for the leader to recognize and acknowledge that personal interests can powerfully influence—and alter—the leader's perception of even the gravest decisions.

The appeal of a death sentence in the case of Ashford L. Thompson presented this issue for Ohio Supreme Court Justice Judith L. French. The Ohio Supreme Court unanimously affirmed Thompson's conviction for the aggravated murder of police officer Joshua Miktarian during a traffic stop. But the court split 4–3 in favor of imposing a sentence of death. Ohio is a state that elects its high court judges, and two of the four judges who voted to uphold the death penalty were in the middle of campaigns to retain their seats. Justice French was one of the two judges.

Justice French had been originally appointed by Governor John Kasich to complete the unexpired two-year term of a retiring judge. This meant that at the time of the Thompson case, she was engaged in her first election and was fighting for her political survival. To retain her seat, Justice French, a Republican, had to compete against Judge John P. O'Donnell, a moderate Democrat, who was also vying for the high court position. Justice French did everything she could to present herself as a conservative "tough on crime" candidate. This had proven an effective strategy in many judicial elections in Ohio. In a political rally at which she introduced Governor Kasich, Justice French made clear that her decisions would be consistent with party politics. She announced to the crowd:

Let me tell you something: The Ohio Supreme Court is the backstop for all those other votes you are going to cast. Whatever the governor does, whatever your state representative, your state senator does, whatever they do, we are the ones that will decide whether it is constitutional; we decide whether it's lawful. We decide what it means, and we decide how to implement it in a given case. So, forget all those other votes if you don't keep the Ohio Supreme Court conservative.[22]

In her campaign material and appearances, Justice French referred to herself as "Judge Judi," seeking to capitalize on the popularity and appeal of Judge Judy, the tough-talking, no-nonsense judge who presides over small-claims disputes on television. Television advertisements extolling candidates as "tough on crime" have a significant effect on elections. That month, American Freedom Builders bought about $600,000 in advertisements for French. American Freedom Builders is a conservative "limited government advocacy group" pursuing politically conservative goals that include the following: "American Freedom Builders was founded to educate and advocate for constitutional principles of limited government and free market economic solutions. We firmly believe in the axiom that less government equals more freedom."[23] The organization launched a commercial reminding voters that French was "tough" and praising her for a previous vote upholding a death sentence. In the same month the advertisement ran, Justice French issued the opinion of the court in the Thompson case. Thompson's lawyers have since asked the U.S. Supreme Court to throw out the Ohio Court ruling arguing, in part, that it was "basically impossible" for Justice French to vote against a death sentence when she was being lauded in her election campaign for imposing death sentences.

The sharp division in the court on the decision regarding whether to impose the death penalty seems to have centered on whether this case, while tragic, presented the sort of aggravated circumstances that warranted capital punishment. Briefly stated, the facts are as follows. In July 2008, Thompson and his girlfriend, Danielle Roberson, went for a drink at a local bar. An hour or two later, Thompson and Roberson drove home. Officer Miktarian followed Thompson's car because he was playing music loudly; he followed Thompson into his driveway for violating the noise ordinance. Miktarian told dispatch that he was engaging in a traffic stop and learned from dispatch that Thompson had a license to carry a concealed weapon. According to Roberson, Officer Miktarian approached the car and asked, "Why are you running through my city with all that boom, boom, boom. I ought to rip all this [s . . .] out of your car." Roberson then explained that Officer Miktarian slammed Thompson onto the hood of his car and the officer reached for his side. The next thing she heard was gunshots, and the officer had been shot four times in the head. In writing for the court, French made clear that a death sentence was appropriate given the facts. Justice William O'Neill, one of the three dissenting judges, did not agree that this was the sort of aggravated murder typically reserved for a death sentence. Instead, he maintained that this event involved a routine traffic stop that went terribly wrong. The dissent further insisted that the death penalty was not warranted given Thompson's lack of a record and law-abiding background. Thompson's conduct seemed totally out of character for a person who had attended college, had worked as a licensed practical nurse, and had no arrests. The opinion upholding the death penalty in Thompson's case was issued on October 29, 2014. Six days later, French was reelected with 56 percent of the vote.

While many factors may have influenced Justice French's decision to vote in favor of the death penalty in a sharply divided court, one source of influence was quite clearly her retention election. What should she have done? When a judge has a personal stake in an outcome, there are options available to forestall improper behavior. For example, she could have recused herself from the decision in the case given the competing interests in play. Such a position might also have proven politically difficult. At the very least, she could have revealed or acknowledged this conflict of interest and addressed it in court with her colleagues. Even indicating an awareness of the appearance of a conflict would have been appropriate and helpful. But that open acknowledgment of the significant personal considerations in play never occurred, likely because she considered such an acknowledgment to be political suicide.

THE RECTOR CASE

One of the least examined tests of leadership at the intersection of ambition and politics is when the executive branch decides whether to grant clemency to a convicted person. By its nature, the choice to extend mercy through a pardon poses difficult balancing questions for the governor or the president. While all executive decisions invite and encounter political and public scrutiny that can prove perilous for the executive, clemency decisions require a level of moral courage in the face of political expediency. Precisely because it is such a profound act of mercy—and likely to be unpopular—the clemency decision offers critical insights into decision making when the choice impacts the decision maker personally. It is against this backdrop that we examine then-governor Bill Clinton's choices and actions in the case of Ricky Ray Rector.

On the eve of the New Hampshire presidential primary in 1992, Clinton was falling behind in the polls. Back home in Arkansas, Rector was scheduled for execution. Clinton's record on crime up until that point was considered an electoral liability. When he had sought reelection for a second term as governor, he had lost, at least in part, because of a perception that he was too soft on crime.[24] So Clinton interrupted his campaigning in New Hampshire to fly home to preside over the execution of Rector. The governor's presence was not required or usual,[25] but Clinton desperately wanted to appear tough on crime.[26]

Events leading up to that execution were both complex and disturbing. On March 21, 1981, Rector fired several shots outside a nightclub after the club had refused entry to one of his friends. The shots killed Arthur Criswell, the bouncer, and wounded two other men.[27] Police searched for Rector for two days. Ultimately, Rector's family convinced him to surrender to an officer, Robert Martin, whom he had known since childhood. When Officer Martin went to Rector's mother's home, as he had arranged with Rector, Rector came into the living room and exchanged a few words with Martin. But when Martin turned his back, Rector drew his pistol and shot him, fatally wounding the officer. Immediately after, Rector attempted suicide, shooting himself in the head. The bullet entered and destroyed Rector's frontal lobe. Rector was left an utterly changed person.

His self-inflicted brain injury had the same effect as a prefrontal lobotomy, causing mild retardation and a lack of emotional understanding.[28] He had an IQ of about 70 and was capable only of engaging in repetitive actions, without emotion.[29] Rector had such limited appreciation of his circumstances that he did not even understand that he had shot himself.[30] Rector asserted several times that he had been in the hospital for surgery on his foot. He maintained this to be the case even after being reminded that he had a scar on his head.[31] His attorneys informed the court that when they spoke with Rector, he sounded like he was repeating what someone else had told him to say. One attorney who represented Rector for the full ten years noted that there was never a friendship between Rector and himself because there was "no one to have a friendship with." One of his other attorneys further explained that Rector just was not there.[32] The doctor who performed the surgery to remove the bullet from Rector's brain told Rector's lawyer and sister that Rector's brain injury had rendered him incompetent and that he could not in any way assist his attorney in his defense.[33] The doctor assumed Ricky would remain institutionalized for the rest of his life.

The trial court saw the issue differently. The court held two separate hearings to determine Rector's competency to stand trial for both murders.[34] Several experts testified for both sides. One of the prosecutor's experts never examined the surgical report, and another reviewed it the morning of his testimony.[35] But the prosecution maintained that Rector was competent to stand trial. One of their experts asserted that Rector was giving a "performance" and faking his mental incapacity. The judge found the evidence "hopelessly in conflict" but still found Rector competent both times.[36] Rector proceeded to trial for each case separately. In September 1981, Rector was convicted and sentenced to life imprisonment for the murder of Arthur Criswell.[37] The Supreme Court of Arkansas upheld that decision on appeal.[38] Then, in November 1982, Rector was convicted of Officer Martin's murder[39] and received a sentence of death.[40]

Rector's lawyers challenged his convictions and sentences in the state supreme court and the federal courts, arguing that he had been incompetent to stand trial and that his mental condition legally prevented him from execution by the state.[41] But the courts were not persuaded and instead upheld Rector's convictions and sentences.[42] In its decision, the Arkansas Supreme Court relied on the fact that Rector's mental condition occurred *after* the crime was committed.[43] The court made clear that this was a not a legal matter but instead was a matter to be considered by then-governor Bill Clinton in exercising the executive clemency function:

In our opinion such circumstances arising after the crime affect the matter of clemency and should properly be addressed to the Governor, who has the facilities for investigating all the facts. Although we may reduce a death sentence to life without parole, and have done so in the past, that action is taken as a matter of law, not as an act of clemency.[44]

One of Rector's attorneys now believes that this was the Arkansas Supreme Court's implicit attempt to call the governor to action to rectify a decision that embarrassed them.[45] The U.S. Supreme Court also refused to grant Rector relief.[46] Justice Thurgood Marshall dissented from the decision to deny Rector a hearing. In dissent, Justice Marshall expressed genuine concern about the state's intention to execute someone who did not understand what was occurring:

The lower courts clearly erred in viewing *Ford* [*v. Wainwright*] as settling the issue whether a prisoner can be deemed competent to be executed notwithstanding his inability to recognize or communicate facts showing his sentence to be unlawful or unjust. Although the Court in *Ford* did emphasize the injustice "of executing a person who has no comprehension of why he has been singled out and stripped of his fundamental right to life," the Court stressed that this was just one of many conditions that were treated as rendering a prisoner incompetent (or insane) at common law. Indeed, the Court quoted with approval Blackstone's discussion of this topic, which clearly treats as a bar to execution a prisoner's inability to recognize grounds for avoiding the sentence: "[I]f, after judgment, [a capital prisoner] becomes of nonsane memory, execution shall be stayed: for peradventure, says the humanity of the English law, had the prisoner been of sound memory, he might have alleged something in stay of judgment or execution."[47]

After the Supreme Court's failure to grant relief, Rector's lawyers had only one course left—an application to then-governor Bill Clinton for a commutation of Rector's death sentence to life imprisonment based on his mental state. Rector's fate would be decided at the intersection of empathy, politics, and one man's ambition to be president.

Bill Clinton returned to Arkansas for Rector's execution day amid a growing controversy over Gennifer Flowers, a woman alleging a twelve-year sexual relationship with Clinton.[48] The media frenzy over his extramarital conduct threatened to derail his campaign. Although Clinton had claimed to return to Arkansas to address the issue of Rector's execution, he actually stayed in meetings all day discussing the "Gennifer Flowers issue" with his staff.[49] Rector's lawyers complained repeatedly in messages left for the governor that despite Clinton's stated intent for returning to Arkansas, he would not take their calls.[50] Finally, when one of Rector's lawyers took that complaint to the press, Clinton spoke with him briefly. In the call, the lawyer described to Clinton why the higher courts had denied the appeal and explained the absurdity of the initial competency findings given that Rector was, in the lawyer's words, "a zombie." The phone call ended without any resolution.[51] Several others talked to Clinton on the issue, including various religious leaders. In one such conversation, Clinton told the Reverend Jesse Jackson that he had researched the issue and there was no way around it: doctors had declared Rector competent.[52] There was a delay in the execution for Rector, and another religious advisor had the chance to speak with Clinton to urge him to grant clemency. But the conversation ended up focusing more on the Gennifer Flowers controversy than the issues involved in the Rector execution.[53]

From all of the evidence, it is painfully clear that Rector was severely mentally disabled at the time of his execution. The death-watch log maintained by prison guards included their observations of his behavior that day.[54] The log entry for January 21, 1992, described Rector as "dancing in his cell. . . . Howling and barking while sitting on his bunk . . . walking back and forth in the Quiet Cell snapping his fingers on his right hand and making noises with his voice like a dog."[55] The *New Yorker*, in 1993, noted that the death-watch log was "sedulously kept," and that Rector had exhibited this sort of odd behavior for the preceding ten years.[56] Rector's family repeatedly testified that Rector had been troubled and solitary and likely had a learning disability even before he committed the murders.[57] But perhaps the clearest indication of his mental disability came at the conclusion of Rector's final meal. Rector had not eaten the slice of pecan pie that he had been served. When asked the reason, he indicated that he was "saving it for later." To make matters worse, the execution team took fifty minutes to find a suitable vein to insert the lethal injection. Rector, not understanding what was happening to him, helped them in their task.[58]

At the time of the Rector execution, the constitutionality of executing individuals who were mentally disabled was not yet settled. Ten years later, the U.S. Supreme Court would decide *Atkins v. Virginia* and would categorically ban the execution of individuals with intellectual disabilities, stating that such executions violate the Eighth Amendment's ban against cruel and unusual punishment. Interestingly, the Court chose to leave to the states the power to define the standard for intellectual disability. But under *Atkins*, Rector's life would likely have been spared.[59] Of course, then-governor Clinton was not expected to foresee this change in the law. But close analysis of Clinton's actions and choices reveals with clarity that he was privileging his personal agenda rather than taking the path that might have been more in keeping with the public good, or even his own values. But it would have presented additional political obstacles.

Clinton's behavior as candidate-governor undoubtedly influenced his perception of the role of executive clemency when he became president. While state governors have routinely injected politics into the clemency decision-making process, perhaps nowhere has the intersection of personal ambition and moral responsibility in executive clemency been starker than in the office of the presidency.

In general, the use of federal executive clemency power has significantly decreased in the past forty years. Between 1932 and 1980, over a hundred federal executive pardons were granted each year; in some years more than three hundred pardons were granted.[60] However, during the entire eight years of President Ronald Reagan's administration, he pardoned 393 individuals and commuted thirteen sentences.[61] During the Clinton administration, standards for obtaining a pardon were made more stringent. Commutation petitions were typically considered not likely to be granted during the Clinton administration.[62] Margaret Colgate Love, during her time as pardon attorney under President Clinton, was directed to "deny all commutation petitions except those in which a member of Congress or the White House had expressed an interest."[63] In addition, regulations enacted in October 18, 1993, still in effect today, codified standards for clemency petitions that include waiting periods.[64] These regulations state that "no petition for pardon should be filed until the expiration of a waiting period of at least five years after the date of the release of the petitioner from confinement or, in case no prison sentence was imposed, until the expiration of a period of at least five years after the date of the conviction of the petitioner."[65]

President Bill Clinton granted clemency in the last years of his term by giving pardons related to unjust prosecutions and also awarding pardons in several political cases. He posthumously pardoned Henry Flipper, who had a court-martial acknowledged as unjust.[66] President Clinton pardoned Preston King, an African American, who lived in exile for many years after he was accused of refusing to report for induction into the military when the military refused to grant deferments as he pursued higher education; racial bias was suspected to be a motivating factor in King's prosecution.[67] However, in addition to granting pardons related to unjust prosecutions, President Clinton's final clemency grants were marked with great political controversy. President Clinton pardoned his brother Roger Clinton and fugitive billionaire Marc Rich on the last day of his presidency.[68] The House Government Reform Committee obtained documents that demonstrated that Denise Rich, Marc Rich's wife, donated $450,000 toward the Clinton presidential library.[69] On January 20, 2001, President Clinton pardoned Roger Clinton for a 1985 cocaine possession for which he had served a year. In February 2001, Roger Clinton was arrested for drunk driving and disturbing the peace in Los Angeles.[70] Many such "political" pardons tend to occur within the last days of a presidency, thereby avoiding real accountability in the electorate.[71]

President Clinton was also troubled at the end of his term with allegations that family members were paid for pardons.[72] Hugh Rodham, President Clinton's brother-in-law, agreed to return $400,000 that he was paid in order to lobby for the pardon of two men who received clemency on President Clinton's last day in office.[73] Roger Clinton also requested clemency for ten individuals but was not given any money for such work.[74]

These examples are not meant to suggest that formally trained lawyers somehow behave any worse than other leaders when operating at the intersection of personal ambition, political aspiration, and moral decision making. But professionalism and principles of leadership ought to mean that leaders will embrace a set of values that will elevate their decisions above base self-interest. Leaders need to develop a robust decision-making compass; law school is in a unique position to expose aspiring leaders to these concepts. Continued failure to do so will perpetuate the practice of politics winning out over public good.

LEADERSHIP LESSONS

The decisions facing Justice French and Governor Clinton teach lessons that are too often unaddressed and unacknowledged.

Leaders must be transparent to themselves and their constituencies when decisions run into their self-interest.

Lawyers understand that under certain circumstances, they may have obligations to reveal when self-interest is in play. For example, professional codes of ethics typically contain provisions governing conflicts of interest and make clear that the lawyer may have a duty to disclose a conflict of interest to clients and relevant parties. Ethics codes may require that lawyers avoid even the appearance of a conflict of interest in the exercise of their legal duties. The rules recognize that such conflicts can interfere with the lawyer's fiduciary obligations. But in the exercise of one's duty as a leader, there may not be any clear rules. Still, the effective lawyer-leader should look to acknowledge and reveal when personal interests or conflicts may be in play. Adhering to a set of personal values and acknowledging tensions that can influence or even alter a decision is critical if a leader intends to make just decisions and to act with moral courage.

Leaders must subordinate their personal interests in the service of the greater good.

Every day, leaders are called upon to make tough choices. Many of those decisions have both direct and indirect personal costs. From the start, the decision to lead means working consciously to make your personal and individual interests secondary to the greater needs of the organization. A willingness to make personal sacrifices signals that the welfare of the group one is leading is of paramount concern. That self-sacrifice may help build a basis for leadership effectiveness that reaches beyond the situation in which the sacrifice is made. The essence of intersectional leadership is the desire to create a culture that serves the greater good. Individual recognition can and should give way to something larger than oneself. That is not to say that good leaders are not often "driven." It means that great leaders can suppress the natural human tendency to put one's own interests first.

Leaders need to redouble efforts to exercise independent judgment.
Personal ambition is only one instance where a leader's individual interest may conflict with his or her obligations as a leader. For example, a leader's decision may potentially benefit people with whom he or she has a personal affinity—family or friends—and adversely affect a larger constituency that the leader represents. When individual interests are in play, it may be difficult for the leader to see their influence or to separate himself or herself from their influence. Leaders must create mechanisms that force them to double check their judgment. This helps resist the temptation to believe that whatever is good for the individual leader must be good for the organization or system.

WHAT EDUCATORS CAN DO
Law schools and educators in practice can better prepare lawyers to address these issues in the following ways.

1) Law schools need to use case studies that illustrate the potential dangers of promoting self-interest over the interests of those the lawyer serves.
To the extent that such conflicts of interest are raised, it is often in the context of a course on professional responsibility, and the examples used tend to exhibit violations of ethical rules on conflicts of interest or the appearance of a conflict. The examination of this issue in this way offers an important beginning of the conversation. Law students need to examine the personal conflicts that arise not only when there is an apparent role conflict but when there is an unspoken conflict known only to the individual. By helping students see the value of identifying and labeling the personal interests in play, they will learn the importance of reflection and transparency.

2) Educators and coaches should work with lawyer-leaders to develop feedback mechanisms to help sort any conflicts.

Lawyer-leaders need to have colleagues and advisors in place around them who specifically act as a sounding board for potential and actual conflicts of interest. Such mechanisms help leaders develop the habit and discipline of checking with others to determine whether their actions and judgments are sufficiently independent or are clouded by personal concerns.

CHAPTER FIVE

If You See Something, Say Something

Leadership Responsibility and Systemic Failures

WHEN SYSTEMS FAIL, everyone rushes to point the finger of blame. Generally, that accusation seeks a single individual at the top whose personal greed, corruption, or indifference led to the failure. As tempting as it might be to believe that a single villain is solely responsible for any systemic failure, that belief is rarely the case. More often than not, catastrophic breakdowns occur when multiple actors in a system fail to act with integrity as they exercise leadership. They witness behavior that raises concern but then fail to say or do anything to intervene. The systemic failure may or may not include an individual ethical lapse, but it generally occurs because of a dangerous leadership lapse across the board.

Plenty of factors may discourage individuals from directing attention toward misbehavior. First of all, whistle-blowers rarely win popularity contests. They may become isolated, may lose their jobs, and may even find a finger of accusation pointed back toward them. Second, fear operates as a powerful disincentive. Fear can take many forms—fear of reprisals, fear of being wrong, or fear of making an accusation against someone with whom you work. Third, some individuals choose not to make waves when others in the organization or system seem, by their own silence, to condone questionable behavior. When the organization seems to give a pass to the person engaging in questionable conduct because he or she is a rainmaker or brings other value, the individuals seeing the misconduct may question the wisdom of complaining. And some individuals may be reluctant to identify wrongful behavior because such oversight falls outside their positional authority, and therefore they do not consider themselves responsible for questioning the conduct of someone who holds a position of authority over them or elsewhere within the organization.

But as we've discussed in previous chapters, leadership does not flow from a title or position. An effective leader has the obligation to speak up when he or she witnesses behavior that is inconsistent with the values the organization espouses. Every member has a role to play in protecting the integrity of a system—even if that threat comes from within the organization itself. Failure to speak up about such threats makes a witness complicit by his or her own inaction. Indeed, this leadership mandate specifically applies to lawyers as leaders, particularly where lawyers hold a formal watchdog or fiduciary role and must monitor actions and identify conduct that could constitute a breach of public trust. This chapter addresses instances where lawyers are not formally tasked with such a role but nonetheless are uniquely situated as leaders to ensure the integrity of a system. In cases where the ethical obligations may be ambiguous, the leadership task becomes all the more critical.

Two examples expose this leadership dilemma and the attendant responsibilities for lawyer-leaders. The first case involves outside counsel in the infamous collapse of Enron. A number of examinations of individual conduct *within* Enron have highlighted the pervasive ethical failures as well as the criminal conduct of key executives within the company. But much less attention has been focused on the role of outside counsel, who saw questionable activity but generally remained silent rather than risk the loss of a major client. The second instance involves another famous scandal—the "kids for cash" conspiracy—arising out of the scheme in which two Pennsylvania juvenile court judges received cash kickbacks over a five-year period for improperly sending children to locked correctional facilities. Again, much has been written about the judges themselves, but the focus of the story here is the leadership lapse involving the lawyer-leaders who operated within the system the judges oversaw. They witnessed the conduct but said nothing.

DOWNPLAYING DANGER OUT OF FEAR

Enron Corporation was an American energy, commodities, and services company based in Houston, Texas. In the late 1990s, Enron was a fast-rising star. Everyone perceived the company as "innovative and sexy," and virtually every major law firm in the country wanted a piece of its business.[1] By 2000, Enron boasted profits of nearly $111 billion.[2] So when Enron hired Vinson & Elkins to serve as outside counsel in the late 1990s, Vinson & Elkins was happy to take them on as a client. Then, in December 2001, the unthinkable happened: Enron collapsed. Investigations later revealed that over the course of five years, Enron and its executives had engaged in fraudulent accounting schemes and improper partnership deals that combined to form an "institutionalized, systematic, and creatively planned accounting fraud."[3] The federal government prosecuted many of Enron's top executives for conspiracy, insider trading, and securities fraud. Its accounting firm, Arthur Andersen, one of the largest accounting firms in the country at the time, faced criminal prosecution and eventually went out of business.

Its outside lawyers, though, did not face prosecution because, technically, they did not violate the law or their ethical obligations. Despite their legal role and the protections it gave them, it is right to question what they should have done in light of what they witnessed. Over a five-year period, chief financial officer (CFO) Andrew Fastow structured ever more complex and problematic finance deals. Vinson & Elkins's lawyers sometimes objected and engaged in shouting matches with Fastow,[4] but the lawyers ultimately backed down and never shared their unease with Enron's most senior executives or with its board. It appears that Vinson & Elkins chose not to disclose their reservations about these deals, at least in part, because of the high stakes involved for their own company.[5] By 2001, Enron was Vinson & Elkins's largest client, paying almost 8 percent of the firm's annual income, amounting to close to $40 million.[6]

Many of the deals that troubled Vinson & Elkins lawyers over the years would come to sit at the heart of the investigations into Enron's collapse. Enron used special-purpose entities—limited partnerships or companies—created to fulfill a temporary or specific purpose to fund or manage risks.[7] By 2001, Enron had used hundreds of these shell companies to hide its mounting debt.[8] Vinson & Elkins was one of the law firms advising Enron on many of these partnership deals.[9] In 1997, when Enron proposed the first of its improper partnership deals, it turned to Vinson & Elkins.[10] At that time, Vinson & Elkins had been losing some of Enron's business because other major firms in Houston and from across the country were vying for, and winning, more of Enron's work.[11] So when Enron asked Vinson & Elkins to advise it on a novel partnership arrangement, Vinson & Elkins jumped at the opportunity.[12] To its credit, Vinson & Elkins's team expressed reservations about the deal to Enron.[13] It appeared that Fastow intended to manage the proposed partnership, and Vinson & Elkins conveyed concern about the conflict of interest of having a company executive in such a role. Vinson & Elkins met with Fastow and convinced him that he could not take this step. Fastow, who would later serve prison time for his role in Enron's collapse, decided to place a lower-ranking employee in charge of the partnership. The board approved this and other novel partnership deals by waiving their conflict of interest provisions.[14] The board did not seek or obtain Vinson & Elkins's advice for this.[15]

Because Vinson & Elkins had initially expressed concern about these unorthodox partnership deals, Enron began seeking the advice of other firms on many of its deals.[16] Within Enron, the view seems to have been that it was difficult to close transactions when Vinson & Elkins lawyers were involved. As a consequence, Vinson & Elkins saw its percentage of Enron's business continue to shrink.[17] Vinson & Elkins received only 20 percent of the work Enron sent to outside counsel in 2001, but they did draw up documents for some of Enron's most problematic deals, known as the Raptors, which allowed Enron to avoid reporting almost $1 billion in losses.[18] According to accounts, the partner at Vinson & Elkins responsible for the Enron account raised concerns to an Enron in-house lawyer about these deals but never elevated those concerns to the general counsel or any senior executives.[19]

Even as Enron reduced its overall legal referrals to Vinson & Elkins, it continued to seek the firm's advice on its most sensitive legal questions. One such matter—and the one for which Vinson & Elkins would later receive the greatest criticism—involved the investigation of allegations of fraud by Sherron Watkins, an Enron vice president and internal whistle-blower.[20] Watkins sent a memorandum warning the chair of the board, Kenneth Lay, of "accounting scandals."[21] Enron decided to hire Vinson & Elkins to investigate the claim. Interestingly, Watkins urged Lay not to assign the job to Vinson & Elkins because the firm had approved some of the precise partnerships that raised questions.[22] But Vinson & Elkins took on the assignment. Despite the law firm's own concerns about some of the deals, it agreed to limit the scope of the investigation into the partnership arrangements.[23] A nine-page report delivered just six weeks before the company collapsed raised no serious alarms.[24] Instead, Vinson & Elkins's report minimized the risks involved.[25] The report made clear that "the facts disclosed through our preliminary investigation do not, in our judgment, warrant a widespread investigation by independent counsel and auditors."[26]

Just as problematic was the approach that Vinson & Elkins took in conducting the investigation. In its review of the alleged illicit partnerships, Vinson and Elkins

lists 11 witnesses it interviewed. Fastow is on the list, as is Watkins. Vinson & Elkins also spoke to one of its own partners, Ronald Astin, for 'general background information.' But two names are conspicuously absent: Kenneth Lay, chair of the board, who, according to Vinson & Elkins's report, approved of many of the transactions, and Jeffrey Skilling, the former CEO who had recently quit the company and whose conduct was explicitly put in question by Vinson & Elkins itself.[27]

Vinson and Elkins's investigation later came to be criticized as a probe "worthy of Inspector Clouseau."[28]

Emphasizing what he would not do, Vinson and Elkins partner wrote: "[It] was decided that our initial approach would not involve second-guessing the accounting advice and treatment provided [by Andersen], that there would be no detailed analysis of each and every transaction and that there would be no full-scale discovery-style inquiry."[29]

No one expects lawyers to police their clients, but failing to say anything that might have warned Enron's executive senior team or board of the extent of the issues Vinson & Elkins saw certainly contributed to Enron's collapse and the reverberating harm it caused throughout the financial world. Reflecting on the decision not to push back on the questionable transactions, Vinson & Elkins's managing partner from the time stated that as long as a transaction was not illegal and had been approved by the client company's management, outside lawyers were expected only to advise on the transaction: "In doing so, the lawyers are not approving the business decisions that were made by their clients."[30] But Vinson & Elkins could have and should have taken their concern to Enron directors.[31] As a legal matter, Vinson & Elkins were insulated by the argument that they were using the protocols that they were given—they simply provided the legal information to those designated to receive it.[32] But from a leadership perspective, they missed an opportunity to press the issue with the real decision makers inside Enron, and they failed to help those executives see the extent of the problems they were facing. The defense that "we utilized the client's protocols," while legally and technically correct, did not fully serve the interests of the client and, ultimately, contributed to a catastrophic organizational collapse.

As this case study demonstrates, lawyers are, at times, uniquely positioned to see issues that might lead to a systemic failure. There are often attendant legal and ethical obligations to act. When such obligations seem murky, leaders may need to say something, at a minimum, to those within the organization making decisions that determine its future, particularly when they may not otherwise know of the information. Lawyer-leaders may need to step up and speak up even when that choice has the potential to threaten their work environment or even their career. The next case demonstrates, in a slightly different context, the cost of saying nothing in the face of misconduct out of fear that one's own situation might become more challenging.

A PERSONAL FIEFDOM IN THE LUZERNE COUNTY JUVENILE COURT

From 2003 to 2008 two juvenile court judges in Luzerne County, Pennsylvania, conspired to deprive thousands of children of their most basic constitutional rights and sent them to detention centers in which the judges had a personal financial interest.[33] The judges effectively ruined the lives of 2,500 children for a financial benefit that exceeded $2 million. The scheme, which involved the perfect storm of greed, opportunity, public indifference, and secrecy, shocked and outraged the country when it was discovered. But the fact that it continued for years without comment from any professionals in the courthouse makes this scandal all the more puzzling and disturbing.[34]

Perhaps one key to the silence is location. Luzerne County, an area that includes the cities of Wilkes-Bare and Hazelton, boasts a long, sordid history of corruption in public administration.[35] Nepotism ran rampant in the county. Politicians handed out jobs to friends and family or simply required bribes to fill positions. Teachers were openly advised to prepare to pay thousands of dollars for jobs in the school districts. The corruption became so deeply ingrained and widespread that residents accepted that this was how business was done in the county. People seemed to forget that paying to play was actually illegal.[36] In the early years of this corruption, politicians at least put money *into* the system, the city and the town infrastructure. Of course, that did not excuse the conduct. But in 2009, even that pretense had evaporated. These corrupt judges just put the money into their own and their friends' pockets.[37]

It is no accident that this conduct occurred in the juvenile court. Juvenile court hearings are governed by statutes that presumptively close court proceedings to the general public. The decision to close out the public stems from a concern for confidentiality of the young offender's identity and a desire to preserve the privacy of the actual hearings themselves. Thus, much of the court's process remains hidden from public view; this helped the judges keep their misconduct secret. Still, juvenile courts do not bar all members of the public. The child's parents and relatives routinely attend. Members of the bar and other authorized employees of the court can typically witness proceedings even when they are not directly involved. But other individuals who might have either a particular or more generalized interest in the proceedings would typically need to apply to the judge for admission. So in these closed proceedings, shielded from public scrutiny, two judges were able to use their power to corrupt the ends of the justice system for personal gain. In the coziness that happens in closed courtrooms, professionals who could see what was occurring watched in silence.

The two judges who sat at the center of this scheme were Mark Arthur Ciavarella Jr. and Michael Conahan. Ciavarella became a member of the Luzerne County bar in October 1975, having received his law degree from Duquesne University in Pittsburgh.[38] He earned a reputation for brashness in private practice.[39] In his campaign for election to the Luzerne County Court in 1995, Ciavarella ran on a platform pledging to get tough on teen crime, emphasizing punishment over rehabilitation. He was elected to a ten-year term in 1995 and won reelection in 2005. Conahan earned his law degree from Temple University Law School in 1977. He became a district magistrate in Hazelton immediately after law school.[40] From 1993 to 1994, he ran for and won election to the Luzerne County Court of Common Pleas. He based his campaign on his proven abilities as a crime fighter.[41] Ironically, at the time, he was already a criminal himself.[42] He had ties to local criminals and organized crime, which led to complaints about his conduct as a judge and even prompted a federal investigation.[43]

Eight months after his appointment to the bench, Ciavarella served as the county's only juvenile court judge, hearing juvenile cases two days a week and on the other three handling criminal and civil cases.[44] The small community of lawyers in Luzerne County who represented clients in juvenile cases also appeared before him regularly in other matters. Ciavarella ran his courtroom as a "tyrant." He encouraged children to waive their right to counsel; he never asked these children if they understood that they had a right to be represented by lawyers. He simply began imposing maximum sentences on juveniles for minor offenses and made parents pay fines when he sentenced kids to locked facilities.[45] He started a zero-tolerance policy for violent offenses on school grounds. The American Bar Association (ABA) five years later would explicitly condemn such policies.[46] The only serious opposition he received at the time was from the Juvenile Law Center (JLC), a Philadelphia-based advocacy group that appealed the case of a juvenile who appeared before Ciavarella without an attorney.[47] In 2001, the Pennsylvania Superior Court agreed with the center, and Ciavarella insisted that juveniles would have lawyers in his courtroom.[48] For the next six years, he continued to reign over his courtroom until he assumed the position of president judge. He took over this position when his friend Conahan took senior status in 2007.[49]

THE CONSPIRACY BEGINS

After a few years on the bench, Ciavarella decided that it was time to replace the county's run-down juvenile detention facility. He approached Conahan and enlisted him to assemble an investor team to build a new for-profit detention facility named PA Child Care.[50] In early 2000, Ciavarella went public with the idea, decrying the current facility as old, leaky, and infested.[51] The county commissioners disagreed with Ciavarella and balked at the construction of a new detention center. Ignoring those objections, Ciavarella turned to another friend, Robert Mericle, a campaign donor and "little brother" to Ciavarella, to build a new facility.[52] Ciavarella put Mericle in touch with Robert Powell, a developer and friend of Ciaveralla, and the two began building a private facility in 2001.[53] Powell enlisted the help of Gregory Zappala, a Pittsburgh attorney-businessman and son of a former Pennsylvania Supreme Court justice. The Powell-Zappala facility became PA Child Care, and the firm offered to lease it to the county for $37 million over three years. The deal included a "finder's fee" of $997,600, about 10 percent of the overall cost, intended for Ciavarella and Conahan.[54]

The two judges still needed the county commissioners to approve the deal. In October 2002, then-president judge Conahan ordered the Juvenile Probation Department to stop sending juveniles to the old facility effective December 31.[55] Conahan and Ciavarella declared the facility unsafe and unfit for further use and focused a media campaign on the inadequacies of the facility, despite the fact that the Public Welfare Department had just inspected and approved it. Conahan eventually choked off funding for that facility,[56] paving the way for PA Child Care to receive juveniles as early as February 2003. He then orchestrated the signing of a Placement Guarantee Agreement between PA Child Care and the Court of Common Pleas of Luzerne County to house juveniles in that facility.[57]

In January 2003, the two judges began to receive their finder's fees through a money-laundering scheme. Mericle disguised the money as a broker's fee and paid it to Powell. The money then reemerged in Conahan's and Ciavarella's bank accounts in installments. Enjoying the new wealth, the Conahans purchased a home next door to the Ciavarellas in Mountain Top, a suburb of Wilkes-Barre. They bought a condominium together in Florida. Still, Ciavarella expected more. He summoned Powell to his office, and Powell learned for the first time that the judges expected payment from him as well. A new scheme developed where Powell funneled cash to the Pinnacle Group, owned by the wives of Conahan and Ciavarella. The payments were disguised as both rental costs for the Florida condominium and fees for docking Powell's fishing boat.[58] When a second facility was built, Powell and Zappala paid a $1 million finder's fee to the Pinnacle Group.[59]

The conspiracy to fill the facility began. A few months earlier, Ciavarella had moved probation officers from cramped quarters in the old facility to county offices downtown and demanded that PA Child Care be "filled at all times."[60] He made clear that he did not care "if we have to bankrupt the county to do it."[61] Three days after PA Child Care opened, Ciavarella expanded his zero-tolerance policy to require automatic detention of any child who skipped school or violated probation.[62] His courtroom was busy and chaotic.[63] On the two days that he heard juvenile matters, he would preside over twenty or more hearings per day.[64] He sent so many juveniles to the new facility that within five months of its opening Powell and Zappala decided to open a second facility, Western PA Child Care in Butler County, 230 miles from Wilkes-Barre.[65] In 2003, Ciavarella ordered 330 juveniles from Luzerne County into placement, an amount that was twice the state average.[66] Luzerne County represented less than 3 percent of Pennsylvania's population, but Ciavarella was responsible for placing 22 percent of juveniles into locked facilities in Pennsylvania.[67]

Ciavarella's courtroom wholly lacked decorum and order. He routinely ignored the rules of juvenile procedure, interrupted defense attorneys without reason, and sneered at juveniles appearing before him, all while wearing a NASCAR hat.[68] He obtained intake files of juveniles from probation officers before the juveniles appeared before him, in direct violation of court procedure and law.[69] He was the antithesis of an impartial judge, and he ruled by a basic rubric: "If you do X, your punishment will be Y. I will send you away. I am telling you ahead of time."[70] But possibly the worst of Ciavarella's offenses involved the routine deprivation of juveniles' constitutional right to counsel. Over 50 percent of juveniles in Ciavarella's courtroom appeared without counsel,[71] despite Pennsylvania's 1972 Juvenile Act, which gave children the right to a lawyer from the time their cases begin until their disposition. Juveniles could waive the right to counsel, but only if that waiver was made "intelligently, knowingly and voluntarily." In October 2005, the Pennsylvania Supreme Court tightened the requirement with Rule 152.[72] The rule requires a juvenile judge to engage in a colloquy with juveniles in open court to ensure that any waiver of counsel met that standard, and the court required the judge to inquire about this waiver in every subsequent court appearance. Only the child could relinquish the right to counsel; the decision could not be made by a parent. An extraordinary number—almost 2,500 juveniles—navigated the system without counsel.[73] Ciavarella ordered probation to set up a table outside the courtroom where juveniles signed forms waiving their right to counsel. Investigation revealed that probation officers routinely advised juveniles that they did not need an attorney or made clear that they would fare better in front of Ciavarella without one. Despite claims to the contrary by police officers, attorneys, and probation officers that kids were better off without attorneys, from 2000 to 2008, 60 percent of juveniles without lawyers were sent to detention, and only 22 percent of those represented by lawyers were placed in such facilities.[74]

Ciavarella handled thousands of juvenile cases during his time as a juvenile judge, and his practices would shock even the untrained observer. Juveniles routinely committed "crimes" that most people would agree did not warrant any level of incarceration, but Ciavarella sent these children away. For example, a sixteen-year-old girl gestured with her middle finger at a police officer who had come to her house because of a custody dispute involving her sister and parents.[75] She was an honor student, a Girl Scout, a YMCA member, and a Bible school attendee with no prior record and no school detentions or suspensions.[76] Her parents, understandably, considered her conduct minor, so she appeared before Ciavarella without a lawyer.[77] He did not even give her the opportunity to speak; he simply sentenced her to detention for six months.[78] A fifteen-year-old boy went joyriding in his mom's car and ran over a barrier. No one was hurt, but his mother needed to file a police report so that insurance would pay for the damage.[79] She thought, as many parents did, that it might be good for her son to appear in court and get a little scare.[80] Her son appeared before Ciavarella without an attorney, since it was his first offense. Ciavarella locked up her son for two years.[81]

AN ENABLING CULTURE OF SILENCE

Silence is an extremely effective form of lying, but most silences are pauses, interludes, breaks in the action.[82] The silence in Ciavarella's courtroom was deep and abiding, six years long, and it was never broken by the people who were closest to it.[83] Although juvenile proceedings are not public, dozens of adults sat in the courtroom every Tuesday and Thursday during Ciavarella's six-year reign. They included court officers, stenographers, prosecutors, public defenders, probation officers, police, and attorneys with other cases. None of them spoke out. Pennsylvania Rules of Professional Conduct require all lawyers in a courtroom to report the judge's misconduct.[84]

None of them did. The rules also required prosecutors to report the huge numbers of children appearing before him without counsel.[85] Not a single prosecutor made a report.

The district attorney of Luzerne County, David W. Lupas, held office from 2000 to 2007 and now sits as a judge of the Court of Common Pleas.[86] While serving as the district attorney, he admittedly did not devote much of his time to juvenile court matters, but he did assign approximately twenty-five prosecutors to juvenile court. Lupas and his first assistant, Jacqueline Musto Carroll, who is now the Luzerne County district attorney, supervised these attorneys.[87] Lupas was adamant that he never received any feedback or complaints about any violations occurring in Ciavarella's court.[88] Thomas J. Killino, a new lawyer working in the DA's office and assigned to the juvenile court in 2004, noticed that the courtroom seemed extremely busy and fast-paced.[89] He observed that the DA's office did not keep records or track dispositions occurring in juvenile court.[90] DAs would later admit that they witnessed the wholesale waivers of counsel and, because no one challenged it, assumed it was proper.[91] They also knew that Ciavarella had enacted his own zero-tolerance policy that ordered probation to seek placement of kids for even minor violations, but again, they claimed to have assumed—without question—that Ciavarella was following the rules.[92]

Among the regular attendees in the juvenile court were the defense attorneys. Interestingly, the public defender's office all but abdicated its constitutionally mandated role in Ciavarella's courtroom. Basil G. Russin served as the chief public defender of Luzerne County for thirty years, from 1980 until 2010.[93] His position was part-time, and he supervised twenty-two public defenders, sixteen part-time and six full-time. During Ciavarella's tenure, Russin assigned only one of the twenty-two public defenders to juvenile court on a part-time basis, averaging just four hours a week. Russin would later claim that he did not have the resources to place a full-time defender in juvenile court. From 2003 to 2008, no more than 250 juveniles had the assistance of public defenders.[94]

Russin's rationale for never objecting to Ciavarella's practices was that no parent or child ever complained to him about Ciavarella's courtroom. Russin knew about the zero-tolerance policy, but instead of challenging this practice, he assumed that this policy fell within Ciavarella's discretion. Russin simply accepted that they were stuck with Ciavarella until he retired, resigned, or was reassigned.[95] Russin also expressed reluctance to lodge any opposition to the zero-tolerance policy because it was popular in the community. But even when he received a complaint, he did nothing. One of his assistant defenders, Jonathan Ursiak, informed Russin about the huge numbers of juveniles going before Ciavarella without counsel. Russin told Ursiak that the office could not do anything and had to assume the court knew and was following the rules about waiver.[96]

The probation department played an "unusually dominant" role in the adjudicatory process.[97] The department took written waivers of counsel from juveniles outside the courtroom on a two-page standard form. The department worked up social histories and made disposition recommendations available only to Ciavarella. The chief probation officer, Sandra Brulo, became a central and controversial figure. Many saw her as an enforcer of Ciavarella's reign of terror. She saw herself as a victim working in an atmosphere of oppression and intimidation, having been called on the carpet by Ciavarella for the slow pace of admissions to PA Child Care.[98] Probation officers testified that Brulo told them that PA Child Care was to be kept full at all times. Essentially, probation perpetuated the system that Ciavarella put in place.

Eventually, someone in Luzerne County found the nerve to file a complaint with the Judicial Conduct Board against Judge Conahan. The eight-page complaint, filed anonymously, accused Conahan of having links to organized crime, engaging in case fixing, and placing unusually high numbers of children into PA Child Care.[99] The reason for the anonymous filing was that "I fear retaliation should my identity be revealed."[100] The complaint listed thirty-three accusations of "glaring violations of ethics which are occurring in the Luzerne County Courthouse"[101] and named Ciavarella and Powell as friends and conspirators.[102] The chief counsel for the Judicial Conduct Board, Joseph Messa, did nothing with this complaint for more than seven months.[103] He finally circulated a memorandum describing the complaint's allegations to the board, but he did not include the actual complaint to the board.[104] Messa recommended a full investigation, but at the June 4, 2007, meeting, the board tabled the matter to be discussed at its October meeting.[105] The complaint never came up again. The board never investigated the complaint, never filed charges, and never took disciplinary action against either judge based on this complaint.[106] Messa later stated that it fell through the cracks and he blamed himself for it.[107]

FINALLY, THE JUDGES ARE CAUGHT

In 2006, Hillary Transue, a bright, witty, and sarcastic eighth-grader, created a mock MySpace profile of an assistant principal.[108] The principal filed a complaint with the police, who traced the wireless account of the post to the Transue household.[109] In March, Transue and her mother were summoned and interviewed by probation officers.[110] Transue received a court date to appear before Judge Ciavarella. Knowing his reputation from friends at school, Transue urged her mother to hire a lawyer, but her mother did not think they needed one. It was, after all, her first offense. Surely no one would send her away. Her mother signed the waiver of counsel, despite the fact that only Transue could legally waive her right to representation. Transue received Ciavarella's standard treatment. She pleaded guilty, and in less than two minutes and 331 words, she was handcuffed and taken from her hysterical mother. Transue's mother and grandfather began calling every organization they could to fight the decision. Finally, the JLC in Philadelphia responded.[111] The center filed a habeas corpus petition to have Transue released and prepared extensively for the case.[112] Ciavarella granted the petition without a fight.[113] The lawyer representing Transue chose to remain in court to watch other proceedings. Ciavarella behaved appropriately for the day, but the lawyer learned from Ursiak that Ciavarella's conduct was atypical.[114]

The JLC proceeded to investigate further. They obtained statistics from the Juvenile Court Judges Commission and learned that in 2003, juveniles waived counsel in 7.4 percent of all juvenile cases in Pennsylvania, but in Ciavarella's courtroom 50.2 percent waived counsel.[115] In 2004, the statewide number dropped to 4.8 percent; Ciavarella's remained the same.[116] Ciavarella placed juveniles in custody at two and a half times the statewide average.[117] Laval Miller-Wilson, attorney for the Juvenile Law Center, went to the courtroom and began interviewing juveniles and their parents.[118] Sealed court records complicated the process of identifying juveniles who had waived counsel. Ursiak would only confirm that unrepresented children appeared in record numbers in front of Ciavarella.

Ultimately, on April 29, 2009, the JLC filed a King's Bench petition, a petition that allows the Pennsylvania Supreme Court to vacate the decisions of lower courts in extraordinary circumstances.[119] The petition alleged that Ciavarella routinely violated juveniles' right to counsel in violation of the Constitution and Rule 152.[120] It focused on the years 2005–2007. Initially, Ciavarella claimed he merely affirmed probation's decisions and stuck to his "placement is great" tune, but three weeks later, he removed himself from juvenile court, although he remained a judge. He called Miller-Wilson, yelling: "What the hell do you want from me now? Why are you breaking my balls?"[121]

His departure from the court resulted in the DA changing its position on the petition. Carroll now had the audacity to contend that the issue was moot without Ciavarella on the bench. The FBI placed a call to the JLC and Marsha Levick, the JLC legal director, inquiring about its investigation. She turned over all of her findings to them. Eight months after filing it, the JLC amended the petition to add more cases. A month later, the court denied the petition without any explanation or comment.

On January 26, 2009, federal prosecutors filed charges against both Ciavarella and Conahan for tax evasion and honest services fraud, the result of a lengthy investigation that began in 2007.[122] Federal officials announced that a plea agreement had been reached between the prosecutors and the judges. The agreement involved the judges' guilty plea to the two counts and the serving of an eighty-seven-month jail sentence.[123] Two days later, the Pennsylvania Supreme Court suspended Ciavarella and revoked Conahan's senior judge certification, rescinding his judicial assignments as well.[124] In July, U.S. District Judge Edwin M. Kosik rejected the plea agreements, ruling that the sentences were too lenient and the former judges had not accepted full responsibility.[125] The judges withdrew their pleas. Ciavarella decided to go to trial, where a jury convicted him of twelve out of the twenty-eight counts in which prosecutors had charged him with crimes related to the scheme.[126] Judge Kosik sentenced him to twenty-eight years.[127] Ciavarella adamantly denies that he placed kids for money; in his mind, it was always in the best interest of the child.[128] He never apologized publicly to the juveniles whose lives he deeply affected. Conahan pleaded guilty and received a seventeen-and-a-half-year sentence.[129] He apologized to everyone at his sentencing.[130]

The judges were not the only people criminally prosecuted because of the massive investigation into the courthouse.[131] Mericle and Powell pleaded guilty for failure to report a felony, and both testified against Ciavarella.[132] Powell received eighteen months in federal prison.[133] Another Luzerne County judge, Michael T. Toole, pleaded guilty to tax and fraud offenses and agreed to cooperate with federal authorities. William T. Sharkey Sr., a former court administrator and cousin to Conahan, pleaded guilty to charges of embezzlement related to gambling. Brulo, the former probation officer, pleaded guilty to a charge of obstructing justice for altering a record of a juvenile respondent.

THE PENNSYLVANIA JUDICIARY REACTS

In light of the federal charges, on January 30, 2009, the JLC asked the Pennsylvania Supreme Court to appoint a special master to review juvenile cases to decide if sentences should be vacated and records expunged.[134] On February 2, the court vacated the previous order denying the King's Bench petition, and three days later, Carroll concurred in the JLC's recommendation for appointment of a special master.[135] On February 11, 2009, the Pennsylvania Supreme Court exercised its King's Bench powers and appointed Senior Judge Arthur E. Grim as special master to review all the cases where Ciavarella placed juveniles.[136] He had 120 days to file an interim report. His interim report reviewed minor-crimes cases where juveniles did not have counsel, and he recommended vacating these sentences and expunging the juveniles' records. On March 26, 2009, the Pennsylvania Supreme Court authorized his recommendation, vacating approximately 360 juveniles' adjudications and expunging the records.[137] On August 7, 2009, Grim filed his final report with a sweeping recommendation to vacate the adjudications and expunge the records of all juveniles appearing before Ciavarella between January 1, 2003, and May 31, 2008.[138] On October 29, 2009, in a nine-page order, the Pennsylvania Supreme Court adopted his recommendation.[139] The ruling affected somewhere between four thousand and six thousand cases.

In approximately six thousand cases, the lives of children were adversely affected by the failure of the prosecutor's office, the public defender's office, and every other lawyer who watched in silence as these judges engaged in gross misconduct.

LEADERSHIP LESSONS

Had the lawyers in Luzerne County and inside Vinson & Elkins operated as intersectional leaders, they would have recognized that they sat in positions where they were able to see actions that threatened the integrity of systems in which they operated. Because of their unique vantage points, they had a responsibility as good leaders to intervene. As a foundational matter, intersectional leaders recognize the importance of maintaining a horizontal view rather than simply a perspective that focuses on their discrete responsibilities within their lane. This is perhaps easiest to see—and easiest to implement—within an organization. But the need to look horizontally applies with equal weight to the intersectional leader's role in a larger ecosystem. If the lawyers in each of these cases had remained alert to the entire system in which they worked, and then had exercised the moral courage to act given what they saw, they would have intervened or at least spoken up about what they witnessed to safeguard the systems from harm.

So, then, what leadership lessons emerge from these examples?

Leaders must recognize that they function as part of a larger ecosystem.
In our more complex and interconnected world, leaders no longer have the option of head-burying when problems arise outside their immediate sphere of influence. In organizations, participants often work in silos that cabin their work and attention. This is often a vertical approach to the work. Leaders need to think horizontally across organizations and systems and see themselves and their work as part of the larger ecosystem in which they exist. In nature, ecosystems depend on the collaborative—and sometimes competitive—efforts of its members to protect the long-term health of the system. If individual members fail to help with that protection, the system will not thrive or evolve. This is true not only in nature but in organizations and in the larger systems in which lawyers operate. In essence, intersectional leaders need to see themselves as part of a connected system that depends on their vigilance and action to survive shocks in the environment.

Leaders must step up and speak up against issues threatening an organization's health and integrity.
The intersectional lawyer-leader recognizes the importance of acting with moral courage. It has often been too easy for leaders to stand silently by when

issues simply did not affect them directly or threatened their own careers from internal or external retaliation. Such a choice was at times applauded as the leader's prudent exercise of discretion. But intersectional leadership challenges that notion. Particularly in times of great moral conflict, the intersectional leader cannot stand mute. This lesson is not a mere platitude. When the intersectional leader witnesses actions that threaten the core values of the system, he or she must find a way to act or draw attention to the danger. By doing so, the intersectional leader both sets the tone for his or her leadership approach and demonstrates to others that courage and principled leadership are expected and are valued within the organization and within the larger system.

Leaders must learn to engage in courageous conversations.
The leader must engage in sustained conversations about difficult issues to get to better outcomes for the organization. Leadership is not easy. Rather it places demands on the individual leader to step into uncomfortable situations in an effort to own his or her piece of the problem and to call out what is wrong. In the case of Vinson & Elkins, a number of courageous conversations did not occur. Lawyers did not escalate their concerns to the board or to the decision makers within Enron who might have been able to raise questions and to stop the fraud before it reached epic proportions. Similarly, leaders within the firm should have engaged in internal conversations about the need to act despite the threat to their bottom line. Open conversations about the conflicts that were playing out might have pushed the firm to act more courageously with its client. Similarly, in Luzerne County, the key institutional players in the juvenile justice system—the chief district attorney, the chief public defender, and the chief probation officer—certainly knew that the practices in that court were at best unusual and at worst unethical or criminal. These organizational heads had a responsibility to the integrity of the judicial system and to the countless children and families who were caught up in it to report their observations and concerns to bodies responsible for assessing judicial performance. While those bodies could easily let an anonymous complaint slip through the cracks—as they did—it would have been more difficult to ignore a joint complaint filed by the principal players in that court. As intersectional leaders, they would have seen themselves as

part of a larger system that required their voices to protect those without a voice in the system.

WHAT EDUCATORS CAN DO

Law schools and educators in practice can better prepare lawyers to address these issues in the following ways.

1) Law schools can teach law students how to engage and sustain a difficult conversation.

Law schools offer plenty of opportunities to teach students to engage in advocacy by making and anticipating arguments with a goal of persuasion. But what they do not often teach is how law students can take a difficult or uncomfortable issue that engages strong emotions and opinions and find ways to engage in a sustained discussion that deepens the conversation even in the midst of deeply felt concerns.

2) Educators in practice and coaches must help leaders recognize that they are part of a larger ecosystem where they encourage employees to speak with candor in the interest of the enterprise.

Too often, leaders focus on their own units and convey to their employees that they simply need to put their heads down to do the work. But leaders at all levels must reiterate that while the people in a particular unit may have specialized duties and contributions, they are also part of a whole. And by virtue of their jobs and vantage points, they may see something that others may miss. Encouraging leaders to convey repeatedly the importance of being interested and in being candid will help ensure the integrity of the enterprise.

CHAPTER SIX

"Keeping Your Head on a Swivel"

Maintaining Multiple Vantage Points

LAWYERS ARE NOT ONLY INTEGRAL PARTS of larger ecosystems, but they also tend to play unique roles within those systems. The complexity of their roles and the accompanying expectations for the performance of those roles can create genuine tensions for the lawyer-leader. In Chapter Four, we sorted through the leadership dilemmas that arise when the lawyer-leader experiences conflicts between his or her personal interests and the greater good—the types of tensions that may occur in a role but are not inherent to the role. This chapter explores the leadership challenges that emerge when conflicts are essentially baked into the role itself. Lawyers who serve as general counsel or work within an organization's legal unit are often expected to serve, broadly speaking, two principal functions: helping to guide the business through its strategic priorities and ensuring that the organization is operating within the law at all times. By design, the lawyer-leader in these roles will need to navigate the conflicting pulls involved in being a business leader (organizational copilot) and being a business protector (organizational rudder). But the role of the general counsel and legal unit today has expanded beyond these two conventional roles. It is multifaceted and involves a greater degree of complexity and tension than previous corporate counsel experienced. So, today, being able to hold *multiple* perspectives simultaneously is critical to effective leadership.

Problems occur when lawyer-leaders favor one of these roles over the others. For example, by envisioning the role as principally involving leading or enabling the business, the lawyer-leader can run afoul of his or her professional, legal, and compliance responsibilities. The choice to downplay legal issues or to ignore questionable conduct because it is viewed as essential to the organization's growth goals can result in considerable problems for the organization and its stakeholders. Those problems have manifested in instances where top executives have profited wildly as shareholders and customers have been bilked out of savings and investments. Problems have also surfaced when the conduct falls short of illegality but still results in damage to the organization's reputation and brand.

On the other hand, the general counsel or member of the legal unit who privileges his or her compliance role may stifle innovation and experimentation that could lead to positive outcomes for the organization and its stakeholders. It is common to hear that the general counsel is perceived as the perpetual naysayer or the traffic cop with a stop sign in hand. The legal unit routinely says "no" to a new idea, strategic redirection, or policy change because it has some risk. This often occurs not because the particular move is illegal or unusually risky but because it is far safer and sometimes easier for corporate counsel to revert to the role of regulatory gatekeeper rather than business leader. By not recognizing and exercising their role as business leader, these lawyer-leaders relegate themselves to the margins instead of helping to guide the decisions of the organization. Choosing not to exercise the business leader role may encourage decision makers within the organization to create workarounds and sidestep the legal unit, soliciting legal advice only after the action has been taken. The effective lawyer-leader keeps his or her head on a swivel, considering issues from multiple vantage points and using those insights to ask "what if."

Over time, the role of inside corporate counsel has undergone dramatic change. Historically, the legal profession did not hold the role of general counsel in high esteem. The general counsel was perceived as technically inferior to lawyers who practiced in large law firms, and the job was considered far less demanding:[1] in-house counsel managed the routine issues of the organization and farmed out the more complex legal tasks to outside counsel. However, beginning largely in the 1970s, the general counsel role experienced a fundamental transformation. General counsels started to join senior leadership teams within large organizations and began to exercise greater discretion in whether and how legal work would be delegated.[2] One of the reasons for this shift was likely the dramatic increase in the price of legal services.[3] Rising costs made organizations reluctant to pay enormous sums to law firms to perform work when in-house counsel could complete the same tasks at much lower prices.[4] Consequently, corporations began to increase the size of their legal departments and to expand the role of inside counsel at least in part as a means of breaking the financial hold outside counsel maintained.[5] But cost was not the only reason for the shift. The corporate counsel role had become more proactive as the advice it provided helped to develop and shape the organization's strategic choices. With the change in focus came an increase in power and prestige.[6]

The next shift occurred as a result of the corporate scandals in the 1990s and in the early part of the twenty-first century. Large corporate failures demonstrated that in-house counsel had a role to play as gatekeeper, responsible for ensuring that corporate officers complied with the law.[7] Outside counsel once had acted as gatekeeper, arguably preventing the corporation from engaging in socially harmful activity. But the scandals in the 1990s involving Enron and WorldCom suggested that outside counsel saw only discrete pieces of the corporate enterprise, which could limit their understanding of the organization's actions or scope of organizational misconduct. Similarly, the financial incentives driving law firms could cause them to downplay or ignore misconduct by the organization.[8] So the role of general counsel once again underwent dramatic change, this time resulting in an exponential expansion of its compliance role.

Today, the role of corporate counsel has taken on tremendous complexity. In-house counsel has at least four interconnected roles. First, it maintains a corporate compliance role, which includes monitoring and ensuring compliance with regulatory frameworks in all markets in which the organization operates. Second, the in-house counsel role includes responsibilities as a corporate officer. The legal unit must advise the organization about its strategic choices given its understanding of the law. This means not only helping the organization to make decisions that will enable its growth but also keeping in mind the fiduciary responsibility to stakeholders. Third, the general counsel plays a role as corporate agent. Legal units cannot manage all of the legal issues confronting their companies and, therefore, must delegate some of the work to outside counsel. But that delegation decision does not mean an abdication of responsibility. Finally, the general counsel has more of a managerial role in running the legal unit. There, the general counsel sets expectations and tone about the role of lawyers within the unit. Setting the expectation that the legal unit will be embedded in the business rather than separate from it can help to guide the organization in real time rather than being solely reactive.

GENERAL COUNSEL AS COMPLIANCE OFFICER

The general counsel office's primary role is to ensure corporate compliance with the law. That compliance function involves three main components: advisory, preventive, and regulatory. As a legal advisor, the general counsel bears the primary responsibility for "all legal matters affecting the corporation."[9] Within this advisory function, the general counsel also advises senior management on major transactions or other situations,[10] as well as advising the corporation's board of directors.[11] The preventive role means educating and alerting the organization about what is proper or improper to guide the organization's actions. This may include developing ethics education programs within the corporation that inform managers and employees of their legal and ethical responsibilities[12] and developing and administering corporate compliance programs, often referred to as "programmatic prevention."[13] All of these efforts are established to prevent violations of the law and to discover them if they do occur.[14] Finally, the regulatory role involves monitoring the organization to ensure that it complies with the law. This can take the form of conducting internal investigations when there is a report of a lack of compliance with the law.

The compliance role has become all the more difficult given that organizations often operate globally and regulatory frameworks are inconsistent, at best, and contradictory, at worst. Even understanding regulatory schemes can prove challenging, so compliance with contradictory provisions may make operations nearly impossible. The general counsel has to understand the technical aspects of compliance and then advise the organization's leadership about actions that may run afoul of those regulations. The compliance role is even more complex in that the legal unit must take the lead in establishing a culture of compliance. Lawyer-leaders cannot see everything or know all that is occurring within today's organizations. This means that they must develop practices and processes that encourage information flow, protect whistle-blowers, and set an expectation that the organization can thrive and abide by the law.

The structure of the organization and the legal unit can make this even more complicated. For example, a centralized legal department has feedback loops from every corporate department working with a single office run by the general counsel.[15] In a decentralized system, the in-house counsel works in individual departments in the corporation, reporting to division heads.[16] This decentralized structure often results in the general counsel having less involvement in day-to-day decision making and may be less informed of legal and ethical problems throughout the company.[17]

GENERAL COUNSEL AS CORPORATE OFFICER

The role of the general counsel includes an organizational leadership function; he or she participates in formulations of corporate strategy at the highest levels of the organization.[18] Because the general counsel and the legal department have a single client (the organization for which they work), there is a concern that that singular focus may cause the lawyers to have difficulty exercising the independence of judgment that is critical in a lawyer-client relationship. While there are examples of such distorted loyalties, the real leadership problem in the exercise of this role may be the tendency to view the client too narrowly, as though the client is only the organizational leadership. The client of the general counsel and the legal team includes not only the senior executives or leadership of the organization but also the organization's customers, shareholders, and other interested stakeholders that may be affected by the organization's choices.

Of course, there have been instances where general counsel have allowed their personal relationship with the company's leadership to blind them to their duty. For example, Franklin Brown, general counsel to Rite Aid, was indicted and convicted for engaging in a pattern of fraud and obstruction of justice spanning six years. Brown schemed with the CEO and CFO of the company to manipulate the company's reported earnings.[19] Brown stated that he felt "an overwhelming sense of loyalty to the company" over the years, deciding to stay on after Rite Aid went public, when many other executives took their money and departed.[20] During his tenure as general counsel, Brown felt considerable loyalty to the CEO and CFO. As the company began to experience some financial difficulties, Brown, the CFO, and the CEO agreed to backdate letters and to take other measures in an attempt to conceal fraudulent accounting practices.[21] Brown told his colleagues he was putting himself "totally on the line for you guys."[22] He chose to engage in illegal conduct because of his relationship to the leaders of the company.

A related problem comes when general counsel, at times, can perceive the leadership team as its sole client: defining the client and the client's interests too narrowly. As an individual, the general counsel may experience some tensions in his or her role. He or she is expected to serve as part of the executive leadership team of the organization and to exercise independent professional judgment about the actions that team seeks to take on behalf of the organization. And the general counsel knows that the role extends beyond the immediate team of which he or she is part. But it is sometimes hard to give full consideration to interests and issues when they are not as tangible and present as one's colleagues.

The legal team may also experience some difficulty in fully grasping its responsibility to see the client as more broadly defined. Much like the general counsel, the legal unit also works with colleagues and supervisors who can be quite adamant about taking actions they think will benefit the organization. Given those relationships, as well as the immediacy of the advocacy for a particular point of view, it may be difficult for members of the legal unit to see and articulate contrary views. But the legal team must develop and maintain processes and practices that are designed to remind them that they also bear responsibility for the customers, shareholders, and other interested stakeholders who may be affected by the organization's choices. The general counsel and the legal team must develop practices that push their thinking to question the ideas of colleagues and to ask "what if" constantly.

GENERAL COUNSEL AS CORPORATE AGENT

General counsel and their legal teams also serve as corporate agents in negotiations with third parties external to the corporation. The most common instance of this arises in the delegation of legal work to outside counsel. Prior to the reinvigoration of general counsel's position in the 1970s, one of the primary roles general counsel served was as a liaison between the corporation's principal outside law firm and managers within the corporation.[23] Since the 1970s, companies rarely have a single relationship with a law firm and, instead, tend to have multiple relationships, often in different countries. This delegation carries challenges. Among the challenges is that the distribution of corporate work among multiple law firms limits the breadth of any one firm's knowledge of the client, empowering general counsel in dealings with firms but reducing the capacity of any one firm to levy judgment when more comprehensive insight into the corporation may be desirable.[24] Also as a result of this delegation, in-house counsel often has insights into the business that any outside firm lacks. Monitoring outside legal services and remaining vigilant about the ways that even discrete choices can have a broader impact remains a responsibility of in-house counsel.

RUNNING THE ORGANIZATION'S LAW OFFICE

Perhaps the most conventional role for the general counsel as leader is the management of the organization's legal department. There, the ability to lead is as important as running any organization. A general counsel functions as the top administrator of the corporation's internal legal department. This position entails overall responsibility for managing the department's budget; establishing and implementing departmental policies; and recruiting, supervising, and inspiring subordinates.[25] General counsel must also establish a culture within the organization recognizing the legal unit's integral role in ensuring overall compliance with the law. In addition, general counsel encourages the development of new approaches and methods of behaving that will comport with legal and regulatory frameworks and will serve the organization and its stakeholders.

Structuring a law department requires leadership in the internal operations of the department. This means paying attention to organizational design. Will there be a command and control structure? To what extent will or should the department operate in a centralized or decentralized fashion? Many law departments use hierarchical internal structures, with multiple reporting levels between the general counsel and the lowest level of staff lawyer.[26] Some corporate law departments have been reorganized to have fewer titles and flatter decision-making structures. These flatter departments often encourage teaming as a way for lawyers to work across functions and

lines of business and to engage with a wider set of people within the organization. These decentralized law departments also place lawyers in closer
physical proximity to the operational managers so that they might have better rapport with those managers and with the specifics of the businesses they
manage.[27] Somewhat counterintuitively, the lawyer within the legal team
who may ultimately be responsible for assessing whether an action comports
with regulations or the law may want to be less separated from the internal
operations to be able to guide the organization better.

Each of these roles has depth and complexity. And these dimensions
place significant demands on the general counsel and legal team. Each of
these roles also broadens the lawyer-leader's vantage points about how best to
serve the organization. What follows are two examples where lawyer-leaders
failed to consider the full set of dimensions in their roles and privileged one
part of the role over another. In the first example, we see an instance where
general counsel at Hewlett-Packard let her personal loyalties to the chair of
the board shape her approach to an investigation; that allegiance blinded
her to the illegality of the investigatory conduct she was expected to oversee.
The second example exposes a failure by the legal team of Wells Fargo to
develop and sustain a culture that encouraged compliance and supported
reporting of misconduct by executives.

PRETEXTING AT HEWLETT-PACKARD

In 2005, Hewlett-Packard (HP) faced a series of embarrassing leaks to the
media from its board meetings.[28] A CNET News.com story featured information about HP's long-term strategic plans, and a front page story in the *Wall
Street Journal* contained sensitive details about the company's CEO search that
could only have come from a member of the board.[29] Board chair Patricia
Dunn was livid and considered it a priority to determine the source of the
leaks and prevent any further unauthorized disclosures. She launched two
sequential investigations of the board members, called Kona 1 and Kona 2,
to determine who among the directors was leaking confidential information.
Midway through Kona 1, at Dunn's request, general counsel Ann O'Neil
Baskins became involved and ultimately assumed responsibility for Kona 2.
At the end of the investigation, it became clear that Baskins had approved
and supervised an investigative strategy that involved a controversial, and

indeed illegal, tactic for gaining access to privileged information. Baskins became so focused on helping the chair root out the leak that she failed to exercise professional judgment in how that investigation was conducted.

As board chair, Dunn recognized the problems that leaks could cause, but she was not sure how to proceed in identifying the sources of the leak. So she sought help. She did not initially turn to HP's general counsel or legal unit but chose first to consult HP's then acting CEO, CFO, and director of administration, Bob Wayman, for advice on how to proceed. Wayman referred her to the head of HP's global security, Kevin Huska, who, in turn, recommended Ron Delia and his outside private investigation firm, Security Outsourcing Solutions.[30] HP had contracted with Delia previously for breaches of confidential information, so Dunn asked Delia to conduct this investigation, called Kona 1, in the spring of 2005. In the course of the investigation, Dunn learned that Delia's organization had accessed phone records of board members but believed that these were obtained as public records. Dunn would later testify to Congress that she had the "clear impression . . . from Mr. Delia . . . that these records could be obtained from publicly available sources in a legal manner."[31]

General counsel did not actually get involved until early in the summer of 2005, in the midst of the Kona 1 investigation. Dunn was not an attorney, so she brought Baskins into the loop. Baskins had risen to the position of general counsel in 2000 and had spent most of her legal career as a lawyer for HP.[32] She felt committed to the company and committed to the board's chair.[33] Later, Dunn would admit that she relied on Baskins's legal expertise and her commitment to ethics in helping her make choices that would be "right for HP." By the end of the summer, Kona 1 appeared to be winding down. Although the investigation had not produced any results or identified the source of the leaks, Dunn was prepared to stop the investigation because the board leaks had stopped.

Or so she thought. In January 2006, a major leak occurred resulting in a CNET feature with details that had come from someone attending an off-site board strategy meeting. Dunn then decided to launch a second investigation, Kona 2. This time, though, Dunn began by consulting Baskins. Dunn proposed to Baskins that they hire Kroll Associates, an outside company that had more of a national reputation, to handle the second phase of the investigation. But Baskins balked at the suggestion. Instead, Baskins urged Dunn to keep the investigation in-house under their supervision and to assign responsibility to Kevin Hunsaker, a member of the legal unit who reported directly to Baskins.[34] The Kona 2 investigation lasted from late January 2006 until March 2006. Over the three-month period, Baskins and Dunn held weekly conference calls to update Dunn on the progress of the investigation. Again, Dunn would later testify that she assumed that because HP attorneys were overseeing the investigation, they were handling it legally.[35] Dunn also testified that she received assurances from Baskins and Hunsaker that the investigation complied with the law and HP's Standard of Business Conduct.[36]

But, in the end, the investigation violated the law. In February, the investigation team proposed a sting operation to determine the source of the leaks. While the matter would be handled in-house, the general counsel decided to bring on a private security company to assist in the operations. The security company had recruited five private investigators nationwide who used a controversial spying technique known as "pretexting." Pretexting, which is illegal in many states, involves the use of deception, misrepresentation, or deliberate withholding of information to obtain information relevant to the investigation.[37] In this case, investigators impersonated HP board members and nine journalists (including reporters for CNET, the *Wall Street Journal*, and the *New York Times*) to obtain their phone records and determine the source of the leak. Not only were Baskins and her legal team generally responsible for the supervision and approval of the investigation, but records indicate that Baskins knew about, and permitted the use of, pretexting.[38]

The ultimate public disclosure of this investigative effort led to a number of state and federal probes. The investigation company faced federal charges in connection with the scandal.[39] Meanwhile, HP settled the spying charges brought against it by agreeing to pay $14.5 million to the State of California. In her testimony before a congressional committee, Dunn remarked, "I never doubted . . . that what they [the investigators] were doing was legal."[40] In retrospect, both Dunn and CEO Mark Hurd made it clear that Baskins had provided "bad legal advice."[41]

The HP scandal focused attention on in-house counsel's responsibilities to maintain legal compliance even when they believe that they are acting for the benefit of the organization. The disclosure of confidential information from HP obviously presented huge problems for the business. No business can operate effectively if its internal strategic choices and considerations end up on the front pages of business journals and newspapers. So it is understandable that Baskins and her team were hoping to contain the problem and to identify the source at any cost. But Baskins and her legal team still had the obligation to examine and assess whether the investigatory techniques were proper.[42] Had Baskins fully understood the multiple roles inherent in her position, as well as the leadership responsibilities that accompany those roles, she would not have been in this position. The general counsel leadership role should have balanced her duties to the various stakeholders, but she betrayed that obligation to balance by focusing inappropriately on only part of her responsibilities. She lost sight of her larger legal and professional duties. In the end, Baskins resigned as general counsel, then stood before a congressional committee investigating the Hewlett-Packard spying scandal. Baskins raised her right hand and swore to tell the truth; then she proceeded to exercise her Fifth Amendment privilege against self-incrimination.[43]

MISALIGNED INCENTIVES AT WELLS FARGO

The preceding case demonstrates the cost of ignoring the general counsel's fiduciary duty and misreading the legal unit's gatekeeping mandate. The next case illustrates what can occur when the legal unit does not establish a culture of compliance and does not take steps to remain in the decision-making loop in order to raise questions about strategic choices and confront leadership when patterns of improper conduct begin to surface.

Wells Fargo continues to find fraudulent accounts. Nearly a year after Wells Fargo's fraudulent account scandal surfaced, the bank turned up more than a million additional accounts that customers may not have authorized.[44] Wells Fargo agreed in September 2016 to pay a $185 million penalty to the Consumer Financial Protection Bureau, the Office of the Comptroller of the Currency, and the city of Los Angeles to settle claims that the bank had opened and charged fees for more than 1.5 million customer bank accounts and another half million credit card accounts without the knowledge and consent of customers.[45] The findings brought the number of potentially unauthorized accounts to 3.5 million—a nearly 70 percent increase over the bank's initial estimate.[46] At the time, Wells Fargo said that 2.1 million suspect accounts had been opened from 2011 to mid-2015; now evidence suggests these problems may have begun earlier, and the company said it would expand its review to include accounts opened from 2009 to 2016.[47] The broader review also uncovered a previously unknown problem: unauthorized enrollments of customers in the bank's online bill payment service. Wells Fargo said that it had found 528,000 cases in which customers may have been signed up without their knowledge or consent, and it will refund $910,000 to customers who incurred fees or charges. Widespread fraud in the Community Banking Division at Wells Fargo dated back to at least 2011. The bank's sales incentive structures seem to have played a major role in inducing employees to commit fraud. The CEO at the helm during this period, John Stumpf, has stepped down. But a question that remains unanswered is this: where were the company's in-house lawyers? Part of the responsibility of the legal unit is to remain alert to threats, to establish and maintain a culture that enables information to surface regarding problems, and to create controls and practices that encourage compliance with the law at all levels. Certainly these policies existed on paper. The problem was that the culture of the company veered away from those policies.

Wells Fargo was one of the largest financial institutions in the world. It was the golden child of the post–financial crisis banking world. Its strategy involved focusing on the consumer side of the business and relying heavily on retail deposits. Not only had that focus enabled the bank to weather the financial crisis, but it emerged from the crisis with a stronger nationwide presence. It had built a reputation for being the banking leader in cross-selling—a practice where the bank markets multiple products to existing customers.[48] The downside to Wells Fargo's strategy? It had to rely on its ability to cross-sell more profitable products to its consumer base to grow profits. From the CEO down through branch management, Wells Fargo leadership placed significant emphasis on selling additional products to existing consumers.[49] In April 2012, Wells Fargo averaged a record-breaking 5.98 products per household. The following year, that figure had risen to 6.1. And, by 2014, it was 6.14—nearly four times the industry average.[50] The increase was no accident. Stumpf set the expectation at earnings calls that Wells Fargo's success at cross-selling retail accounts was one of the principal reasons to buy shares in the company.[51] Top Wall Street analysts during the period consistently made the case to acquire Wells Fargo shares largely because of their strong cross-sell numbers.[52] And Stumpf set the tone internally, establishing a goal of eight accounts per customer, repeating the mantra to bank employees that "eight is great."[53] Other major banks averaged less than three accounts per customer.[54]

Stumpf's cross-selling ambition shaped incentive structures in the company, establishing bonuses for success and penalties for failure. Wells Fargo provided various "incentive pay programs designed to support specific business objectives."[55] In a number of branches, those pay programs assumed the form of bonus packages conditioned on satisfying product sales goals.[56] Tellers earned approximately 3 percent of their salary in incentive pay linked to sales, while personal bankers typically relied on sales bonuses for 15–20 percent of their annual compensation. For tellers and bankers—who made an average of $11.81 and $17.22 per hour before any bonus, respectively—sales bonuses had become a crucial source of income.[57] Daily sales performance at the branch level was closely monitored by branch managers, who were themselves closely watched by district and regional managers. Branch managers reported sales numbers up the chain of command as often as seven times per day, and the progress of managers, tellers, and personal bankers was often monitored hourly.[58] If a branch began to lag, its manager risked being "chastised and embarrassed in front of 60-plus managers in your area by the community banking president."[59] Managers heard the message from their supervisors that sales were expected to increase at any cost, and then managers pressed their employees with the least job security to meet those goals.[60] Employees were encouraged to make sales pitches at bus stops and retirement homes to boost their numbers, and some were required to make a minimum of 100 calls per day to prospective customers.[61]

Falling behind often snowballed—any shortfall in daily sales at some branches would be added to the next day's target.[62] Once behind, some employees were pressured to open accounts for friends or family members.[63] "Laggards"[64] sometimes received written and verbal admonishments and had their sales numbers posted for colleagues to view in branch offices.[65] A number of employees were threatened with termination for failure to meet their goals,[66] and a "significant number" were fired.[67] Low-paid workers in this high-pressure environment may have resorted to targeting vulnerable populations—such as the homeless[68] and the elderly[69]—just to make their quotas and keep their jobs. Employees who pointed out the fact that the sales goals were unrealistic or that their consumer base was already saturated with Wells Fargo products were often berated or fired.[70]

Although much of this activity occurred at the branch level, the leadership team and general counsel should have been aware that the incentive structure had the potential to encourage fraud. Wells Fargo leadership maintained, though, that because these incentives were new, they could not have foreseen this misconduct. But the bank had a history of questionable practices that should have put leadership and the legal unit on notice. A consent order issued by the Federal Reserve in July 2011, directing Wells Fargo to cease and desist various fraudulent practices in its mortgage lending division, found the following:

[Wells Fargo's] internal controls were not adequate to detect and prevent instances when certain of its sales personnel, *in order to meet sales performance standards and receive incentive compensation*, altered or falsified income documents and inflated prospective borrowers' incomes to qualify those borrowers for loans that they would not otherwise have been qualified to receive.[71]

Moreover, there was some evidence for leadership that sales goals were providing incentive for employees to commit fraud as early as 2011.[72] In early 2011, incentive-driven fraudulent practices began to emerge in the Community Banking Division of Wells Fargo.[73] Stumpf testified before a congressional subcommittee that he could not rule out systemic fraud in community banking before 2011, and Wells Fargo agreed to investigate incidences of fraud dating back to 2009.[74] However, allegations of fraud predate even that period, as aggressive sales goals were a part of Wells Fargo culture well before 2009.[75]

IGNORING COMPLAINTS AND PATTERNS

Stumpf maintained that he had no knowledge of the fraudulent practices employed in the banking division until late 2013.[76] Stumpf further claimed not to remember precisely when in 2013 he was informed of the fraud permeating his former company.[77] But a number of disclosures suggest that he may have known far earlier than 2013. A letter to Stumpf in 2007 warned of widespread "unethical (and illegal) activity" inside Wells Fargo and the "routine deception and fraudulent exploitation of our clients."[78] The employee who had written the letter had been transferred from the branch after raising sales concerns and later won a federal whistle-blower retaliation case against Wells Fargo. Also in 2007, the Sales Quality Manual for the Community Banking Division was updated with Stumpf's executive guidance. Among other changes, the manual contained a proviso reminding employees that they needed to obtain a customer's consent before opening accounts in the customer's name.[79] In 2011, an email to Stumpf from a branch manager detailed the practice of moving money to new accounts for the same customer for the purposes of artificially inflating growth numbers.[80]

According to Stumpf, the board of directors "was made aware generally of issues [concerning fraud] in committees at high levels in the 2011–2012 timeframe."[81] Stumpf claims that in 2011, the board commissioned a team to employ data analytics to monitor sales practice violations.[82] In 2012, the board began reducing sales goals for team members to qualify for incentive compensation.[83] In 2013, the board initiated corporate-wide oversight of sales practices.[84] In 2014, they further aligned compensation plans in an attempt to ensure that pay was commensurate with ethical performance.[85] In 2015, training materials were altered to target fraudulent sales practices, sales goals were lowered again, and Stumpf began conducting town hall–style meetings to address sales fraud.[86] On October 1, 2016, sales goals were eliminated entirely.[87]

Throughout this period, fraud firings continued at a steady clip, peaking in 2013.[88] The bank indicated that it fired 5,300 workers, including some managers. The firing of thousands of employees should have raised flags for the legal department; these numbers indicated that the situation went beyond rogue employees engaging in misconduct, pointing to deep, systemic problems within the bank. The legal department should have been at the table at the first discussions on the strategic choice to link incentives to cross-selling. But even if the lawyers were not at the initial discussions of the cross-selling strategy, once the firings began to take place they were on notice. They should have had processes installed to alert them to such patterns and to help them see connections between the fraud and the incentive structure. The legal unit should have posed "what if" scenarios to examine what might be causing these missteps and to explore options for responding to problems in the Community Banking Division. However, at no point prior to the public disclosure of the fraud do we see any evidence that the legal unit took any action to investigate this fully or that bank leadership took steps to abolish sales goals.

Why did the fraud occur? Representative Sean P. Duffy (R-Wisc.) echoed a sentiment pervasive among his colleagues in the House and Senate about the reasons that Wells Fargo failed to stem fraudulent practices earlier: "Wells Fargo was making a lot of money off of [fraud] . . . was hoping that it wouldn't get caught . . . and kept the practice in play because they were making big profits."[89] Stumpf's personal holdings in Wells Fargo stocks increased by over $200 million during the period of known fraud—in large part due to fraudulently inflated cross-selling numbers that he pitched to shareholders as the reason to buy in.[90] In late October 2013, however, Stumpf sold $13 million in Wells Fargo stock on the open market, which was by far the largest such sale he made during his tenure.[91] Stumpf maintains that the sale had nothing to do with his discovery of fraud in the banking division, and that the timing was coincidental.[92] Stumpf resigned his post at the helm of Wells Fargo and, under mounting pressure from Congress, forfeited some $41 million in stock awards and much of his salary from 2016. However, Stumpf still departed with nearly $250 million of Wells Fargo stock, much of which was generated during the period of rampant fraud in his organization.[93]

All told, Wells Fargo's community banking officials used numerous fraudulent practices to meet sales quotas. An analysis commissioned by Wells Fargo indicates that between 2011 and 2015, community banking employees opened 1,534,280 deposit accounts "that may not have been authorized and that may have been funded through simulated funding, or transferring funds from consumers' existing accounts without their knowledge or consent."[94] Many employees forged customer signatures for the purposes of opening these unauthorized accounts.[95] Approximately 85,000 of the fraudulent accounts incurred about $2 million in fees, which Wells Fargo is currently in the process of refunding.[96] The fees assessed against the fraudulent accounts may be just the tip of the iceberg in terms of consumer harm. Opening deposit accounts can negatively impact the credit scores of consumers, which increases interest rates on a variety of loans and can also impair employment prospects. Consumers who had fake accounts opened in their names could pay heightened interest rates on home mortgages, potentially costing them tens of thousands of dollars.[97]

General counsel and the balance of the executive team were aware, or should have been aware, that these incentive policies and the enforcement tactics that accompanied them resulted in inappropriate and illegal conduct. It was apparent to anyone who looked that fraud had become a normal sales practice. The in-house lawyers were, at best, willfully ignorant of what was occurring in community banking because the company was profiting from these practices. Had the legal unit established and sustained a culture of compliance at all levels of the company, these fraudulent practices would have been less likely to take place because it would have been clear they were not tolerated. Instead, the legal unit disregarded and failed in its fiduciary duties to the bank's customers.

As the preceding case study demonstrates, lawyers are expected to create a set of processes and practices that can surface patterns of improper conduct and alert the team to illegal actions taken by their companies. So what is the leadership imperative in such cases? Lawyer-leaders need to keep their heads on a swivel, watching for signals that actions taken by individuals within the company may be threatening stakeholders and threatening damage to the brand. Representing the company may mean that the legal unit needs to look at the behavior of colleagues, and even superiors, to ascertain whether they are establishing a culture that encourages improper conduct. It is uncomfortable to imagine that one's colleagues may be engaging in improper, let alone illegal, conduct. But the leadership responsibility of the lawyer-leaders involves asking themselves hard questions, exploring "what if" scenarios to assess pervasive problems fully, and then engaging in courageous conversations.

LEADERSHIP LESSONS

Both the Hewlett-Packard and Wells Fargo case studies serve as cautionary tales for the leadership pitfalls that can take place when in-house counsel distill their roles and ignore the need to maintain a broader perspective.

Holding multiple *perspectives simultaneously is critical to effective leadership.*
The reality of today's lawyer-leaders is that they often must take into account
a number of different perspectives. Relationships that tack too closely to one
constituency may cause leaders to develop an inappropriately narrow view
of their role. When lawyer-leaders recognize that their role involves leading
from the intersection of stakeholders, perspectives, and ideas, they are better able to bring the judgment that the role expects.

Each of these cases exposes us to general counsels and legal units that
were reluctant to rock the boat or challenge the company's practices. But
that may be the role of the intersectional leader who is positioned to protect a wide-ranging set of interests. The intersectional leader who adopts a
mind-set that is suspicious of easy agreement recognizes that the role involves
second-guessing decisions that others comfortably accept and then asking
probing questions to see and expose the full range of implications and options. The lawyers at HP and Wells Fargo stifled that inquiry, which led to a
broader set of problems for the organizations they wanted to help and protect.

The lawyer-leader must embrace optionality.
The complexity of the issues that companies face today place great demands
on the in-house lawyer-leader. This complexity requires a spectrum of options and approaches that stretch beyond the route that the organizational
leadership may wish to pursue. Intersectional lawyer-leaders need to engage
in "what if" scenarios, constantly recognizing that there may not be a single
established course or a single perspective that should control the direction.
By pushing the examination of issues and exploring alternatives, lawyer-
leaders can bring a level of rigor to the decision making they must engage
or advise others to take. Lawyer-leaders also push against the tendency to
favor one perspective because colleagues or those close to the leader prefer a
particular course. Debate and critical thinking are tools that lawyer-leaders
must sharpen to be effective.

The lawyer-leader must develop and nurture a culture of inclusion and integrity.
Much of the work ensuring compliance with the law at all levels begins with
the culture of the organization. If the organization sets an expectation of
conformity with the law, aligning its incentives with the legal expectations,

then the role of the lawyer-leader is that much easier. But the intersectional framework also teaches that the lawyer-leader needs to nurture that culture by actively seeking out views skeptical about the organization's practices or course. Listening to those views and being willing to consider their validity can create an environment that is actively open to examination and criticism. And establishing a cultural norm that invites divergent thinking may actually help the lawyer-leader engage in the sort of dichotomous thinking the role demands.

WHAT EDUCATORS CAN DO

Law schools and educators in practice can better prepare lawyers to address these issues in the following ways.

1) Law schools should teach law students to take an active role in discussions rather than being passive learners.

Law firms, nonprofits, companies, and prosecutors' and defenders' offices can all benefit from having newer lawyers provide input from a perspective that is fresh, that does not take the culture for granted, and that may grow out of a different geography or practice. In their summer and term-time internships, law students will likely encounter supervisors who insist that there is only one way to perform certain tasks: "It has always been done like that here." Law students should be taught to question that reflexive response because the familiar path may impede a thoughtful new approach. Even the most established organizations benefit from a different perspective at times. Teaching law students to speak up and challenge convention as part of their law school experience will help them develop that discipline for practice.

2) Educators in practice and coaches need to help leaders build a proactive culture in their organizations.

The behavior of leaders sets a standard for the organizations or units they lead. To create an environment that is proactive rather than reactive means that the leader must ask far-reaching questions to push employees to think about options. The leader must create spaces to have conversations that are not simply focused on the short-term goals or the particular interests of the unit. The leader should set the expectation that he or she will want employees to think about how issues they face affect the entire enterprise, the market, and stakeholders and to develop approaches and solutions that take these broader interests into account. All too often, organizations become so focused on day-to-day operations that they fail to create room for broader conversations about vision and possibilities.

CHAPTER SEVEN

What Got You Here Won't Get You There

Pulling Together the Leadership Lessons for Lawyers

LAWYERS CAN AND DO PLAY central roles in almost every field simply by virtue of being lawyers. But the volatility, complexity, and uncertainty that characterize today's environment have combined to raise the stakes for being an *effective* lawyer-leader. Lawyer-leaders currently face questions that are infinitely more complex than those typically encountered by their predecessors, and the environment in which they must address those questions is far less forgiving of errors in judgment. The decisions lawyer-leaders make—and advise others to make—often have wide-ranging implications that may prove nearly impossible to anticipate at the moment of the decision or advice. Adding to the role's difficulty is the increasing frequency with which behaviors and attitudes that leaders once believed could be kept within the confines of offices are finding their way into the public domain. The lawyer-leader must acknowledge the public nature of his or her role and must take steps to embrace values and attributes that are above reproach and can withstand public scrutiny.

Quite simply, more is required of today's leader than the "business as usual" thinking and purely pragmatic judgment that flows from a reliance on conventional models. Both the nature of the problems and the speed at which change erupts compel leaders to find ways to develop and maintain a broader perspective so that they can exercise the necessary judgment to guide the organization forward. This means that lawyer-leaders must be inclusive with regard both to the teams they assemble and the perspectives they seek. They will need to surround themselves with other, often competing, perspectives to help identify trends, to articulate pressing issues, and to facilitate the development of viable solutions. The broader perspective today's leaders need will emerge only if they decide to position themselves with access to the views of key stakeholders who hold different and diverging perspectives. From that nodal position, the lawyer-leader can become an intersectional leader.

Being an intersectional leader involves more than being an individual contributor to the enterprise. It is fairly common for leaders to believe that what enabled them to rise in the ranks will be enough to sustain them in the leadership role. But, time and again, that belief has proved untrue. That is not to suggest that all the legal experience and expertise that lawyer-leaders have accumulated and have used to their and the organization's advantage somehow becomes irrelevant at the point at which they are elevated to a formal position of leadership. Rather, it means that subject-matter expertise does not form the sum total of what they will need to lead. Instead, to be effective, lawyer-leaders will need to move from being an individual contributor to one who connects people and networks for the good of the enterprise. They will need to supplement their technical knowledge with a host of other skills and capabilities to help them discern the best courses of action in the midst of uncertainty so that they can be the kind of inspirational and stabilizing force as the organization moves forward through change. As intersectional leaders, they will need to tap into the collective viewpoints of people whose experience and expertise may differ. They will need to collaborate and, at times, step out of the way to let others take the lead. They will need to invite skepticism that forces them to examine and challenge their own assumptions and orthodoxies. These practices form the core of intersectional leadership.

KEY ATTRIBUTES AND SKILLS FOR THE INTERSECTIONAL LAWYER-LEADER

To understand what intersectional leadership entails, one must recognize that it is far more than a leadership theory. It is a set of behaviors that can be taught, learned, and practiced. To understand intersectional leadership more fully, one must identify the attributes and skills that characterize the intersectional leader. The preceding chapters exposed some of the dangers that occur when lawyer-leaders fail to understand their leadership task. Those case studies produced a number of individual lessons for the lawyer-leader who hopes to avoid similar leadership lapses. When we distill those lessons to their essence, five key leadership attributes are foundational to the intersectional lawyer-leader:

1. The lawyer-leader cultivates and invites diverse views.
Intersectional leaders recognize that leadership is shared. They continuously seek out and value diversity of thought in their teams, inviting skepticism to challenge their own and their team's assumptions. They recognize that they can and will learn from perhaps unexpected sources that fall outside familiar teams and have less familiar vantage points.

2. The lawyer-leader acts with moral courage even out of public view.
Intersectional leaders set the behavioral example, signaling their commitment to integrity in private and in public settings. That example sets the tone for the team and the culture to bring their best.

3. The lawyer-leader subordinates his or her personal ambition to the good of the whole.
Intersectional leaders operate transparently, exposing instances when their personal interests may be in play. They actively work to understand and subordinate their personal ambition to the good of the whole by instituting processes and disciplines that check personal motivations. They collaborate with others, which may mean giving up something important to them for the good of the whole.

4. The lawyer-leader embraces his or her role as guardian of the system's integrity.
Intersectional leaders accept that they function as part of a larger ecosystem that may experience internal and external threats. Seeking information from a wide array of sources and networks enables intersectional leaders to have a wider lens about the issues that threaten the system's integrity. That wide lens also enables intersectional leaders to spot and address issues, better understanding both the potential benefits and negative implications of decisions they make.

5. The lawyer-leader adopts a mind-set that embraces optionality.
Intersectional leaders question constantly and set an expectation that they and their teams will hold multiple thoughts simultaneously to push their own

thinking. Even when dichotomous thinking is not an explicit requirement of the role, intersectional leaders use "what if" scenarios to understand the nature of the problem and the range of potential resolutions.

These five attributes distinguish intersectional leaders from other leaders by changing the way that leadership is practiced and the way that lawyer-leaders engage their people. Of course, a variety of skills underlie these traits. To provide some measure of stability and guidance in the midst of uncertainty and volatility, lawyer-leaders will need to do more than rely solely on their technical legal expertise. They will need to hone and tap into a set of skills that enable them to be emotionally intelligent,[1] cognitively competent, culturally competent, and broadly connected.

EMOTIONAL COMPETENCIES

Emotional intelligence, unlike IQ, can be taught and learned.[2] Critics often suggest that people are "born with certain levels of empathy."[3] Others believe that individuals "acquire empathy as a result of life's experiences."[4] Research suggests that *both* are true.[5] This research has important implications for legal education and leadership. Traditionally, emotional intelligence (EQ) has been defined as the ability to recognize and understand emotional information about oneself and others. Emotional intelligence means having awareness of one's own emotions and of the emotions of others, and then using that awareness to manage oneself and to influence the behavior of others.[6] Studies suggest that individuals with high emotional intelligence competencies, IQ being equal, have a more developed ability to persuade, influence, and communicate compared with individuals with less developed competencies.[7] It is, therefore, not surprising that emotional intelligence has emerged as an important benchmark for effective leadership.[8] However, while the conventional definition has merit and continuing significance, it does have some key shortcomings. The intersectional leader will need to add more dimensions to this skill set to exercise the kind of EQ that today's diverse environment demands.

As a first step, let's briefly examine the basic components of emotional intelligence. Self-awareness is one of the essential elements and happens to be a particularly important competency for lawyers. It encompasses knowing your motivations, drives, and idiosyncrasies. Self-awareness also requires that the lawyer-leader understand the ways that certain external factors affect one's own performance and productivity. While this sounds simple on the surface, it really demands a level of reflection that can prove difficult and disconcerting. Leaders must examine and come to understand not just their personal goals but the *values* that drive their choices.[9] The most obvious manifestation of the emotional intelligence attribute is the ability to engage in candid self-assessment.[10] Emotionally intelligent leaders tend to be motivated by more than prestige, money, or power. They tend to be moved and influenced by a "deeply embedded desire to achieve."[11] This often manifests as an overriding sense of purpose—that extends well beyond individual self-interest—as well as a deep and abiding passion for the work itself.

The second component of emotional intelligence is self-regulation. This dimension expects leaders not only to be aware of their own feelings but to manage those feelings in ways that uplift rather than derail others.[12] A leader who possesses emotional intelligence knows how to control impulses and feelings that otherwise would lead to unfiltered displays of emotion. These displays can unsettle and disrupt others' ability to function well within the organization. If, for example, a crisis occurs within the organization, the emotionally intelligent leader does not engage in the sort of behavior that amplifies the stress of the crisis. Instead, he or she operates as a calming force in the face of turmoil. Similarly, if an organization is led by individuals who lack self-regulation, others within the organization may be reluctant to raise questions or to alert leaders to problems out of an understandable fear that the leader will fly off the handle when hearing bad news. Or, in a legal organization, associates may not want to work for a partner who deals with the stress of deal making or litigation by screaming at and threatening associates and staff.

The importance of self-regulation in leadership goes beyond the daily operations of an organization. Adherence to some measure of self-regulation sets the tone for how the organizational culture operates and is understood. The integrity of the organization is enhanced when it is clear from the top that uncontrolled outbursts and disrespect for dissenting views will not be tolerated. To be clear, self-regulation does not mean an absence of passion. In the right circumstances, demonstrating one's passion for leadership and the organization can prove energizing for others within the organization

and can galvanize the group toward common goals. However, displays of
negative emotion tend to make environments toxic for others and threaten
the overall productivity and health of the organization.[13]

Perhaps the most important aspect of EQ is empathy.[14] Empathy in leadership is the ability to understand and feel what others experience by stepping into their shoes and seeing the situation from their perspective. At first
blush, it may appear that empathy is in conflict with what many perceive
as the role of the leader: to be tough and clear-minded to make the tough
calls. But empathetic leaders often make the difficult calls better than other
leaders. Empathetic leaders start from the premise that they must gather information and understand the implications of a problem before acting and,
through empathy, often enable their people to weather the tough call. Evidence suggests that in times of turmoil or fundamental change, empathetic
leaders are often more capable of guiding their organization because they
anticipate the range of emotions from those within their organizations and
can get the most from them.

Let me offer a personal example. As a consultant, I worked with a large
professional services organization just after the passage of the Sarbanes-
Oxley legislation. This legislation was Congress's response to the fallout
from the collapse of Enron and its accounting firm, Arthur Andersen. The
legislation was far-reaching and wholly transformed the way professional
services were allowed to operate. Almost overnight, the accounting industry
underwent a colossal change: it moved from an industry that experienced
little if any oversight to one that had strict regulatory controls. The training that I had been hired to conduct focused on some of the operational
changes the organization would have to make under Sarbanes-Oxley. But
the leadership team was acutely aware of—and sensitive to—the pervasive
anxiety within both the industry and the organization about the sweeping
changes that were occurring. My job was to facilitate a Socratic dialogue
using hypotheticals from the way business had been done and then to examine the way the organization would have to function in the new regulatory
environment. The leadership could have chosen to limit the hypotheticals
and ensuing discussion to the technical changes the new regulations would
require and impose. Instead, the leaders specifically asked me to conduct a
wide-ranging dialogue that would bring to the surface both the operational

and emotional implications of the changed environment. The conversations were not always straightforward or easy, but the participants made clear that they appreciated the opportunity to air and address some rather thorny issues in an open and empathetic manner. The result was that the transition to the new regulatory and operating world was almost seamless for that organization.

Finally, EQ seems to include what we generically call social skills. Leaders who possess good social skills tend to be able to relate to people from a wide range of backgrounds and life experiences.[15] They tend to be adept at managing relationships and, perhaps as importantly, often exhibit optimism and resilience. At one time or another, most of us have had the good fortune to collaborate with or to have been led by people with this EQ trait, who stand out for having many leadership arrows in their quivers and knowing when to use the right one. They understand the social component of a work environment and find ways to tap into what is common among all, aligning viewpoints in order to move the organization forward toward a shared goal. Even in an organization where different people will respond to different motivations, they can develop and produce a unifying message of purpose that touches people and rallies them in a common direction. So social skills combined with self-awareness, self-regulation, and empathy take the leader a long way toward being effective.

But not all the way. The traditional formulations of EQ fall short of what today's leader needs. They do not typically address or sufficiently emphasize the sort of emotional intelligence that leaders must have in a more diverse world and work environment. The intersectional leader must be sensitive to— and appreciative of—difference: he or she must *value* the racial, cultural, and gender diversity within our environments because true growth and change comes from the dynamic exchange and robust engagement that flows from difference. What the conventional emotional intelligence formulation leaves out, intersectional leadership considers key: intersectional leaders must be able to admit that their own race, culture, and gender frame how they perceive the world, and they must be willing to put their perceptions aside in order to be educated by people whose experiences and reactions differ. This means not only including on one's team individuals who see and experience the world differently. It means being willing to recognize and concede that the leader's experience is not the norm or the only model from which he or she should try to make sense of the world or the issues presented. Intersectional leaders step out of the narrow confines of their experience and expectations to step into the shoes of others. They let others guide and teach. By embracing and assigning value to that learning experience, intersectional leaders are more willing to conclude that these varied experiences or viewpoints may enrich their understanding of an issue. They also realize that their perspective should never be the sole consideration and may not even be the most helpful data point in understanding an issue. They must be rigorously open-minded.

Again, a personal example, this time in the negative, may be in order. In my first job after law school, I worked as a young public defender in the county in which I was raised. The county was plagued by racial strife, and the public defender department operated offices in three parts of the county. When budget cuts loomed, the chief defender decided to close the office located in the west end of the county. That office served a population that was predominantly African American, Asian, and Latino. The chief defender's decision was prompted by both financial concerns and political considerations: while many of the office's clients came from the west end of the county, the political "center of gravity" existed in the center of the county. Therefore, closing that office to save money seemed not only a financially expedient choice but one he could make without political consequence. He simply could not imagine that anyone would have doubted the correctness of the decision. So the chief defender did not discuss his decision to close the office with stakeholders in the community. He did not publicly acknowledge that he was planning to close the office and, instead, intended to announce the closure simply as a fait accompli. But the decision could not be kept secret in such a small community. People of color in the west end of the county viewed such a move as a slap in the face to the community. The media picked up the story and echoed their discontent. Articles appeared in the local paper quoting local elected officials who were quite candid in their critiques of the insensitivity of his decision. The move became so volatile that the chief defender ultimately reversed his decision and allowed the office to remain open. But his initial insensitivity and basic unwillingness to consider and respect alternate perspectives created a problem from which he was never able to recover in that community.

COGNITIVE COMPETENCIES

Another way of looking at the chief defender's behavior is through the lens of cognitive science. His behavior revealed a form of "naïve realism,"[16] which is the "unshakable conviction that he or she is somehow privy to an invariant, knowable, objective reality—a reality that others will also perceive faithfully, provided that they are reasonable and rational."[17] Naïve realism often leads individuals to believe that those who disagree with them "misperceive" reality and are unreasonable or irrational. We tend to see our own views as more common and widely shared than they really are.[18] All of us are prone to naïve realism, but through awareness and education, we can work to reduce its impact. If these types of personal, political, and professional assumptions go unchallenged through professional school and one's professional career, it is likely that upon being cast into a leadership position, an individual will be less open to divergent views and less effective as a leader.

As we examined in detail for the U.S. Attorney's Office in New Orleans, lawyers in leadership positions do not tend to surround themselves with individuals from diverse backgrounds who will question the leader's policy choices and his or her judgment. The problems that ensue from insularity make clear that intersectional leaders ought to create and expect their team to be a team of rivals. Perhaps one of the best-known examples of this concept is found in the cabinet of President Abraham Lincoln.[19] Lincoln included three men in his cabinet who had run against him for president. Given the context and the disparate personalities, it is perhaps not surprising that Lincoln's cabinet meetings rarely, if ever, represented a cozy consensus. But he recognized the importance of having access to wide-ranging views and that having to address conflicting viewpoints often sharpened his own thinking.

In looking to lead more effectively and less dangerously, intersectional lawyer-leaders need to turn to cognitive science for important insights into their own leadership behaviors. They need to develop a set of cognitive competencies. Lawyers are rarely exposed to cognitive science concepts that might help them understand human behavior better. But becoming conversant with concepts such as confirmation bias and fundamental attribution error may help intersectional lawyer-leaders become aware of practices that they may not consciously see or fully appreciate that can severely hamper their effectiveness. So, let's discuss each in turn.

Confirmation bias is the act of favoring information that confirms one's beliefs or hypotheses.[20] The stronger the belief, the stronger the effect. People display this bias when they gather or remember information selectively, or when they interpret it in a way that is biased. Confirmation bias also manifests in the way individuals interpret ambiguous evidence as supporting their existing position.[21] Lawyers are perhaps most susceptible to this type of bias because of their legal training. Law school teaches students to interpret existing data in ways that support their arguments and to convince decision makers or listeners that any contrary data is either irrelevant or unpersuasive. This can lead to the polarization of attitudes, in which a disagreement can become more extreme and the parties more opposed as they evaluate evidence on a particular issue. As differing parties explore ambiguous evidence, a confirmation bias can result in a situation where evidence reinforces existing attitudes, expanding, rather than narrowing, the disagreement between them.[22] The intersectional leader must learn and make use of these cognitive issues in order to take steps to control their impact. Deliberately creating discomfort in the lawyer-leader's team may seem counterintuitive, but it does help to combat the presence of confirmation bias.

Fundamental attribution error is another cognitive science concept that is important for intersectional leaders to acknowledge and understand. The concept explains the ways that individuals tend to assume or infer that an actor's personality dictates his or her behavior.[23] This bias often occurs when people underestimate the power of the situation to shape behavior.[24] Fundamental attribution error, more simply, is the cognitive function that causes us to blame the individual rather than the circumstances or situation for certain behaviors. The tendency to underestimate the situational impact and to overestimate personal intentionality is exacerbated when we do not know much about the other person. Research suggests that this bias may be culturally based and culturally driven. For example, researchers have found that Westerners tend to view themselves as independent agents and believe that individual choice and motivations drive their own actions. Given that view, it is perhaps not surprising that Westerners focus more on the individual than context in their efforts to explain and understand choices and behavior.[25] Today's leaders need to be sensitive to the existence of the fundamental attribution error because it often leads them to assume intentionality when clients do not appear for meetings with counsel or team members are late for meetings. More often than not, we seek to blame the individual for this behavior without having inquired sufficiently to understand the circumstances that led to the undesirable outcome. The intersectional lawyer-leader needs to develop practices that encourage such an inquiry to be automatic.

CULTURAL COMPETENCIES

An equally important corollary to the development of cognitive competencies is the promotion of cultural competency, a set of skills, knowledge, and attitudes that leaders use when interacting with culturally diverse team members.[26] These are, at their core, cognitive competencies, which relate to the ability to perceive and interpret information.[27] Greater cognitive competency increases the capacity for understanding individuals of different cultures.[28] In an increasingly globalized world, work teams are often composed of individuals from different cultures.[29] Therefore, the ability to increase cognitive competency is more likely to put leaders in a position where they can increase the range of information they have about members of a diverse team; this in turn reduces reliance on simplistic stereotypes. Researchers have suggested that this form of competency also enhances leaders' ability to "anticipate the thinking and perceptions of others and to adjust their actions accordingly."[30]

Social scientists and cognitive psychologists have studied the manner in which people make sense of themselves and others. When we encounter the complexities of our daily lives, all of us attempt to reduce the world around us into categories to create a more manageable structure. When our minds look to understand conduct, we look to salient cues, such as race and ethnicity, and then draw on culturally embedded understandings to evaluate behavior. We engage in categorization. One problematic form of categorization is stereotyping. Stereotypes have been defined as the "general inclination to place a person in categories according to some easily and quickly identifiable characteristics such as age, sex, ethnic membership, nationality, or occupation, and then to attribute to him or her qualities believed to be typical of members of the category."[31] We cluster information into categories, which often leads to prejudgment based on our perception of those groupings. Stereotypes tend not to be any more accurate than any other type of generalization.

Many biases we hold toward different groups may be unconscious. The concept of implicit bias has come to be viewed as a significant factor in understanding our attitudes toward individuals or groups who may be different from us.[32] Implicit bias is defined as the "attitudes or stereotypes that affect our understanding, actions and decisions in an unconscious manner" automatically and without any conscious thought.[33] Even individuals who see themselves as "racially egalitarian" and take active steps to conduct themselves without prejudice can engage in biased behavior automatically. Implicit associations between groups (social groups, racial groups) and traits occur outside an individual's conscious awareness and may not even align with the beliefs that individual openly endorses.[34] What leads to the development of implicit biases are the often stereotypic images that pervade our culture. Implicit biases are activated under circumstances where an individual is operating under time constraints, is confronting some degree of ambiguity, is cognitively taxed, and is being asked to exercise discretion—conditions often present in our work environments.

What can be done to reduce the influence of bias? Research reveals that positive exposure to individuals from other cultures and racial groups can help us develop counterstereotypic experiences and can, therefore, reduce the bias. In essence, intersectional leaders must acknowledge their own biases and actively work toward changing negative assumptions or attitudes that may interfere with their ability to lead across lines of difference. Actively engaging with others from different backgrounds helps to break down stereotypes.

Working in culturally diverse teams, either in a leadership position or as a team member, can show people that they lack the requisite knowledge to act quickly in response to team dynamics. This can result in frustration and some level of interpersonal hostility.[35] Developing the ability to adapt and find a comfort level with some degree of ambiguity is one of the hallmarks of good leadership. Individuals with a high tolerance for ambiguity rely more heavily on objective information and are more likely to experiment and seek a variety of approaches and opinions before acting.[36] This helps leaders to understand that people are, in many ways, different from them and thus, in turn, to seek the information necessary to avoid the stressful situations described earlier.[37]

The ability to "recognize, understand and acknowledge the identity, experience and position of a culturally different person without denying one's own cultural identity"[38] is essential for effective leadership of diverse groups. When team members feel they belong to a group that respects diverse views, they tend to perform well. They recognize that together they are more effective than apart and can be more creative and productive. Trust, group efficacy, and identity propel teams to engage wholeheartedly and do together what they could never do individually.[39]

BROAD CONNECTIVITY

Building diverse teams can expose intersectional lawyer-leaders to different perspectives and ideas, but leaders must do more: they must develop and maintain broad connections beyond their own team. Lawyers come into practice often specializing in a particular area, talking to those in their area, and thinking about only their field of specialization. While it is important for lawyers to think deeply about the practice of law and to develop a deep expertise, it is equally important for lawyer-leaders to develop broad networks within their organization that reach beyond the legal team. Lawyers within larger organizations are too often siloed, experiencing and encouraging their units to maintain some distance from the rest of the organization. And lawyers within legal units often view their work as more solitary than they should. The intersectional lawyer-leader must learn to develop diverse teams within the legal unit and must connect into multiple networks outside both the unit and the organization.

Organizational analyses have revealed the often-unrecognized vitality and power of networks.[40] Businesses and firms are divided into units often within a matrixed power structure. The structural design is intended to facilitate efficiency and effectiveness of operations. But despite the intentionality of the design, information rarely flows according to the organizational chart. Instead, individuals who have achieved a level of seniority lose touch with much of the day-to-day operations, so ideally there are reporting lines that, at least in theory, help channel the information flow. Companies gather and disseminate information formally and informally, and the informal mechanisms rarely have anything to do with position or seniority. There are networks that develop and function within organizations where people outside authority—perhaps even on the periphery—may be the go-to for information and ideas. Similarly, individuals can be part of multiple networks. The intersectional lawyer-leader should be alert to these patterns of information and seek to be part of multiple and wide-ranging networks, gaining access to perspectives and ideas that can improve his or her own approaches and thinking. The breadth and depth of the leader's network can expose the leader to new opportunities and potential threats.

Leaders must be able to conjure a vision about the organization—where is it now and where might it go? The ability to plan for an ever-changing future is linked to the leader's ability to notice faint signals on the horizon that may affect the organization. He or she must also be able to sift through noise within the organization to understand issues that may cause problems internally. To do this, lawyer-leaders need to position themselves in networks, both internal and external, that may help them extend their perspectives and insights. From those nodal positions, the intersectional leader will need to ask questions. Asking "what if" and engaging in scenario planning and optional thinking can help the intersectional leader think more broadly. By inviting ideas even from outside the leader's area of expertise and from novices within an organization, the leader signals an openness to new ways of thinking that are not constrained by technical training.

Given the volatility and complexity of the contemporary context, lawyer-leaders must distill and learn lessons from their predecessors who have failed. Today's lawyer-leader must commit to developing and embracing a set of attitudes and skills that will help him or her connect perspectives and learn from the intersection of divergent groups and networks. As discussed at the outset, intersectional leadership can be taught, learned, and practiced. But it requires a fundamental shift on the part of legal educators and members of the legal profession: they must willingly accept that the mantle of leadership confers a responsibility that involves more than technical, legal expertise. Both law schools and lawyers must be intentional and rigorous in learning how to adapt to today's environment and to be an active leader across the differences within it.

CHAPTER EIGHT

Reducing the Danger Ahead

Teaching Lawyers Leadership

IN THE TWENTY-FIRST CENTURY, the lawyer will need to think not just "like a lawyer," but "like a leader." Legal education trains lawyers to trust their own judgment and to place considerable faith in their ability to tackle complexity independently, given the rigor of their technical, legal training and expertise. But as we have seen in previous chapters, more is required to be an effective lawyer-leader. Intersectional lawyer-leaders will need to appreciate the dynamics of the world in which they are operating and to accept that no single individual can have all the answers given the complexity of the decisions they will be expected to make.

Lawyers who misunderstand the need to learn how to lead in today's environment will likely continue to engage in the dangerous behaviors highlighted in the preceding chapters. But the good news is that leadership can be taught experientially in law schools and imparted to executives and lawyers in executive education and practice. Exposing law students to intersectional leadership education is an important first step toward reducing the danger posed by ill-prepared lawyer-leaders. Providing leadership education to individuals early in their careers can lead to the development of practices and attitudes that they will have the opportunity to refine and improve over the course of their careers. If law schools seriously intend to prepare the next generation of leaders, they must recognize and embrace the duty to start this process of learning by exposing law students to leadership concepts and lessons through their pedagogy and substantive discussions. Similarly, practicing lawyers who currently function as leaders or have ambitions to such roles will also need to train for this new form of leadership. Through a greater exposure to leadership, lawyer-leaders will be better able to reduce the practices that would otherwise prove quite disruptive and destructive. Ideally, leadership for lawyers ought to be conceived as an ongoing continuum of lessons and practices that begins in law school and continues throughout the lawyer-leader's career. But for the sake of clarity, the ensuing discussion is divided into two parts: teaching intersectional leadership in law schools and then exposing lawyers in practices to intersectional leadership concepts and skills.

"THINKING LIKE A LEADER" IN LAW SCHOOLS

So what might law schools do to adopt leadership as a substantive focus? They can start by thinking seriously about what it means to provide a scaffolded learning opportunity that enables students to step into, perform, and reflect on the role of the lawyer-leader in its many dimensions. Leadership concepts can be taught in the law school curriculum beginning in the first year. In large doctrinal courses as well as in smaller lawyering and clinical classes, law professors can model leadership behaviors and create opportunities to test- drive leadership concepts such as inclusion and collaboration. Law schools should also develop and offer upper-level leadership seminars that build on those initial experiences and deepen exposure to cognitive and emotional concepts and competencies.

Leadership learning can and should begin as early as the orientation sessions that law students must attend. For example, the law school where I teach, New York University School of Law, has recently chosen to introduce issues of leadership at this formative stage. Every first-year law student is administered the Myers-Briggs Type Indicator (MBTI)[1] personality inventory prior to orientation. The MBTI is an introspective, self-report questionnaire that gives insights into an individual's psychological preferences in the ways that he or she perceives the world and makes decisions. The inventory focuses on four broad areas of inquiry: (1) whether the individual is inward- or outward-focused; (2) how the individual prefers to take in information; (3) how the individual prefers to make decisions; and (4) how the individual prefers to live his or her outer life. The results tend to demonstrate to the individual that what might seem to be random variation in one's behavior is actually quite orderly and consistent and track the ways the individual prefers to use her perception and judgment.[2] NYU Law students take the MBTI and are then provided an overview of what the inventory measures and what the results mean for them as lawyers and as leaders. Students learn early that

perception involves all the ways of becoming aware of things, people, happenings, or ideas. Judgment involves all the ways of coming to conclusions about what has been perceived. If people differ systematically in what they perceive and in how they reach conclusions, then it is only reasonable for them to differ correspondingly in their interests, reactions, values, motivations, and skills.[3]

Engaging the conversation about judgment, perception, and personal development helps law students recognize that these are important considerations as they begin their journey to becoming lawyers and leaders in their profession.

The MBTI gives law students a foundation for thinking about themselves as a lawyers and as potential leaders in a diverse environment. This test and the ensuing discussion about the results create a great launching pad for intersectional leadership education. I also encourage law schools to administer the Implicit Association Test (IAT),[4] which offers yet another opportunity for personal insight. The IAT is a testing instrument within social psychology that probes unconscious attitudes and associations. It does this by detecting the strength of a person's automatic association between pairs of concepts and gives insights into emotion-laden types of attitudes. One of the most well-known IATs is the Race IAT, which measures attitudes toward racial groups by examining the speed with which individuals categorize Black and White faces with positive and negative words. Most people will tell you that they know their opinions and views on issues such as gender and racial equity. We believe we know our own minds and are able to assess others fairly and accurately. But the IAT suggests that we may have hidden biases or attitudes that trigger without our awareness or conscious control and cause us to diverge from the views we consciously espouse. The IAT helps surface these otherwise hidden attitudes. The IAT was introduced in the scientific literature in 1998 by Anthony Greenwald, Debbie McGhee, and Jordan Schwartz and has proven relatively resistant to manipulation. It may even have predictive validity.[5]

The IAT helps us better understand our own implicit biases. Biases and the stereotypes on which they are based often operate as blind spots for lawyers. These biases are stored in our brains and influence our behavior in ways that we might not even realize. For example, narratives about strong lawyers and strong leaders are overwhelmingly White and male. We may simply make positive associations with leadership and White males because we have been socialized to accept that connection. The IAT recognizes that most Americans are socialized with some degree of bias. The negative effects of that bias are more often engaged in times of stress and quick decision making. So the IAT is an excellent vehicle to identify and address this unconscious behavior. Rather than labeling entering law students "racist" or "sexist," which engages defenses and often shuts down any meaningful discussion about bias, the IAT helps students see that we all have these unconscious attitudes, but they can be consciously and actively addressed. Because the results often surprise the test taker, that experience creates a teachable moment that can help law students become more aware of the ways that we acquire stereotypical views and the steps they must take to overcome them.

Against that backdrop, leadership lessons should be developed pervasively in doctrinal courses in the first year. This may involve professors using methods that emphasize inclusion, signal the importance of diverse viewpoints, and draw students' attention to context. The ways that the professor manages classroom participation can demonstrate an important leadership lesson on diversity and inclusion. Research has shown that female students and students of color do not respond to questions posed to the entire class as immediately as White male students.[6] Evidence suggests that they will take a longer time to respond largely because they wait to formulate a complete answer in their heads before raising their hands. Evidence suggests that White male students are often more willing to think aloud in the course of making an answer. A professor's willingness to wait a moment before calling on a student in class—rather than calling on the first hand raised—will often result in a more diverse set of viewpoints contributing to the doctrinal analysis and the conversation. Similarly, the professor's commitment to withholding her point of view on an issue until a full discussion has occurred will likely encourage students to listen to and consider viewpoints that differ from their own. Once the professor—the leader in the room—stakes out a position, it may make students less willing to test their own ideas and to consider alternative ways of viewing the same set of facts and legal issues. Finally, openness to full discussions of the underlying circumstances that lead to the articulation of a particular rule of law may help law students begin to track how context matters and can help them shape decisions.

First-year teachers can also look for ways to teach teamwork and collaboration. In many ways, the first-year curriculum encourages and rewards individualized performance and pays little, if any, attention to teaming or group work. Many law students leave professional school having been taught to operate solely as individual contributors without ever having learned anything in their substantive courses about the dynamics of working in teams. The problem with that singular focus is that following graduation from law school, most lawyers will work as part of teams throughout the rest of their professional careers. First-year professors can look for opportunities to introduce group work into the curriculum while still covering the substantive material.

Let me offer an example. One of my colleagues teaches Criminal Law, a required course, to first-year law students. A course in Criminal Law routinely addresses questions of violence, personal responsibility, and punishment, and those issues often evoke strong emotions. The law school course challenges students to do more than offer visceral reactions. They must learn to analyze volatile issues by critically reflecting on underlying theories and competing goals of the criminal justice system. In many courses, this is an individualized process, but this colleague has deliberately incorporated teamwork and group learning to help students grapple with some of the more difficult components of the course. In coverage of the crime of rape, which tends to be an emotionally freighted conversation, she has found a way to engage the students in small-group discussions of the issues that sets the stage for the larger in-class discussion. She asks a class of ninety students to divide into groups of ten in order to draft a rape statute. She further instructs them to assume that they know the victim and, therefore, want to build in protections to safeguard the victim's concerns. At the same time, she asks them to imagine they know and care for the accused and, therefore, want to make sure to include provisions that will protect the interests of the person charged. The small-group discussions tend to be challenging and have the potential to get bogged down in endless debate. But because the assignment is to submit a statute to the professor, they must work through their differences (both stated and unspoken) to deliver a group product. Students routinely report that the exercise was difficult but, in the end, helped them see—and not caricature—other viewpoints on an issue that they entered the room seeing from only one perspective.

Moving outside the doctrinal courses, law schools should include leadership concepts in first-year lawyering courses (sometimes called Research and Writing) and into legal clinics. Research and Writing classes often focus on teaching basic lawyering skills such as trial and appellate advocacy, interviewing skills, and negotiation. Many of these courses introduce concepts related to the need for empathy and self-awareness. Similarly, clinical courses typically devote a great deal of attention to the task of helping students learn to operate at the intersection of interests. In clinics that include individual representation, law students must learn to confront their own differences from their client (racial, ethnic, gender, class) and must bridge the gap to gain a client's trust. To their credit, clinical teachers often expose students to the idea that intersectionality can help them become better lawyers for their clients. They miss the mark, though, in not making the connection that these skills are leadership skills and not just practical lawyering skills. Clinics and lawyering classes could teach and underscore that good leadership is also good lawyering.

Finally, there is an opportunity in a range of other law school classes to expose students to leadership skills. For example, brainstorming is an exercise that happens at some point in nearly every law school classroom. Students in a clinic may be asked to brainstorm the types of conduct that deserve punishment in a first-year criminal law classroom, or they may be asked to identify strategies for advocacy regarding housing for formerly incarcerated individuals. In each case, allowing students or the professor to critique ideas as they are suggested limits input and discussion. The professor should, instead, make clear that brainstorming is designed to generate ideas first before evaluating and assessing the strength of suggestions. By encouraging broad participation in idea generation, the students and the professor may uncover unexpected ideas or perspectives. This, in turn, signals the value of robust engagement of all voices.

ONE EXPERIENCE IN TEACHING
LEADERSHIP TO LAW STUDENTS

Building on these foundations, a law school should offer a stand-alone seminar devoted to leadership. Such a course would enable law students to take a deeper dive into the various concepts that undergird intersectional leadership. It can also provide law students with an opportunity to test in a small, interactive setting some of the skills associated with leadership. I have developed and teach a seminar on leadership at NYU School of Law. The course sets as an ambition the task of exploring the responsibilities and challenges of lawyers in leadership in the public, private, and nonprofit sectors. Readings for the course review theories and case studies of leadership with a specific focus on circumstances in which lawyers have failed in exercising effective leadership. The seminar is interactive and sets the expectation that the class conversations will continue outside the classroom in a closed electronic forum established for the class to discuss further the issues addressed in class. An in-depth examination of the class is one possible starting point for leadership classes taught in law school.

Setting the ground rules for the conversations is a critical first step. Class discussions intentionally cover issues of race, gender, diversity, economic status, and students' concerns about the challenges they may face in thinking about what it means to lead and to follow. It is important to establish the rule that we will be respectful in our exchanges, listening and looking to understand different viewpoints. The design of the course involves exposing students to interdisciplinary materials on leadership, psychology, and bias to help ground their discussions. We use case studies to surface and converge on particular problems that lawyer-leaders encounter. The case studies allow me to place the students in leadership positions, asking them to decide how they would confront various challenges that arise in both private- and public-sector settings. For many students, this course is the first time that they have been given a full opportunity to discuss these topics in a law school course, and their efforts to articulate issues and insights are often hampered initially by inexperience. But the closed online forum enables deeper discussion after students have had the chance to reflect on topics raised in class by giving them an opportunity to organize their thoughts and then add or adjust their insights.

The class begins with a discussion of leadership and how it is defined. Students are encouraged to offer their own working definitions of leadership, using examples from when they have led and examples of good leadership that they have observed. This conversation allows us to identify some common components of effective leadership and to begin working toward a shared definition of leadership, a definition that will be revisited and refined over the course of the semester. One of the pedagogical goals that this first meeting reflects and attempts to achieve is the participation of all of the students. I want them to become comfortable engaging with the materials and with each other. Of the twenty-five students in the class, almost one third of the students are LLM students with the remaining two thirds being JD students. The LLM students are often from countries outside the United States, and their legal experience ranges quite broadly. For many of the U.S. JD students, this is a wholly new experience. So making room for all voices is critically important.

Preliminary discussions about leadership also allow the professor to introduce basic concepts of leadership theory to law students. Students gain exposure to forms of leadership that dominated in the past, such as command-and-control forms of leadership.[7] Then, the class examines other models of leadership including intersectional leadership. As importantly, the early classes are vehicles through which the professor can introduce the process of sense-making.[8] Sense-making in this context means exploring and understanding the shifting legal, cultural, and political landscape within organizations, communities, and movements. It also means learning about how we identify and map changes that affect our ability to lead. While some lawyers and law students are exposed to the use of experts in the law, these are often characterized as functional relationships where the lawyer focuses on extracting the necessary information from the substantive-area expert. In the leadership context, it means developing networks both inside and outside the law context. It means recognizing that the lawyer-leader may not have all of the answers and should conceptualize a process and a team that provides perspectives different from your own.

Let me spend a moment on pedagogy. Working with case studies involves more than the conventional practice of conducting a leadership postmortem. So rather than limiting the discussion to an analysis of the mistakes the leader made and the actions he or she should have taken, our discussion uses an intersectional analysis. Students determine what interests were at stake. What perspectives were considered and missed? Who should have been on the team? How might the leader have anticipated these issues? How did the leader analyze the problem and the context? The students then, in real time, are asked to develop methods of team communications, an action plan, and an implementation strategy to craft an approach that might avoid these and other mistakes. The students will then present their ideas to the class and respond to questions. This "stand and deliver" model prepares students for one of the key leadership and legal challenges: working with a team to create a problem-solving narrative. Over the course of the semester, I emphasize group work so that students can develop some comfort working in teams. I also mix the groupings, being alert to race, gender, and national origin.

The course exposes students to the interplay of diversity and leadership to help shape their understanding of intersectional leadership. Many courses that introduce concepts of diversity simply add single classes on race, gender, and diversity as separate and distinct from the topics being taught. I include readings from and discussions about women and people of color as leaders throughout the course, as a way of normalizing the conversation about race and gender as a critical part of all discussions. By the time I want the class to engage in a deeper discussion of gender and leadership, for example, the students have already been thinking about the ways that gender dynamics influence our views of leadership. Against the backdrop of earlier readings and discussions, a conversation on masculine notions of leadership in popular culture then gains considerable traction. Not only do the issues of gender spark interesting conversations among the students, but they can lead to broader conversations of work-life balance and purpose that are often not discussed in a law school setting. Students are asked to take the lead in creating the type of environment that has balance and respect for different working styles. These discussions then set the stage for a conversation about global fluency, leadership, and broad notions of diversity.

The course then looks at the ecosystems in which lawyer-leaders operate and how we might address and learn from failure. Students engage with the fact that learning from failure in a legal context involves actual clients who may suffer harm as a result of that error. But even when a mistake has been costly, the students must recognize that hiding from failure does little more than ensure that other failures will follow. Lawyer-leaders have to learn to take on the tougher task of looking failure in the face and trying to glean lessons. It is difficult to institutionalize a systematic way to learn from their failures. Legal organizations find it particularly hard. The seminar discusses the tension between not wanting to reward failure and wanting to create processes that enable us to face it rather than hiding from it. It also encourages students to think about the ways that a team leader might benefit from taking personal responsibilities for failures of the team and sharing the credit for successes with the team.

The final set of classes focuses on students as leaders, exploring how they can develop a leadership style, exercise leadership in law school, and set a personal leadership agenda. They begin this module with a class and readings about leading without authority. This class helps underscore that leadership is not necessarily conferred as a result of obtaining a certain level. Leadership can and must be exercised at all levels. This concept has formed the backdrop of all of the preceding classes, but in the final modules, we bring these questions to the foreground and expect students to think critically about their roles as leaders where they will be working as new lawyers. We examine the types of behaviors, attitudes, and skills they can exercise and exhibit as the newest employees in an organization. The seminar then helps them develop a leadership style that is authentic, consistent with the leaders they consider themselves to be and the leaders others experience.

The class next explores the practical application of the lessons and leadership concepts they have learned over the course of the semester. They begin with a simulation that launches a robust debate about the role that law schools can and should play in preparing lawyers to lead. Following the debate, the students begin to develop ideas on ways they might take a leadership role in the law school to create opportunities for leadership to be exercised by law students. As part of the process of understanding how one might move an institution to change, we bring in a lawyer-leader to discuss issues that have arisen in his or her organization that required intersectional leadership. In particular, I have brought in lawyer-leaders who have been willing to share their insights on how leadership has shifted in current political and economic conditions. Students often ask about how the leader embraces innovation, learns from failure, or engages in team building to enhance his or her thinking about complex problems. This interchange of ideas allows students to test some of their ideas about intersectional leadership and to hear the perspective of an effective lawyer-leader. The lawyer-leader often helps to ground their ideas in real-life examples, and both the students and the lawyer-leader have often come to see the issues raised in a new light.

The course ends with the students laying out a leadership learning agenda that they can use as they begin their career as lawyers. To ground the leadership agenda, it helps to ask the students to imagine themselves at the end of their careers. I then ask them to develop a retirement speech about their lives as leaders, looking back on their careers and assuming they implemented everything they learned about leadership. In drafting the speech, I remind them that this is not about what job they ultimately held but what kind of leader they became. The process of developing that speech pushes them to set personal goals and enables them to reverse-engineer the steps they would like to take to ensure that they will become the type of leader we have studied.

The legal profession has come to accept that legal education continues after law school. We have bar requirements that mandate continuing legal education. The same holds true for leadership education. Finding ways to create learning opportunities for leadership in law school and in the profession will help prepare future lawyer-leaders for the roles they will assume. Obviously, some of the exercises that I employed in the leadership seminar for law students would be useful for practicing lawyers who have not been exposed to leadership concepts in law school. But what follows are some suggestions for ways that intersectional leadership could be taught to lawyers in practice.

TEACHING LAWYERS
INTERSECTIONAL LEADERSHIP

Top businesses have come to realize that executive education and leadership training are crucial tools for aligning an organization and moving it in new directions. They have also recognized that investing in employees' development can have a positive impact on the company's performance and bottom line.[9] Typically, when these organizations offer executive education and leadership training, they include leaders from across the business and internal functions to participate in the programs. The benefit of having all leaders engaged in a joint executive education program is that the organization can better ensure an alignment in message and behaviors among its leaders following the program. But even where the leadership training is tailored to the particular organization, further customization may be needed; education that specifically targets lawyer-leaders would be an important addition. This is partly because lawyer-leaders are often not running businesses like their colleagues attending the training session. Instead, lawyer-leaders typically occupy roles that cut across businesses and functions. So helping lawyer-leaders see the roles that they can play as intersectional leaders in strategy execution or innovation could prove helpful—and profitable—to the business.

While businesses do not typically carve out leadership training for their legal units, they at least recognize the value of leadership training in general. Law firms and law offices typically do not. Legal organizations regularly invest in training to help their lawyers develop and hone legal skills. They help new lawyers develop trial skills, negotiation skills, and transactional skills. But when it comes to leadership, law offices still tend to assume that if you are a good lawyer, you will automatically be a good leader. They simply do not see how leadership factors into the bottom line for them. Consequently, it is not unusual to see law offices promoting to leadership positions the firm's rainmaker or the lawyer who excels at combat in an adversarial setting. But such offices are missing the critical interim step that businesses have already recognized: leadership must be learned and developed. And since lawyers often play unique roles as leaders, their leadership training should prepare them for the challenges and opportunities they will likely face.

So what should the leadership training address? Previously, I distilled the leadership lessons into five key leadership attributes that are foundational to the intersectional lawyer-leader:

1. The lawyer-leader cultivates and invites diverse views.
2. The lawyer-leader acts with moral courage even out of public view.
3. The lawyer-leader subordinates his or her personal ambition to the good of the whole.
4. The lawyer-leader embraces his or her role as guardian of the system's integrity.
5. The lawyer-leader adopts a mind-set that embraces optionality.

Leadership training that is specifically designed for lawyer-leaders needs to teach these concepts and enable participants to examine their behavior in light of these attributes. How might organizations effectively deliver this training to lawyer-leaders? Research has shown that adults learn best and embrace change more consistently when they are engaged in experiential learning; presenting them with opportunities to learn and practice in context helps them see and implement new ways of thinking and behaving. What follows are a series of approaches and methods that organizations can employ to help lawyer-leaders learn and practice intersectional leadership.

MAKING THE CASE FOR DIVERSITY

The first attribute—cultivating and inviting diverse views—is critical to the intersectional lawyer-leader. But developing that attribute may be dependent, at least in part, on the organization's commitment to diversity and inclusion. It is therefore critical for lawyer-leaders—and their organizations—to make and understand the business case for diversity and inclusion. Building on that case, intersectional lawyer-leaders will then need to find ways to develop practices and engage in experiences that enable them to learn about cultures different from their own. Two ways that this might be taught experientially are through a trial simulation and through a study tour in a different country.

A simulation where leaders put themselves on trial for failing to cultivate and invite diverse views is a powerful mechanism to enable lawyer-leaders to reflect critically on their behavior as leaders. The exercise divides the participants into a defense team, a prosecution team, and a judicial team (presided over by an instructor who will play the judge). The defense and prosecution will prepare their case, gather evidence, and build a coherent argument for their side. As part of this stage, the participants examine documents and prepare to present and cross-examine witnesses in court. The legal process is a familiar model to lawyers, which is a benefit in this simulation, but it also forces participants to focus on factual evidence rather than opinion. The process of building a persuasive case means bringing forward information from different parts of the company and then telling a story about what the company is doing to enable and cultivate diversity. Being forced to take a position contrary to one's own beliefs is a good way to challenge the assumptions of experienced leaders.

As evidence, the lawyer-leaders examine research that documents how having racial, ethnic, and gender diversity at the top of the house is good for business. For example, evidence shows that companies in the top quartile for racial and ethnic diversity are 35 percent more likely to have financial returns above their national industry medians.[10] Similarly, companies with the highest representation of women on their top management teams experienced better financial performance than companies with the lowest representation of women.[11] Research further shows that ethnically and gender-diverse top teams offer companies more problem-solving tools, broader thinking, and more innovative solutions. The group then considers their own organization's data on diversity and how well they promote women and people of color. By placing themselves on trial, the lawyer-leaders can examine their behavior critically based on evidence and then discuss and debate what they might do differently as leaders to engage diverse perspectives. Finally, the judicial team, led by the instructor, hears the evidence and delivers a verdict based on the cases presented.

The trial process is an exceptional learning vehicle because it permits the examination of their own behavior through the evidence and arguments presented in court. Perhaps even more important, the postverdict discussion about the implications for the group as leaders—given the evidence and outcome—is instructive for the participants. In my experience as a consultant, this simulated experience often generates deeper debate about challenges in creating genuine diversity and the steps that leaders can and must take to ensure greater diversity of thought and experience in their own units and teams.

Similarly, organizations that operate globally may want to find ways to enable lawyer-leaders to understand and appreciate the value of global diversity. As the world becomes increasingly interconnected and businesses, law firms, and nonprofit organizations become more global, the need to develop true global fluency becomes all the more important. Global fluency requires developing an appreciation of and respect for cultural nuances, norms, and approaches. By seeing the value of practices born of a different culture or set of experiences, the intersectional leader can learn and adopt new ways of behaving that might enable diverse groups to find common ground and work toward shared goals.

But what does it mean to be truly global? Following the global financial crisis, many U.S. businesses and firms looked for growth opportunities through new business in emerging markets. That choice meant that U.S. companies and firms needed to become fluent in practices and regulatory frameworks with which they had little previous experience. The standard due diligence involves hiring technicians, local legal experts, and local political consultants from emerging markets to facilitate entry into the new market. More often than not, the process also involves exporting the company's practices and views and trying to fit them into the new market. It is not unusual to see U.S. companies tapping young, high-potential employees to lead the business in the emerging market. It is far more unusual to see U.S. firms hiring leaders from emerging markets and bringing them back to the United States so that the company might learn from them.

I once consulted for a company that set a strategic goal to operate as one organization rather than as a U.S.-centric organization with offices in other countries. My job was to interview the various country heads and to highlight concerns, challenges, and opportunities involved in the new global strategy. In the course of the consultancy, I interviewed a country leader in Eastern Europe and asked him when he would believe that the company was serious about its new global strategy. He responded: "When they start sending me emails in my own language." His comment drove home quite poignantly that until the organization stepped out of its U.S.-centric frame, it would not be able to understand what it meant to be truly global. Lawyer-leaders in global businesses, who at times are grappling with foreign regulations that differ from U.S. frameworks, may lose opportunities by comparing and contrasting schemes without fully understanding why the differences might make sense culturally.

To be fluent globally and to make decisions that are culturally alert, leaders must develop an understanding of their markets by understanding the dynamics of cultural diversity. To develop global fluency, the intersectional lawyer-leader will focus on emotional intelligence, empowerment, and self-awareness for the entire leadership team. Immersion into a different culture or country through a study tour is a great way to raise these competencies in a group. In my leadership consulting, I have led tours of leaders to visit other countries where they intend to do business. The key to such experiences is not just placing these lawyer-leaders in the field to visit other countries and environments. Rather, it involves creating an intensive, interactive, and reflective learning experience. It is important to expose lawyer-leaders to their counterparts in these other markets, but also to have them engage with different businesses and political decision makers, regulators, and bankers to begin to understand the environment and the ways law and regulation operate in that context. For these immersive experiences, I encourage journaling and reflective conversations about what lessons they can learn from this cultural environment.

SOCRATIC DIALOGUES ABOUT MORAL COURAGE

The second key leadership attribute for the intersectional lawyer-leader involves acting with moral courage even when his or her actions and decisions take place out of public view. One methodology that can examine dilemmas that lawyer-leaders face—but find difficult to discuss—is the Socratic dialogue. A Socratic dialogue is an interactive conversation with a group of participants that addresses some of the challenges that leaders within an organization face but are reluctant to discuss. The format looks to engage a group of panelists in a lively conversation focused on what they would do if they confronted a particular issue or problem rather than focusing simply on what they think about the topic. The format pushes the panelists to go deeper and to consider behaviors as well as mind-sets that might enable or inhibit their engagement with the issue being discussed.

The moderator develops a hypothetical scenario loosely based on real issues within the organization; for our purposes, this might be a conflict or series of conflicts that arise when the lawyer-leader sees something that threatens the organization and is not sure what responsibility he or she might have to address the problem. The participants serve in roles based on their day-to-day expertise. The moderator assumes a role in the scenario and invites the panelists to advise him or her, to comment on his or her choices, or to react to another panelist's statements to say what they would have done differently. To prompt the conversation, the moderator typically sets himself or herself as the person encountering the dilemma. The participants are expected to comment on the moderator's choices, discuss what they would do, or advise him or her about steps to take in light of the situation he or she encounters. To deepen the discussion, the moderator typically introduces a simple problem and then adds layers of complexity to the issue. That progressive development of the problem tends to lead to a robust dialogue about a complex set of issues and decisions.

The point of the dialogue is to help the participants see themselves and their dilemmas from a variety of vantage points. By framing the discussion using a hypothetical, participants gain sufficient distance from the problem to discuss it and see options for addressing it. The power of the methodology is that we generally are not asking what they should do in a specific set of circumstances, but rather, what would they do in this situation. And as we unfurl the problem, the moderator models the actions that help them make choices and reflect on those choices. By asking provocative questions in the hypothetical, we enable participants to engage issues that might otherwise remain unspoken. In the end, through a fast-paced discussion, participants and the moderator have engaged in a vibrant, candid, and structured dialogue with peers and colleagues that can broaden perspective and reveal vantage points not previously considered.

COLLABORATION TRAINING AND THE IMPORTANCE OF SUBORDINATING PERSONAL GOALS

Engaging lawyer-leaders in collaboration training can teach the importance of subordinating personal interests to the good of the enterprise. Collaboration training can be an effective vehicle to raise questions and spark discussions of ways that we tend to privilege our own goals over larger goals.

During my work as a consultant for the past twenty years, it has become clear that we no longer live in a world in which businesses or other large entities have command-and-control structures, where the leader makes the call and teams fall in line with that choice. Now the leader must learn to collaborate with others across businesses or departments and find ways to influence actions without having the power to dictate the choice. Because the twenty-first-century organization tends to be matrixed with multiple reporting lines, it is often quite challenging to move others toward a goal across an organization. Organizations are often siloed and have separate and some-times competing unit goals. These enterprises often compensate employees and provide incentives for them to focus on their individual goals or unit goals rather than on the larger enterprise interests, which further complicates the process of acting toward shared goals. An organization cannot function well or achieve goals as well when the organization is working against itself.

We all know that disciplined collaboration can help us generate better results than we might achieve as separate units. If we can properly identify opportunities where we can leverage capabilities and practices, we can be more than the sum of our parts. Leaders need to learn that collaboration typically means sacrifice—subordinating a personal interest like credit, re-sources, or talent in service of the greater good. Training on collaboration can use case studies to help lawyer-leaders understand when it makes sense to collaborate and when it might not. Lawyer-leaders can learn and practice a process that leads to disciplined collaboration: assessing the opportunity for a collaboration, being alert to barriers that might derail the effort, and developing strategies as a leader to address those barriers to keep the col-laborative effort moving forward.[12] The true goal is not just to get people to work together but to generate better results.

VISIONING EXERCISES ENCOURAGE A FOCUS ON INTEGRITY AND OPTIONALITY

The final two attributes of the intersectional leader are perhaps best taught and practiced in visioning exercises. The effective intersectional lawyer-leader must learn to engage his or her role as guardian of the system's integrity and must also adopt a mind-set that embraces optionality. An exercise that focuses the lawyer-leader on both attributes is a visioning exercise that the lawyer-leader can conduct with his or her office, team, or unit. The exercise involves identifying a shared vision for the group that addresses where the group is going and why. This exercise is not the same as developing a strategic plan. It is instead an aspirational road map for the group that assesses both the destination and the current reality and encourages the group to iden-tify possible scenarios as they make choices that will affect the organization.

Here's how the exercise unfolds. A lawyer-leader assembles his or her en-tire office (lawyers, staff, investigators, administrative personnel). The group is asked to imagine that they have arrived at a point five to seven years from the current time. They are then asked to describe the future picture of the office. What is the office's focus? Why? How is it conducting its work? What is the nature of that work? How does it function? In what ways is it serving its purpose? What do clients say about it? What do employees say about the company? The intention of the exercise is to be positive and aspirational, identifying what the group wants for the office, not focusing on what they believe is possible. The teams must be pushed to describe this future state in sufficient detail that they could know and recognize when they achieved it. Once the group has articulated the future destination and purpose, they will examine their current reality across the same dimensions. By exploring current reality in this way, the group can see what is missing, what needs to change, and what options they might need to consider now to get the group to the future destination.

Understanding one's role in an organization relies on being able to ask the questions that push one's thinking and to see issues differently. The lawyer-leader sits at the intersection of networks and must help the group navigate toward a shared purpose. Having a wide cross-section of individuals participating in the visioning exercise helps the lawyer-leader to step outside the confines of his or her own perspective in order to see the system in which he or she operates from multiple vantage points. It is incredibly difficult to guard a system's integrity if the lawyer-leader cannot see it fully. Similarly, it is easy to miss threats if the lawyer-leader does not put processes and practices in place that actively engage in a regular routine of asking "what if" questions that force the leader and the team to consider options. Planning for an ever-changing future and the skills necessary to lead in that future requires leaders to develop such an approach. Intersectional leadership depends on the lawyer-leader's ability and willingness to develop and participate in broad networks. The purpose of these networks is to help broaden the lawyer-leader's understanding and ability to detect weak signals on the horizon. By seeing them early and interpreting them, the lawyer-leader can better determine the direction and context in which his or her organization operates.

Where Do We Go from Here?

The Future of Lawyers, Law School, and Leadership

QUESTIONS ABOUT THE NATURE and responsibility of leadership have taken center stage given the electoral results in 2016. The U.S. presidential election and the United Kingdom's "Brexit" vote ushered into power a brand of "populist" leaders whose rhetoric, practices, and approaches come into direct conflict with the key lessons of this book. These newly elected leaders ran on platforms that played to and exacerbated divisions and suspicions, offering to help their supporters "take back control" of government by wresting power from those associated with the status quo. The success of their appeals came from their ability to tap into and seize upon atavistic sentiments and deep-seated resentments largely of an aging set of voters. These constituents felt overlooked and disempowered by politicians who had espoused many of the views and behaviors that this book advocates as essential to effective leadership: embracing empathy, being inclusive, and valuing multicultural perspectives. Instead, these newly elected leaders campaigned on, and their supporters approved, rhetoric and policies that promoted nativism, protectionism, and xenophobia. Time will tell whether voters will be happy with what they have chosen.

These reactive leadership models will likely enjoy short-term success only to collapse in the end. Here's why. Effective leadership means having vision—a long view—that is positive and motivating. Appealing to the basest instincts may work as a short-term campaign tactic, but such divisive entreaties will not empower or enable these officials to *lead*. Effective leadership—

no matter what one's politics may be—depends on uniting, inspiring, and moving others toward a greater common goal.

Let me offer a few examples. First, *uniting* people who previously disagreed with you is critical to effective leadership. Whether an organization must blend after a merger or a country must heal after a contested election, the leader must find ways to unify conflicting or different perspectives. This means reaching across political ideologies, personal difference, and strategic divides to find and build commonality. Kenneth Chenault, the CEO of American Express since 2001, offers an illustration of this point. With a law degree and just over two years of consulting experience at Bain & Company, Chenault joined American Express and for the next twenty years methodically took on a series of jobs and roles that allowed him to learn the business. He made a point of working with people whom he viewed as competitors, seeking their advice and learning from them. He engaged in straightforward conversations with his rivals, encouraging them to move beyond personal stakes by focusing on "what is best for the company."[1] When Chenault became CEO, the top ten executives, many of whom had been rivals, stayed on to work under his leadership. As CEO, his leadership style continued this theme. He assembled a team of rivals—a group with diverse styles and backgrounds—to push his thinking. He famously stated, "Whenever I think about an issue, I always argue the opposite side of it. So, when I ultimately decide on a course of action, I've already been through all the conceivable scenarios, and I'm going to go for it."[2] He not only brings people to the table who disagree with him but embraces their arguments as his own so that he fully understands opposing positions before he makes a choice. Inclusion combined with the aspiration to do what is best unites his people.

Second, a leader must *inspire* those whom he or she leads, meaning the entire enterprise, its stakeholders, and its clients. To do that, the leader must set as an ambition advancing the needs of the whole, not just his or her personal interest or the partisan concerns of a select few. No one would have been surprised if the political priorities of Nelson Mandela, president of South Africa from 1994 to 1999, had been not simply to dismantle South Africa's system of apartheid but to punish White Afrikaners who had been the architects and beneficiaries of one of the world's most brutal separatist regimes. Mandela had organized and led resistance efforts against the forced relocation of Black people to townships. As a young lawyer, he fought against state-sponsored violence in every form and brought cases against the government for routinely engaging in police brutality. But his legal career came to an end when he was convicted of sabotage against the apartheid government. Mandela would ultimately serve twenty-seven years in prison. Shortly before his release, tensions in South Africa had reached a boiling point, leaving many fully expecting a racial civil war. But Mandela's vision was not one of revenge, where one pits one group against another. Instead, when he served as president of South Africa, he united the country around a single compelling idea: dismantling the legacy of apartheid by fostering racial reconciliation.

Finally, once the leader has united the organization, enterprise, or country, his or her job is to *move it toward a shared vision* of a greater good. Janet Reno, former Attorney General of the United States, offers a prime illustration of this leadership capability. Reno was the first woman to hold the position, serving for two terms, which was longer than any other Attorney General in the previous 150 years. In many ways, her tenure as Attorney General was contentious, and many to this day remember only her most controversial moments. But what few outside the criminal justice system recognize is that she single-handedly transformed the operations of that system by inviting a wide-ranging set of stakeholders to co-create a vision of community-oriented justice that worked with communities to prevent crime. Reno worked hard to engage often opposing criminal justice actors—police, prosecutors, judges, and defense lawyers—in refashioning their respective roles to develop a community orientation in their practices. She was the first Attorney General to address the fate of people returning from custody and reentering communities. She helped found specialized courts focusing on drug usage as a public health issue. By reimagining how the criminal justice system might function, Reno, unlike any Attorney General before or since, united a fractious criminal justice community behind a new vision for that system even though it placed her directly in conflict with the more punitive policies embraced by her boss at the time, President Bill Clinton. As a lawyer-leader, Reno sat at the intersection of disparate groups and connected them in ways that they never imagined possible.

These are the practices that anchor intersectional leadership and have been exhibited by many transformational lawyer-leaders. The latest wave of political leaders, however, seems intent on ignoring these examples by reaching back for an older model of leadership where the leader simply tells others what to do—the command-and-control leadership model. As noted earlier, this leadership model dominated industries and enterprises throughout the twentieth century. It assumed that leaders could operate singularly and decisively. Command-and-control leaders expected those whom they led to pursue avenues that the leaders identified, to gather information as directed, and then to follow a course of conduct determined by the leaders. This hierarchical form of leadership, marked by a centralized top-down leadership structure, was built on the premise that the leader at the apex of the organization or unit was all-knowing or had special access to inside information. Such leaders were expected to make decisions by relying on their own judgment and being selective when soliciting viewpoints or input. The command-and-control model often witnessed leaders engaging in a process of hoarding knowledge and then controlling the timing of the release of that information to enhance the command structure and to legitimize the leader's decisions. Its success depended on an environment or marketplace that did not produce many unplanned variables.

Today, command-and-control models have become anachronistic and, consequently, are experiencing a dramatic decline. The problems with this form of leadership may be obvious, but perhaps it is worthwhile to identify a few concerns. The individual leader typically does not have special knowledge that others cannot retrieve and learn. Technology has increased the breadth of information available to and accessible by other employees and stakeholders. The powerful image of the all-knowing leader has been weakened. Further undermining this notion is the complexity of today's economic, political, social, and legal challenges. Identifying the right course of action and anticipating the full range of ramifications that might flow from that chosen path has become all the more difficult, particularly given the speed at which decisions need to be made. To develop strategies and solutions that match the velocity of the environment will require leaders to engage and coordinate an array of individuals and groups, each tackling particular angles of problems to increase the likelihood that the decision makers will have more information available to help them choose an appropriate course. Leaders and employees co-create opportunities and options. Organizations in the public and private spheres have recognized that decentralized, interconnected, and information-distributing structures are far more capable of identifying and addressing the sorts of dilemmas that arise today. Those structures demand a different kind of leader.

Leaders who commit to intersectional leadership exhibit the sorts of traits that thrive in decentralized environments. They intentionally engage others in a collaborative process of imagining, defining, and working toward a common cause or greater mission that is meaningful for the enterprise and for its stakeholders. They recognize that they do not, and cannot, hold all the answers. Instead, they actively seek out a wide range of ideas and viewpoints to challenge their assumptions and to force them to think critically about issues and solutions. They have a broad orientation that comes from developing and participating in expansive internal and external networks to tap into multiple and varied streams of information and ideas. Intersectional leaders thrive in the midst of this creative tension because they recognize that the competition and collision of ideas can stretch them and enable them to imagine a richer set of options. All individuals who aspire to positive forms of leadership can benefit from intersectional leadership. Intersectional leadership emanates from a principled position that dissimilar voices can bring value to one's thinking. It is forward-looking because it seeks to motivate and inspire, rather than divide and cast blame. And because it encourages involving multiple perspectives, it is inclusive. This model is also sustainable because the leader works with employees and stakeholders to create a shared vision.

Intersectional leadership is particularly important for lawyer-leaders because of where they sit and how they operate. Lawyer-leaders are often situated at the junctures of structures: between separate units in an organization, between management and stakeholders, between systems and clients. From that nodal position, lawyer-leaders can see and tap into varied perspectives and interests if they consciously choose to listen, inquire, and learn. Moreover, their function within organizations and firms quite often demands a degree of comfort with ambiguity and optionality. Fortunately, lawyer-leaders do, at times, operate in situations where the answers and dividing lines are clear: the law or regulations dictate or prohibit a particular action, for example. But more often the real value of lawyer-leaders comes to light where they make or enable decisions when there is no clear path or where the circumstances, rules, and regulations are open to different interpretation. In these moments, lawyer-leaders play critical roles within the larger ecosystem. Their unique access to information, their broad orientation, and their ability to have insight into all parts of an organization's operations position lawyer-leaders to be guardians of the entity's integrity. These are all critical features of the intersectional leadership model. But lawyer-leaders need to be prepared and trained to practice and adopt these practices and leadership behaviors.

LAW SCHOOLS NEED TO RECOGNIZE THE DANGER AND THE OPPORTUNITY

The time has come for the legal profession to take leadership education for lawyers seriously. Perhaps before the trends were as clearly defined as they are now, the case had not yet been made for the legal academy to incorporate leadership development. But we have reached a point of maturity in both the discipline and the profession that demands a reset in the mission of legal education. Law schools must acknowledge that they produce leaders and must then focus on educating them so that they can perform well in roles they will likely hold. It is far easier to assume that lawyers will be ready to lead simply by virtue of their legal training, and that employers will fill whatever leadership gaps exist on the job. But the previous chapters highlight the flaws in that assumption. The legal academy needs to think not just about what they teach but how they teach. In the end, law schools and educators who focus on improving practice will need to map both the substance and pedagogy to the demands of the current environment. They can do this by teaching and reinforcing intersectional leadership concepts.

Quite frankly, it is in the interest of law schools to teach intersectional leadership. First, it would make them more competitive. Law schools are becoming less attractive to young professionals, and the net result is that law school applications have declined in recent years. According to the American Bar Association, law student enrollment numbers dropped by approximately 9,000 between 2013 and 2014. About 43,500 students were admitted to accredited schools for the 2014–2015 school year. By contrast, 60,400 were admitted to law schools in the fall of 2010. That represents a drop of 28 percent in a five-year period. The number of people who applied to law school for the fall 2015 semester hit the lowest point in fifteen years. Countless experts have attempted to interpret this trend, typically concluding that the expense of the education and the lack of confidence in employment opportunities in an uncertain economy are the principal reasons for the reduction. But what is hidden in these numbers is a worry about the lack of relevance of a legal education. Young people who are looking to find purpose in their careers are turning to other fields. If law schools want to continue attracting students who bring the sort of intellectual curiosity and ambition to tackle the most pressing problems in the world, these schools will need to recast their mission. With the addition of a leadership focus, law schools will become more relevant to young people with leadership ambitions.

For generations, law schools have attracted such students. What typically has appealed to law students has been the social justice mission of legal education. Law students expect to be taught about the law's actual operation. But at the same time, they expect to challenge its boundaries and to discover ways that the law can and should be an instrument of social, political, and economic change. Even beyond the social justice mission, law schools teach that lawyers can and should rise to the top of whatever system or organization they join because they are among the brightest intellects. One can certainly quibble with whether that assessment is accurate, but law schools tend to believe it and instill that certainty in their students. Whether a lawyer is litigating a large-scale merger or acquisition, suing for medical malpractice, or representing an indigent defendant accused of a violent crime, the basic message to law students is that their work is contributing fundamentally to key systems in organizations and the world.

That message misleads internally and externally. Students who arrive at law school expecting to lead have their beliefs in their fitness for such roles confirmed. And some who never considered leadership roles prior to law school often discover that the law school environment lights a leadership flame in them. The problem is that law schools typically do nothing with this opportunity, and law students lose the ambition or graduate with the mistaken impression that they know enough to lead effectively. In addition to the internal gravitational pull on lawyers to become leaders, there is also an external push. Often, the lawyer in the room is expected to be the leader. The person who can articulate his or her positions clearly, argue forcefully against those with opposing viewpoints, and intuit how to order arguments so that they flow logically and persuasively is often the person nominated to lead. Law schools have an obligation to prepare their students to engage these roles better to help them and a trusting public have confidence that they will be effective leaders.

The second reason that law schools and educators in practice should have an interest in teaching intersectional leadership is that it will make lawyers better *lawyers*. The five key components that constitute intersectional leadership are also skills that, if taught to lawyers, will improve both their leadership potential and their day-to-day lawyering abilities. Here's how. The first component, developing a team that brings traits, styles, and experiences dissimilar to one's own, is a core capability for a lawyer. Too often, lawyers gravitate toward and spend time almost exclusively with other lawyers. Breaking out of that pattern and forcing oneself to partner with individuals with different expertise, mind-sets, and skills helps the individual practicing lawyer see issues and recommend action that may have an impact on broader interest groups (clients, stakeholders, and regulators, for example). Lawyers often need to reach and persuade audiences (jurors, opposing parties, witnesses) to move in directions that are beneficial to the lawyer's client. Helping the lawyer develop arguments and anticipate concerns of a variety of stakeholders through discussions with a broader team can enhance the lawyer's ability to achieve the desired outcome for his or her client.

A second component of intersectional leadership, and one with which lawyers can have great difficulty appreciating, is that learning often comes from unlikely sources. Seeking out viewpoints from those with the least amount of legal experience or expertise is simply not a practice that occurs with any frequency in legal environments. Whether we are talking about the district attorney's office or a corporate law firm, we rarely see more-experienced lawyers soliciting the views of the least-experienced members of the firm. But doing so could produce real benefits. Seeking input from those other than the legal organization's "established experts" will provide a unique perspective. Legal organizations are notorious for answering the question

"Why we do it this way?" with the answer "Because we have *always* done it that way." But engaging those with less experience can be eye-opening and transformative. New lawyers and legal interns often have no more than a vague understanding of what can or cannot be done in the law. They have not yet learned the limits with which practicing lawyers are often painfully familiar. That familiarity, though, can lead established lawyers to think conventionally and to forget how to imagine ways that stretch what appear to be solid, immovable boundaries. Lawyers who supervise law school interns often say that having a fresh set of eyes looking at issues helps to push their own thinking about issues and practices they no longer question.

The third component of intersectional leadership is learning to engage in true collaboration rather than teaming. Lawyers who subordinate their personal interests for the greater good get better-quality work from their teams. Giving up credit, resources, or talent to the larger objective may ultimately garner more satisfying outcomes for clients and, as a corollary, may bring praise to the firm or office. This is often difficult for lawyers to do because of the individualistic training they currently receive in law school; there is a resulting reluctance to give up recognition or credit. But collaboration often leads to results that help clients. For example, a collaborative model in a law firm could lead to a better allocation of work assignments. Rather than shifting work to the individual or group that has time or is idle, the firm would consider who has the best level of experience or expertise for this particular part of a project. It may also lead to farming out work where others have better expertise—collaborating with nonlawyers to bring a full-service solution to the client. In a public defender's office, the lawyer may need to include a social worker or educational specialist and empower him or her to work with the client on needs that may or may not be directly related to the legal issue. Being willing to give up exclusive control over every part of the legal case is challenging but important.

Fourth, intersectional leadership teaches the importance of developing an active and intense suspicion of agreement. Lawyers who gain agreement easily may miss questions or objections that could arise later in the process when it is more difficult to shift strategies or arguments. A lawyer who embraces the practice of questioning each assumption will be able to challenge and push his or her own ideas. It will also help lawyers be better prepared for questions and rebuttal arguments posed by adversaries, clients, or other interested parties. Creating an environment that is suspicious of agreement and invites candor should be comforting to lawyers given that this does comport with their basic training in adversarial lawyering. But making sure that the lawyer continues to see the value of robust discussion even in practice will be critical.

The last intersectional leadership dimension exhorts lawyer-leaders to act with moral integrity. This may mean subordinating personal ambition to the good of the organization, which can also enhance lawyering. Lawyers can develop processes and create groups to serve as sounding boards so that lawyers can better avoid the types of behaviors that lead to potential moral or ethical conflicts even in individual cases. Looking for conflicts of interest that may not rise to the level of a professional ethical conflict but could make the client uncomfortable, enables the lawyer to enhance the level of trust experienced by the client in the lawyer-client relationship. The ability to recognize those potential conflicts and to be open about them occurs not only at the leadership level but at the day-to-day practice level as well.

So, in the end, law schools and educators have real interests in teaching leadership. It is encouraging that some major law firms and some of the most established U.S. companies are beginning to recognize the need to teach lawyers leadership. Managing partners in law firms have in recent years looked to initiate formal leadership programs within their firms or have sent some of their lawyers to established general leadership programs. U.S. companies in every industry have recognized the value of leadership training for their leaders and executives who demonstrate high potential for such positions. Typically, they include lawyers in these general leadership programs. But a select few have begun to construct and deliver specialized leadership training for their legal units that builds on the more generalized concepts they can glean from the leadership courses that other executives within the organization take. These are all positive steps that can be enhanced by sharpening the focus of that training to intersectional leadership concepts.

What has led many of these organizations to make the novel decision to offer specialized leadership training to lawyers is not the sort of dramatic leadership breaches highlighted by the preceding chapters. Rather it has been the missed opportunity to gain a strategic advantage by helping lawyer-leaders function even better in role. It is good business to do so, and lawyer-leaders are uniquely able to lead once trained. They are critical thinkers. They have to understand a broad range of issues and possibilities to be able to advise a client well. They have to be quick studies themselves and must find ways to engage others to gather data and to pull information that will be critical to a thoughtful approach to a given question. These capabilities also serve them well in leadership. It is not surprising that we are beginning to see more lawyers who have served as general counsels in business leaving those positions to assume a role as CEO. The general counsel role requires lawyers to understand the many facets of a large organization and to help it make decisions that enhance the interests of the enterprise and its stakeholders. The general counsel's ability to keep his or her head on a swivel provides an opportunity to think across the organization and to stay in front of issues before they become problems. It is just as important for a lawyer to be able to recognize and appreciate a good argument but also understand that the organizational direction may rest in the path less argued.

REASONS FOR HOPE

Looking ahead in the twenty-first century brings me great hope as we think about preparing law students and lawyers to lead. In the first two decades of this century we have seen increased attention paid to leadership education. Law schools, law firms, and legal organizations are increasingly discussing leadership, thinking deeply about the law school and law firm business model to better prepare lawyers. And finally, the public continues to look to lawyers to lead; indeed, in many state legislatures, we see a large percentage of lawyers. In New Jersey, Louisiana, Virginia, South Carolina, Texas, Florida, and Mississippi, the percentage of lawyer-legislators remains high, at more than 25 percent, and the highest is in New Jersey, where 36 of 120 legislators, or 30 percent, are lawyers, according to the Stateline-NCSL survey.[3]

Legal education has also been willing to evolve from the narrow view that those from practice have little to contribute to the pedagogical enterprise. While leadership can be taught and learned without law professors having actually been leaders, experience in practice environments does help contextualize some leadership lessons. In addition to being more open about leadership pedagogy, increasingly, legal education has come to value interdisciplinary approaches. Some law schools are now requiring courses teaching financial literacy, so that lawyers can leave law school able to read and understand profit-and-loss ledgers and have some rudimentary knowledge around budgeting. This pivot to broader thinking about what legal education should include will only enhance the preparation of lawyers to lead. Some schools are similarly beginning to examine the role of technology in legal education. Again this move to include technology, whether cybersecurity, data protection, or data retention, will help lawyers think more broadly than the narrow technical aspect of lawyering. This gives me hope because as we acknowledge that legal education is producing a large number of leaders, broadening law students' perspectives on what it means to be a lawyer may help to contribute to a new understanding of the roles that lawyers play, including leadership roles in different fields.

But perhaps the reason for the greatest hope is this generation of law students and young leaders. In past generations, legal professionals and even leaders themselves often viewed work focused outside the primary mission of the organization as being important but supplementary. This approach often left the social mission as an afterthought to the day-to-day operational functioning of the organization. Millennials have come of age during a time of rapid and dramatic technological changes. They get their news differently than preceding generations (88 percent report getting their news from Facebook).[4] They are more connected; they check their smartphones on average forty-three times a day,[5] and they stay connected with each other on social media. The connectedness is for social and social justice issues. Their generation has demonstrated a selflessness that has embraced such wide-ranging social concerns as marriage equality and the Black Lives Matter movement. Millennials have focused on making the organizations that they work for support and reflect equality and inclusiveness. While the tech industry continues to wrestle with this challenge, the issues of social justice and equality seem to be hard-wired into the DNA of many of this generation. A World Economic Forum study of five thousand millennials in eighteen countries revealed that their top priority for business was that it should "improve society."[6]

This combination of a laser focus on social justice coupled with the desire that their day-to-day work provide a tangible connection to social justice issues provides new challenges for professional schools and for organizations that employ millennials. Having taught and practiced law for more than three decades and having spent half that time also in the world of executive education focusing on leadership development and pipeline issues, I see this as is a clear sign of change and hope looking out to the horizon.

Finally, as we think more broadly about legal education, legal organizations, and leadership more generally, this is an exciting time. There is a focus on experiential education but also on teaching a much broader range of professional competencies. There is an increased focus on preparing students to be part of a connected and global-practice world. And while we continue to grapple with the extent to which we will teach values, many institutions are rethinking what the core values of legal education should look like. Fundamental conversations will lead to more discussions about leadership. These conversations include how we will think about and guarantee access to justice, how we prepare law students and lawyers to succeed and balance their personal and professional lives, and how we continue to perpetuate experimentation and innovation in curriculum and practice.

Addressing profound issues of inequality, race ethnicity, and leadership is the challenge of this generation, especially the future lawyer-leaders that emerge from it. It is an exciting time to be a part of this challenge and to continue to push our thinking for the future.

Notes

INTRODUCTION

1. Jake May, *Still Standing: Flint Residents Tell Their Stories About Living with Poisoned Water*, MLIVE, http://www.mlive.com/news/index.ssf/page/still_standing_flint_residents .html (last visited Dec. 20, 2017).

2. Matt Pearce, *A "Man-Made Disaster" Unfolded in Flint, Within Plain Sight of Water Regulators*, L.A. TIMES (Jan. 22, 2016), http://www.latimes.com/nation/la-na-flint -water-20160122-story.html.

3. *Flint Water Crisis Fast Facts*, CNN (Nov. 28, 2017), http://www.cnn.com/2016 /03/04/us/flint-water-crisis-fast-facts/index.html.

4. Kevin Monahan, Hannah Rappleye, Stephanie Gosk, & Tim Sandler, *Internal Email: Michigan "Blowing Off" Flint over Lead in Water*, NBC NEWS (Jan. 6, 2016), https:// www.nbcnews.com/storyline/flint-water-crisis/internal-email-michigan-blowing-flint -over-lead-water-n491481.

5. *Id.*

6. Ron Fonger, *General Motors Shutting Off Flint River Water at Engine Plant over Corrosion Worries*, MLIVE (Oct. 13, 2014), http://www.mlive.com/news/flint/index.ssf/2014/10 /general_motors_wont_use_flint.html.

7. Ron Fonger, *GM's Decision to Stop Using Flint River Water Will Cost Flint $400,000 per Year*, MLIVE (October 14, 2014), http://www.mlive.com/news/flint/index.ssf/2014 /10/gms_decision_to_stop_using_fli.html.

8. *State of Emergency Declared in the City of Flint*, CITY OF FLINT, MICHIGAN, https:// www.cityofflint.com/state-of-emergency/ (last visited Dec. 20, 2017).

9. *Id.*

10. *How the Flint Water Crisis Investigation Led to Manslaughter Charges*, MLIVE (June 15, 2017), http://www.mlive.com/news/flint/index.ssf/2017/06/investigation _leads_to_manslau.html.

11. Jessica Durando, *How Water Crisis in Flint, Mich., Became Federal State of Emergency*, USA TODAY (January 19, 2016), https://www.usatoday.com/story/news/nation-now /2016/01/19/michigan-flint-water-contamination/78996052/.

12. Paul Egan, *These Are the 15 People Criminally Charged in the Flint Water Crisis*, DET. FREE PRESS (June 14, 2017), http://www.freep.com/story/news/local/michigan/flint -water-crisis/2017/06/14/flint-water-crisis-charges/397425001/.

13. Brady Dennis, *Four More Officials Charged with Felonies in Flint Water Crisis*, WASH. POST (Dec. 20, 2016), https://www.washingtonpost.com/news/energy-environment /wp/2016/12/20/four-more-officials-charged-with-felonies-in-flint-water-crisis/?utm _term=.ee101dfab596.

14. Bain Insights, *The Potential Impacts of Brexit on the Global Economy*, FORBES (June 29, 2016), http://www.forbes.com/sites/baininsights/2016/06/29/the-potential -impacts-of-brexit-on-the-global-economy/#7049d2020e00/; *Greece's economic debt crisis affecting global economies*, https://www.brookings.edu/opinions/why-the-greek-debt-crisis -is-a-problem-for-the-entire-world-economy/.

15. Mike Myatt, *30 Outdated Leadership Practices Holding Your Company Back*, FORBES (July 28, 2013), http://www.forbes.com/sites/mikemyatt/2013/07/28/30-outdated -leadership-practices-holding-your-company-back/; Chuck Bayne, *3 Key Aspects of Leadership Training for the Modern World*, WYO. L. ENFORCEMENT ACAD. (Feb. 6, 2015), http://www.wleacademy.com/leadership/3-key-aspects-of-leadership-training-for-the -modern-world/; Timothy B. Corcoran, *Ten Things I'd Do Differently as a Law Firm CEO*, CORCORAN CONSULTING GROUP (March 28, 2013), http://www.corcoranlawbizblog .com/2013/03/10-things/; Claire Warren, *Employers Held Hostage by Outdated Management Model, Warns Hamel*, CHARTERED INST. PERSONNEL & DEV. (June 27, 2014), http:// www.cipd.co.uk/pm/peoplemanagement/b/weblog/archive/2014/06/27/employers -held-hostage-by-outdated-management-model-warns-hamel.aspx.

16. Daniel Goleman, *What Makes a Leader?*, HARV. BUS. REV. (Jan. 2004), https://hbr .org/2004/01/what-makes-a-leader; William Gentry, Jennifer J. Deal, Sarah Stawiski, & Marian Ruderman, *Are Leaders Born or Made? Perspectives from the Executive Suite*, CTR. FOR CREATIVE LEADERSHIP (Mar. 2012), http://www.ccl.org/Leadership/pdf/research /AreLeadersBornOrMade.pdf; Stanford GSB Staff, *Colin Powell: "Never Show Fear or Anger,"* STAN. GRADUATE SCH. BUS. (Nov. 1, 2005), https://www.gsb.stanford.edu/insights/colin -powell-never-show-fear-or-anger; Ekaterina Walter, *5 Myths of Leadership*, FORBES (Oct. 8, 2013), http://www.forbes.com/sites/ekaterinawalter/2013/10/08/5-myths-of-leadership/; "... leaders are made, not born, and made more by themselves than by any external means. Second ... that no leader sets out to be a leader per se, but rather to express himself freely and fully."—Warren Bennis, *On Becoming a Leader*. Bennis, one of the leading executive educators of our time, concludes that leadership is a body of skills and knowledge that can be learned and developed, as opposed to some "preordained set of attributes."

17. *How Many Law Schools Are in the US?*, MAGOOSH LSAT BLOG (Sept. 26, 2016), https://magoosh.com/lsat/2016/many-law-schools-united-states/.

18. Jeff Jacoby, *US Legal Bubble Can't Pop Soon Enough*, BOSTON GLOBE (May 9, 2014), https://www.bostonglobe.com/opinion/2014/05/09/the-lawyer-bubble-pops -not-moment-too-soon/qAYzQ823qpfi4GQl2OiPZM/story.html.

CHAPTER ONE

1. Dan Slater, *Barack Obama: The U.S.'s 44th President (and 25th Lawyer-President!)*, WALL ST. J. (Nov. 5, 2008), http://blogs.wsj.com/law/2008/11/05/barack-obama-the -uss-44th-president-and-24th-lawyer-president/.

2. *State of the Congress 2013*, MEASURE OF AMERICA, http://www.measureofamerica .org/113-congress-infographic/ (last visited Dec. 20, 2017).

3. Menachem Wecker, *Where the Fortune 500 CEOs Went to Law School*, U.S. NEWS & WORLD REP. (June 26, 2012), http://www.usnews.com/education/best -graduate-schools/top-law-schools/articles/2012/06/26/where-the-fortune-500-ceos -went-to-law-school.

4. *See, e.g.*, Derek Handova, *How Can Lawyers Become Tech Company CEOs?*, IPWATCHDOG (Sept. 22, 2016), http://www.ipwatchdog.com/2016/09/22/lawyers -become-tech-company-ceos/id=72651/; *Ten Current CEO-Lawyers*, BITTER EMPIRE, http://bitterempire.com/ten-current-ceo-lawyers/ (last visited Dec. 20, 2017).

5. *Ten Current CEO-Lawyers.*

6. *Id.*

7. *Id.*

8. Benjamin Spencer, *The Law School Critique in Historical Perspective*, 69 WASH. & LEE L. REV. 1949 (2012), http://papers.ssrn.com/sol3/papers.cfm?abstract_id=2017114.

9. *Id.*

10. Nancy L. Schultz, *How Do Lawyers Really Think?*, 45 J. LEGAL EDU. 57 (1992).

11. Wayne S. Hyatt, *A Lawyer's Lament: Law Schools and the Profession of Law*, 60 VAND. L. REV. 385, 389–390 (2007).

12. Robert W. Gordon, *Lawyers, Scholars, and the "Middle Ground,"* 91 MICH. L. REV. 2075, 2108–2109 (1993).

13. *Id.* at 2109.

14. WILLIAM M. SULLIVAN ET AL., EDUCATING LAWYERS: PREPARATION FOR THE PROFESSION OF LAW 127–128 (2007).

15. MAX WEBER, THE THEORY OF SOCIAL AND ECONOMIC ORGANIZATION (A. M. Henderson & Talcott Parsons, trans., 1947) (describing rational-legal leadership which would come to be known as transactional leadership).

16. JAMES DOWNTON, REBEL LEADERSHIP: COMMITMENT AND CHARISMA IN THE REVOLUTIONARY PROCESS (1973); JAMES MCGREGOR BURNS, LEADERSHIP (1978); BERNARD BASS, LEADERSHIP AND PERFORMANCE (1985).

17. Andy Boynton, *Are You an "I" or a "T"?*, FORBES (Oct. 18, 2013), https://www .forbes.com/sites/andyboynton/2011/10/18/are-you-an-i-or-a-t/#c2585a66e888.

18. Vivian Hunt et al., *Why Diversity Matters*, MCKINSEY & COMP. (Feb. 2015), http:// www.mckinsey.com/business-functions/organization/our-insights/why-diversity-matters.

19. *Id.*

20. *Id.*

21. *Id.*

22. *Id.*

23. *Id.*

24. Deborah L. Rhode, *Law Is the Least Diverse Profession in the Nation. And Lawyers Aren't Doing Enough to Change That*, WASH. POST (May 27, 2015), https://www.washingtonpost .com/posteverything/wp/2015/05/27/law-is-the-least-diverse-profession-in-the-nation -and-lawyers-arent-doing-enough-to-change-that/?utm_term=.e779419888e5.

25. *See generally* THOMAS FRIEDMAN, THE WORLD IS FLAT: A BRIEF HISTORY OF THE TWENTY-FIRST CENTURY (2005). *See also* John Gray, *The World Is Round*, N.Y. REV. BOOKS (Aug. 11, 2005), http://www.nybooks.com/articles/2005/08/11/the-world-is-round/.

26. John Coleman & Bill George, *Enhance Your Overseas Experience*, HARV. BUS. REV. BLOGS (Mar. 6, 2012), http://blogs.hbr.org/2012/03/enhance-your-overseas-experience/.

27. Susan Bryant, *Collaboration in Law Practice: A Satisfying and Productive Process for a Diverse Profession*, 17 VT. L. REV. 459 (1993); David Chavkin, Matchmaker, *Student Collaboration in Clinical Programs* 1 CLIN. L. REV. 199 (1994).

28. Rick Lash, *The Collaboration Imperative*, IVEY BUS. J. (Jan./Feb. 2012), https://iveybusinessjournal.com/publication/the-collaboration-imperative/.

29. Daniel Goleman, *Leadership That Gets Results*, HARV. BUS. REV. (Mar.–Apr. 2000), https://hbr.org/2000/03/leadership-that-gets-results (identifying affiliative leadership as one of six leadership styles).

30. ROBERT K. GREENLEAF, SERVANT LEADERSHIP (1977).

31. Nathan Bennett & G. James Lemoine, *What VUCA Really Means for You*, HARV. BUS. REV. (Jan.–Feb. 2014), https://hbr.org/2014/01/what-vuca-really-means-for-you.

32. Scott Berinato, *A Framework for Understanding VUCA*, HARV. BUS. REV. (Sept. 5, 2014), https://hbr.org/2014/09/a-framework-for-understanding-vuca.

33. *The Unpopular, Successful Auto Bailout*, AM. PROSPECT (May 24, 2011), http://prospect.org/article/unpopular-successful-auto-bailout.

34. John Cassidy, *An Inconvenient Truth: It Was George W. Bush Who Bailed Out the Automakers*, NEW YORKER (Mar. 16, 2012), http://www.newyorker.com/news/john-cassidy/an-inconvenient-truth-it-was-george-w-bush-who-bailed-out-the-automakers.

35. Mitt Romney, *Let Detroit Go Bankrupt*, N.Y. TIMES (Nov. 18, 2008), http://www.nytimes.com/2008/11/19/opinion/19romney.html.

36. Jon Greenberg, *Did President Obama Save the Auto Industry?*, POLITIFACT (Sept. 6, 2012), http://www.politifact.com/truth-o-meter/article/2012/sep/06/did-obama-save-us-automobile-industry/.

37. Jonathan Cohn, *Somebody Forgot to Tell Bush, Cruz and Rubio the GM Bailout Worked*, HUFFINGTON POST (June 7, 2015), http://www.huffingtonpost.com/2015/06/07/2016-gm-bailout_n_7523248.html.

38. Jay Gilbert, *Millennials at Work Reshaping the Workplace*, PWC, https://www.pwc.com/gx/en/managing-tomorrows-people/future-of-work/assets/reshaping-the-workplace.pdf.

39. *Id.*

40. Peter F. Drucker, *The Theory of the Business*, HARV. BUS. REV. (Sept.–Oct. 1994), https://hbr.org/1994/09/the-theory-of-the-business.

CHAPTER TWO

1. *See* Cynthia Burton & Adrienne Lu, *Christie Names Several Senior Aides*, PHILA. INQUIRER, Dec. 4, 2009.

2. Michael Symons, *Christie Cabinet Stocked with Ex-Prosecutors*, ASBURY PARK PRESS (N.J.), May 22, 2011.

3. *Id.*

4. Mark Magyar, *All the Governor's Prosecutors*, NJ SPOTLIGHT (Mar. 11, 2004), http://www.njspotlight.com/stories/14/03/11/all-the-governor-s-prosecutors/.

5. Salvador Rizzo, *Christie Announces That David Samson Resigned as Port Authority Chairman*, NJ.COM (Mar. 28, 2014), https://www.dailykos.com/stories/2014/1/29/1273407/-NYT-Christie-Profile-Direct-Line-to-the-Governor.

6. *See* Magyar, *All the Governor's Prosecutors*.

7. *Id.*

8. *Chris Christie Aide Tied to "Bridgegate" is a Longtime Government Worker*, NJ.COM (Jan. 8, 2014), http://www.nj.com/politics/index.ssf/2014/01/chris_christie_aid_tied_to_bridgegate_is_a_longtime_government_worker.html.

9. Katie Zernike & Marc Santora, *"Very Sad" Chris Christie Extends Apology in Bridge Scandal*, N.Y. TIMES, Jan. 10, 2014, at A1.

10. Jenna Portnoy, *Chris Christie Bridge Scandal Takes Down Governor's Campaign Manager*, NJ.COM (Jan. 10, 2014), http://www.nj.com/politics/index.ssf/2014/01/im_sorry_christie_responds_to_bridge_scandal_e-mails_with_rare_apologetic_side.html#incart_river.

11. *Id.*

12. *See id.*

13. *See* Gibson, Dunn & Crutcher LLP, *Report of Gibson, Dunn & Crutcher LLP Concerning Its Investigation on Behalf of the Office of the Governor of New Jersey into Allegations Regarding the George Washington Bridge Lane Realignment and Superstorm Sandy Aid to the City of Hoboken*, WALL ST. J. (Mar. 26, 2014), at 3, http://online.wsj.com/public/resources/documents/nybridge0327.pdf.

14. *Id.*

15. *Id.*

16. *Id.*

17. *Id.*

18. *Id.*

19. *Id.* at 3–4.

20. *Id.* at 4.

21. *See id.*

22. *Id.*

23. *Id.* at 4, 61.

24. *Id.* at 68–70.

25. *Id.* at 4–5.

26. *Id.* at 5.

27. *Id.*

28. *Id.* at 6.

29. *Id.* at 31.

30. *Id.* at 31–32.

31. *Id.*

32. *Id.*

33. *See* Zernike & Santora, *"Very Sad" Chris Christie*.

34. *See* Gibson, Dunn & Crutcher LLP, at 35. (The firm interviewed more than seventy witnesses and reviewed over 250,000 documents in its investigation.)

35. *See* Michael Barbaro, *Report Details Ex-Ally's Claim about Christie*, N.Y. TIMES, Mar. 28, 2014, at A1.

36. Adam Edelman, *Gov. Christie's Internal Bridgegate Review, "Not Conclusive," Former NYC Mayor Rudy Giuliani Says*, N.Y. DAILY NEWS (Mar. 30, 2014), http://www.nydailynews .com/news/politics/gov-christie-internal-bridgegate-review-conclusive-nyc-mayor-rudy -giuliani-article-1.1739586.

37. *See* DORIS KEARNS GOODWIN, TEAM OF RIVALS (2012).

38. *See* Gibson, Dunn & Crutcher LLP, at 128.

39. *Id.*

40. *Id.* at 129.

41. *Id.*

42. Brent Johnson, *Chris Christie Responds to New Bridge Scandal Allegations*, NJ.COM (Feb. 1, 2014), http://www.nj.com/politics/index.ssf/2014/01/chris_christie_responds _to_new_bridge_scandal_allegations.html.

43. *Timeline: New Jersey's George Washington Bridge Scandal*, NBC NEW YORK (Nov. 1, 2016), http://www.nbcnewyork.com/news/local/Timeline-George-Washington-Bridge -Scandal-Chris-Christie-Fort-Lee-Bridgegate-239431091.html#ixzz4QhIFwbAO.

44. Dustin Racioppi, *Verdict: Kelly, Baroni Guilty on All Counts in Bridgegate Trial*, APP.COM (Nov. 4, 2016), http://www.app.com/story/news/local/courts/2016/11/04 /bridgegate-jury-deliberation-fifth-day/93280730/.

45. Ted Sherman & Tim Darragh, *David Samson, Close Confidant of Christie, Pleads Guilty in Airline Shakedown*, NJ.COM (July 14, 2016), http://www.nj.com/news/index.ssf /2016/07/david_samson_port_authority.html.

46. *See* NJTV NEWS, http://www.nj.com/politics/index.ssf/2014/03/david_samson _resigns_as_port_authority_chairman.html.

47. *Id.* at 12:47–13:01.

48. Laura Maggi, *Radio Call of Cops "Down" Summons Police to Danziger Bridge*, TIMES-PICAYUNE (Feb. 18, 2007; updated Dec. 9, 2009), http://www.nola.com/crime/index .ssf/2007/02/radio_call_of_cops_down_summo.html.

49. Laura Maggi, *NOPD Probe of Danziger Bridge Lacks Key Proof, Witnesses*, TIMES-PICAYUNE (May 18, 2007), http://blog.nola.com/tpcrimearchive/2007/05/nopds _bridge_probe_full_of_bla.html.

50. *Id.*

51. *Id.*

52. *Id.*

53. *Id.*

54. *Id.*

55. *Id.*; *see also* Laura Maggi, *Teenage Danziger Bridge Victims Were in Wrong Place at Wrong Time*, TIMES-PICAYUNE (June 20, 2011), http://www.nola.com/crime/index.ssf /2011/06/teenage_danziger_bridge_shooti.html.

56. Dan Swenson, *What Happened on the Danziger Bridge*, TIMES-PICAYUNE, http:// media.nola.com/crime_impact/other/What-Happened-On-The-Danziger-Bridge.pdf (last visited Jan. 24, 2013).

57. *Id.*

58. Maggi, *Radio Call of Cops "Down,"* 1.

59. *Id.*

60. *Id.*

61. *Id.*

62. *Id.*

63. *Id.*

64. *Id.*

65. *Id.*

66. *Id.*

67. Swenson, *What Happened on the Danziger Bridge.*

68. Laura Maggi, *Charges Rejected Against Danziger Bridge 7*, TIMES-PICAYUNE (Aug. 14, 2008), http://www.nola.com/crime/index.ssf/2008/08/charges_rejected _against_danzi.html.

69. Laura Maggi, *NOPD Probe of Danziger Bridge Lacks Key Proof, Witnesses*, TIMES-PICAYUNE (May 18, 2007), http://blog.nola.com/tpcrimearchive/2007/05/nopds _bridge_probe_full_of_bla.html.

70. *Id.*

71. TIMES-PICAYUNE, *Update: Third New Orleans Police Officer Pleads Guilty in Danziger Bridge Case* (Apr. 7, 2010), http://www.nola.com/crime/index.ssf/2010/04/nopd_officer _pleads_guilty_i.html.

72. Maggi, *Charges Rejected Against Danziger Bridge 7.*

73. Mary Foster, *Feds to Investigate Post-Katrina Bridge Shootings*, USA TODAY (Sept. 9, 2009), http://usatoday30.usatoday.com/news/nation/2008-09-30-1534544418_x.htm.

74. TIMES-PICAYUNE, *Retired Officer's Guilty Plea in Danziger Bridge Case a Blow to Struggling NOPD* (Feb. 25, 2010), http://www.nola.com/crime/index.ssf/2010/02 /retired_officers_guilty_plea_i.html.

75. *Id.*

76. TIMES-PICAYUNE, *Danziger Bridge Shooting Plea, Second in Case, Provides New Cover-Up Details* (Mar. 11, 2010), http://www.nola.com/crime/index.ssf/2010/03/danziger _bridge_shooting_plea_1.html.

77. TIMES-PICAYUNE, *Update: Third New Orleans Police Officer Pleads Guilty in Danziger Bridge Case* (Apr. 7, 2010), http://www.nola.com/crime/index.ssf/2010/04/nopd_officer _pleads_guilty_i.html; Laura Maggi, *4th Former New Orleans Cop Pleads Guilty in Danziger Bridge CoverUp*, TIMES-PICAYUNE (Apr. 28, 2010), http://www.nola.com/crime/index .ssf/2010/04/4th_former_new_orleans_cop_ple.html; Ramon Antonio Vargas, *Fifth NOPD Officer Pleads Guilty in Danziger Bridge Case*, TIMES-PICAYUNE (June 4, 2010), http:// www.nola.com/crime/index.ssf/2010/06/hills-plea.html.

78. Laura Maggi, *Civilian Pleads Guilty in Danziger Bridge Case*, TIMES-PICAYUNE (Apr. 28, 2010), http://www.nola.com/crime/index.ssf/2010/04/civilian_pleads_guilty _in_danz.html.

79. TIMES-PICAYUNE, *Update: Third New Orleans Police Officer Pleads Guilty.*

80. Brendan McCarthy, *Danziger Bridge Coverup Brings 3-Year Sentence for Former NOPD Officer Jeffrey Lehrmann*, TIMES-PICAYUNE (Sept. 22, 2010), http://www.nola.com/crime /index.ssf/2010/09/jeffrey_lehrmann_ex-nopd_offic.html.

81. Brendan McCarthy, *Former NOPD Officer Michael Hunt Sentenced to 8 Years in Danziger Bridge Civil Rights Case*, TIMES-PICAYUNE (Dec. 1, 2010), http://www.nola.com /crime/index.ssf/2010/12/former_nopd_officer_sentenced.html.

82. Brendan McCarthy, *Ex-NOPD Officer, Danziger Bridge Cooperator Ignatius Hills Sentenced to 6½ Years*, TIMES-PICAYUNE (Oct. 5, 2011), http://www.nola.com/crime /index.ssf/2011/10/ex-nopd_officer_danziger_bridg.html.

83. Laura Maggi, *Former New Orleans Police Officer Sentenced to 5 Years in Danziger Bridge Case*, TIMES-PICAYUNE (Dec. 1, 2011), http://www.nola.com/crime/index.ssf /2011/12/former_new_orleans_police_offi_3.html.

84. Laura Maggi, *Danziger Bridge Cooperating Witness, Former NOPD Lieutenant, Will Serve 4 Years in Prison, Judge Decrees*, TIMES-PICAYUNE (Nov. 2, 2011), http://www.nola .com/crime/index.ssf/2011/11/danziger_bridge_cooperating_wi.html.

85. *U.S. v. Bowen et al.*, Docket No. 10-204 (E.D. La. July 12, 2010), http://media .nola.com/news_impact/other/danziger-indictment.pdf.

86. Pierre Thomas, *Katrina Cover-Up: Cops May Face Death Penalty*, ABC NEWS (July 14, 2010), http://abcnews.go.com/GMA/orleans-police-face-death-penalty -hurricane-katrina-bridge/story?id=11160077.

87. TIMES-PICAYUNE, *5 NOPD Officers Guilty in Post-Katrina Danziger Bridge Shootings, Cover-Up* (Mar. 15, 2011), http://www.nola.com/crime/index.ssf/2011/08/danziger _bridge_verdict_do_not.html.

88. Caterina Gouvis Roman, Seri Irazola, & Jenny W. L. Osborne, *After Katrina: Washed Away? Justice in New Orleans*, URBAN INST. REP. (August 2007).

89. *Id.*

90. *Id.* at 1, 4.

91. *Id.* at 4.

92. *Id.* at 5, 8, 9. See also Brendan McCarthy, *Sweeping NOPD Reform Strategy Outlined in Federal Consent Decree*, TIMES-PICAYUNE (July 24, 2012), http://www.nola.com/crime /index.ssf/2012/07/federal_consent_decree_outline.html.

93. *Id.*

94. Thibodaux Rotary, *Jim Letten US Attorney* (Oct. 3, 2011), http://thibodauxrotary .org/jim-letten-us-attorney/.

95. Robertson Campbell, *Crusading New Orleans Prosecutor to Quit, Facing Staff Misconduct*, N.Y. TIMES (Dec. 6, 2012), http://www.nytimes.com/2012/12/07/us/jim -letten-new-orleans-us-attorney-resigns.html?_r=0.

96. Clancy DuBos, *Jim Letten Leads a Team of Modern-Day Untouchables*, BESTOFNEWORLEANS .COM (Jan. 4, 2010), http://www.bestofneworleans.com/gambit/jim-letten-leads-a-team -of-modern-day-untouchables/Content?oid=1254794.

97. *Id.*

98. TIMES-PICAYUNE, *"Mencken1951" Unmasked: It Is Federal Prosecutor Sal Perricone* (Mar. 15, 2012), http://www.nola.com/politics/index.ssf/2012/03/letten_announces.html.

99. Brendan McCarthy, *Danziger Bridge Convicts Seek Sentencing Delay Because of Perricone Scandal*, TIMES-PICAYUNE (Mar. 28, 2012), http://www.nola.com/crime/index .ssf/2012/03/attorneys_for_officers_convict.html.

100. *Id.*

101. *Id.*

102. Elizabeth Murphy, *New Orleans AUSA Admits to Posting Hundreds of Online Comments*, MAIN JUST. (Mar. 16, 2012), http://www.mainjustice.com/2012/03/16/new-orleans-ausa-admits-to-posting-hundreds-of-online-comments/.

103. Brendan McCarthy, *Judge Imposes Stiff Sentences on 5 NOPD Officers Convicted in Danziger Shootings*, TIMES-PICAYUNE (Apr. 4, 2012), http://www.nola.com/crime/index.ssf/2012/04/judge_imposes_sentences_on_5_.html.

104. Gordon Russell, *Federal Prosecutor Sal Perricone Resigns*, TIMES-PICAYUNE (Mar. 20, 2012), http://www.nola.com/crime/index.ssf/2012/03/federal_prosecutor_sal_perrico.html.

105. McCarthy, *Judge Imposes Stiff Sentences.*

106. ASSOC. PRESS, *Danziger Bridge Cover-Up Convict Seeks New Trial* (May 19, 2012), http://www.nola.com/crime/index.ssf/2012/05/danziger_bridge_cover-up_convi.html.

107. *Id.*

108. *Id.*

109. *Id.*

110. Elizabeth Murphy, *Inside the Scandal That Toppled the New Orleans U.S. Attorney*, MAIN JUST. (Dec. 7, 2012), http://www.mainjustice.com/2012/12/07/inside-the-scandal-that-toppled-the-new-orleans-u-s-attorney/print/.

111. ASSOC. PRESS, *Federal Judge Seeks Records Related to Danziger Bridge Leaks Probe* (June 12, 2012), http://www.nola.com/crime/index.ssf/2012/06/federal_judge_seeks_records_re.html.

112. John Simerman, *Jim Letten Demotes Second-in-Command, Tries to Quietly Weather Scandal*, TIMES-PICAYUNE (Nov. 8, 2012), http://www.nola.com/crime/index.ssf/2012/11/letten_demotes_second-in-comma.html.

113. Murphy, *Inside the Scandal.*

114. *U.S. v. Bowen*, 969 F. Supp.2d 526 (2012).

115. *Id.* at 527.

116. Murphy, *Inside the Scandal.*

117. Gordon Russell, *Landfill Owner, Probe Target Fred Heebe Sues Jan Mann, Top Federal Prosecutor*, TIMES-PICAYUNE (Nov. 2, 2012), http://www.nola.com/crime/index.ssf/2012/11/landfill_owner_probe_target_fr.html.

118. Murphy, *Inside the Scandal.*

119. *Id.*

120. *Id.*

121. *Id.*

122. *Id.*

123. *Id.*

124. *Id.*

125. *Id.*

126. The *Times-Picayune* referred to it as "an order that excoriates U.S. Attorney Jim Letten's office." Laura Maggi, *Federal Judge Reorders U.S. Attorney's Office to Investigate*

Leaks in Danziger Bridge Case, Times-Picayune (Nov. 26, 2012), http://www.nola.com /crime/index.ssf/2012/11/federal_judge_re-orders_us_att.html.

127. *Id.*; Murphy, *Inside the Scandal.*

128. "Moreover, the Perricone matter has been under investigation for eight months (since March), and yet it comes as a complete surprise to everyone at DOJ and the U.S. Attorney's Office that another 'poster' exists, especially one maintaining as high a position in the U.S. Attorney's Office. It is difficult to imagine how this could possibly have been missed by OPR, and surely raises concerns about the capabilities and adequacy of DOJ's investigatory techniques as exercised through OPR. In any event, the Court has little confidence that OPR will fully investigate and come to conclusions with anywhere near the efficiency and certainty offered by suitable court-approved independent counsel. The Court strongly urges DOJ to do so post haste. Should DOJ determine not to proceed accordingly, the Court is left to proceed as it sees fit." And in a footnote to this paragraph, "It would seem obvious that, upon news of Perricone's activities, among the first questions to be answered were: (1) Is anyone else in the U.S. Attorney's Office posting inappropriate and/or compromising online comments? and (2) Did anyone in the U.S. Attorney's Office know or suspect that Perricone was posting prior to his admission in March 2012? (Even if OPR asked the first question in March, one shudders to imagine what answer was given by First AUSA Mann. Either she confessed to such activity, or falsely denied it.) Regardless, had the DOJ proactively and independently investigated and carefully analyzed the online comments in March 2012 as did the expert who uncovered Perricone and Mann, the answer to the first question would have been known months ago." *U.S. v. Bowen et al.*, Docket No. 10-204 (E.D. La. Nov. 26, 2012), http://media.nola.com/crime_impact/other/engelhardtorder.pdf.

129. Murphy, *Inside the Scandal*; *Perfidious Prosecutors*, N.Y. Times (Dec. 2, 2012), http://www.nytimes.com/2012/12/03/opinion/perfidious-prosecutors.html.

130. Rick Jervis, *Top Federal Prosecutor in New Orleans Resigns*, USA Today (Dec. 6, 2012), https://www.usatoday.com/story/news/nation/2012/12/06/us-attorney-louisiana -letten/1751153/; see also Robertson, *Crusading New Orleans Prosecutor.*

131. Gordon Russell, *Jan Mann, Jim Mann Have Retired from U.S. Attorney's Office*, Times-Picayune (Dec. 17, 2012), http://www.nola.com/crime/index.ssf/2012/12 /jan_mann_jim_mann_have_retired.html.

132. Murphy, *Inside the Scandal*; *Perfidious Prosecutors.*

CHAPTER THREE

1. *Houston DA Controversy*, Newsweek (Feb. 25, 2008), http://www.newsweek.com /houston-da-controversy-94067.

2. *Id.*

3. *Id.*

4. *Id.*

5. Brian Rogers, Alan Bernstein, & Matt Stiles, *More E-mails Emerge in Harris County DA Scandal*, Hous. Chron. (Jan. 9, 2008), http://www.chron.com/news/houston-texas /article/More-e-mails-emerge-in-Harris-County-DA-scandal-1754858.php.

6. *Id.*

7. *Id.*

8. *Id.*

9. *Id.*

10. Lisa Falkenberg, *A Lonely Feeling in the DA's Office*, HOUS. CHRON. (Feb. 7, 2008), http://www.chron.com/news/falkenberg/article/A-lonely-feeling-in-the-DA-s-office -1629965.php.

11. *Id.*

12. Priscila Mosqueda, *Death Row Inmate Appeals, Cites Report Showing Racial Bias in Harris County*, TEX. OBSERVER (Mar. 14, 2013), http://www.texasobserver.org/study -minorities-more-likely-to-get-death-sentence-in-harris-county/ (last visited June 1, 2016).

13. *Id.*

14. Leslie Casimir, *Black Leaders Urge Rosenthal to Step Down*, HOUS. CHRON. (Jan. 12, 2008), http://www.chron.com/news/houston-texas/article/Black-leaders -urge-Rosenthal-to-step-down-1777192.php (quotations omitted).

15. Council Member Jolanda Jones, *Case Against Rosenthal Couldn't Be More Convincing*, HOUS. CHRON. (Jan. 20, 2008), http://www.chron.com/opinion/outlook/article/Case -Against-Rosenthal-Couldn-t-be-more-convicing-1791958.php; *see also* Thom Marshall, *Marshall: DA Faces Music from Ministers*, HOUS. CHRON. (Dec. 13, 2002), http://www .chron.com/news/article/Marshall-DA-faces-music-from-ministers-2128840.php. (Black ministers in Houston had a conversation with Rosenthal about the problems of "all-White" juries.)

16. *Id.*

17. *See also* Scott Phillips, *Continued Racial Disparities in the Capital of Capital Punishment: The Rosenthal Era*, 50 HOUS. L. REV. 131 (Abstract), Oct. 2012.

18. *Id.*

19. *Id.*

20. *Id.*

21. *Id.*

22. *Id.*

23. 4 Bl. Comm. 353. Challenge for cause is distinguished from a peremptory challenge. *See Turner v. State*, 114 Ga. 421; 40 S.E. 30S Cr. Code N.Y. 1903, 5 374; *Challenge for Cause*, BLACK'S LAW DICTIONARY (2d ed. 1910).

24. That means that in most jurisdictions the juror can be sent to another trial department to sit in another case.

25. *Batson v. Kentucky*, 476 U.S. 79, 89 (1986) ("the component of the jury selection process at issue here, the State's privilege to strike individual jurors through peremptory challenges, is subject to the commands of the Equal Protection Clause"). This memorandum does not examine the use of peremptory strikes by civil litigants or criminal defendants, though the equal protection clause also applies to peremptory strikes in those contexts. *See Edmonson v. Leesville Concrete Co., Inc.*, 500 U.S. 614 (1991) (concerning civil litigants); *Georgia v. McCollum*, 505 U.S. 42 (1992) (concerning criminal defendants).

26. *Id.* at 85; *see also Strauder v. State of West Virginia*, 100 U.S. 303, 305 (1879) (finding no right for a defendant to a "petit jury composed in whole or in part of persons of his own race").

27. 476 U.S. at 89 ("the Equal Protection Clause forbids the prosecutor to challenge potential jurors solely on account of their race or on the assumption that Black jurors as a group will be unable impartially to consider the State's case against a Black defendant.").

28. *Batson v. Kentucky*, 476 U.S. 79 (1986).

29. *Id.*

30. *Id.* at 82.

31. *Id.*

32. *Id.*

33. *Id.* at 85.

34. *Id.* at 86.

35. *Id.*

36. *Id.* at 86, 88.

37. *Id.* at 87. According to the majority, race discrimination in the courtroom "is most pernicious because it is 'a stimulant to that race prejudice which is an impediment to securing . . . equal justice'" for Black Americans. *Id.* at 87–88 (quoting *Strauder v. West Virginia*, 100 U.S. 303, 308 [1879]).

38. Kellie Slappey, *Racial Justice Act*, N.C. HIST. PROJECT (2016), http://northcarolinahistory.org/encyclopedia/racial-justice-act/.

39. North Carolina Racial Justice Act, SB461, § 15A-2011, b, 3 (2009), http://www.ncleg.net/Sessions/2009/Bills/Senate/PDF/S461v6.pdf. Studies on the death penalty from Dr. Isaac Unah and Professor John Boger, both from UNC-Chapel Hill, provided the basis for the act. Their study found that a defendant in North Carolina is 2.6 times more likely to be sentenced to death if at least one victim is White and that of the 159 people on death row, 31 defendants had all-White juries, and 38 defendants had only one person of color on the jury. The Court in *McCleskey* considered and rejected McCleskey's comprehensive statistical data establishing that race was motivating the discretionary choice to charge a case as a capital offense and exposing the defendant to a potential death sentence. The defense offered data compiled by David Baldus that established that an African American man accused of killing a White victim was seven times as likely to face capital punishment compared to a White defendant. The Court rejected the claim that this data amounted to a violation of McCleskey's constitutional right to equal protection under the law.

40. *Id.*; Samuel R. Gross, *David Baldus and the Legacy of* McCleskey v. Kemp, IOWA L. REV. 97 (2012), at 1906–1924, https://repository.law.umich.edu/cgi/viewcontent.cgi?article=1181&context=articles.

41. SB461, § 15A-2011 (2009).

42. SB461, § 15A-2011, b, 1, 2, 3 (2009).

43. The key component of the *McCleskey* decision, that proof of intentional or purposeful discrimination must be proven in the defendant's individual case, is not a requirement under the RJA, although it would be sufficient to support a claim.

44. Sommer Brokaw, *Challenge to Racial Justice Act*, CHARLOTTE POST (N.C.) (Nov. 23, 2011), http://www.thecharlottepost.com/index.php?src=news&srctype=detail&category=News&refno=4153.

45. The letter was addressed to North Carolina senator Phil Berger (D-Guilford), president pro tempore, on November 14, 2011, on behalf of all forty-four district attorneys. *Id.*; John Hinton, *District Attorneys Call for End to Racial Justice Act*, WINSTON-SALEM J. (Nov. 19, 2011), http://www.journalnow.com/archives/district-attorneys-call -for-end-to-racial-justice-act/article_0410b610-d498-5929-a6d1-f74159a10abe.html.

46. Jorge Rivas, *NC: Governor Vetoes Repeal of Racial Justice Act*, COLOR LINES (Dec. 14, 2011), https://www.colorlines.com/articles/nc-governor-vetoes-repeal-racial-justice-act.

47. ACLU, *North Carolina v. Robinson—Hearing Transcripts*, https://www.aclu.org/legal -document/north-carolina-v-robinson-hearing-transcripts (last visited June 2, 2016).

48. *Id.*

49. *Id.*

50. *Id.*

51. BARBARA O'BRIEN & CATHERINE M. GROSSO, MICH. ST. U. C. L., REPORT ON JURY SELECTION STUDY 11 (2011), https://www.aclu.org/other/michigan-state -university-college-law-report-jury-selection-study.

52. ACLU, *Michigan State University College of Law—Report on Jury Selection Study*, https://www.aclu.org/other/michigan-state-university-college-law-report-jury-selection -study?redirect=capital-punishment-racial-justice/michigan-state-university-college -law-report-jury-selection-study (last visited June 2, 2016).

53. Such a disparity was consistent over time in four five-year periods or ten twenty-year periods. The probability of this disparity occurring in a race-neutral jury selection process varied based on the time period from less than one in 10 million to less than 1,000,000,000,000,000,000,000,000. The court went on to find similar disparities in the judicial divisions, in Cumberland County, and in Robinson's own case. ACLU, *North Carolina v. Robinson—Order*, https://www.aclu.org/legal-document/north-carolina -v-robinson-order (last visited June 2, 2016).

54. *Id.*

55. *Id.*

56. *Id.*

57. *Id.*

58. *Id.*

59. *Id.*

60. *Id.*

61. ACLU, *North Carolina v. Tilmon Golphin, Christina Walters, and Quintel Augustine*, https://www.aclu.org/cases/death-penalty/north-carolina-v-tilmon-golphin-christina -walters-and-quintel-augustine (last visited June 17, 2015).

62. *Id.*

63. Order Granting Motions for Appropriate Relief, No. 97 CRS 47314-15, 7–8 (N.C. Sup. Ct. 2012), http://www.law.msu.edu/racial-justice/Golphin-et-al-RJA-Order.pdf.

64. *Id.*

65. *Id.*

66. *Id.*

67. *Id.*

68. *Id.*
69. *Id.* at 49.
70. *Id.*
71. *Id.*
72. *Id.*
73. *Id.*
74. *Id.*
75. *Id.*
76. *Id.*
77. *Id.*
78. *Id.*
79. *Id.*
80. *Id.*
81. *Id.* at 69–70, 85.
82. *Id.*
83. *Id.*
84. *Id.*
85. *Id.*
86. *Id.*
87. *Id.*
88. *Id.*
89. *Id.*

CHAPTER FOUR

1. WILLIAM M. SULLIVAN ET AL., EDUCATING LAWYERS. PREPARATION FOR THE PROFESSION OF LAW (2007); AMERICAN BAR ASSOCIATION SECTION OF LEGAL EDUCATION AND ADMISSIONS TO THE BAR, LEGAL EDUCATION AND PROFESSIONAL DEVELOPMENT: AN EDUCATIONAL CONTINUUM REPORT OF THE TASK FORCE ON LAW SCHOOLS AND THE PROFESSION: NARROWING THE GAP (1992).

2. *See* Timothy Casey & Kathryn Fehrman, *Making Lawyers Out of Law Students: Shifting the Locus of Authority*, 20 PERSP.: TEACHING L. RES. & WRITING 96, no. 2, 3 (2012) (discussing California Western School of Law's second-year STEPPS Program to teach knowledge, skills, and values necessary for a legal career); Symposium, *The Future of Public Interest Law: Meeting Legal Needs in the Twenty-First Century, a Symposium in Celebration of the 15th Anniversary of the CUNY School of Law*, 3, Y. CITY L. REV. 139, 150–151 (2000) (discussing a new course at Yale Law School, Professionalism in the Public Interest, teaching firm-bound lawyers about pro bono work and allowing them to develop a practice to carry with them to their firm job); Charity Scott, *Collaborating with the Real World: Opportunities for Developing Skills and Values in Teaching*, 9 IND. HEALTH L. REV. 409 (2012); Dean Donald Burnett, *A Pathway of Professionalism—The First Day of Law School at the University of Idaho*, 52 ADVOCATE (ID.) 17 (2009) (discussing the Day One program at Idaho to put students' legal education into perspective from the first day of orientation, centering it on professionalism); Margaret Martin Barry, *Are We Practice Ready Yet?*, 32 B.C.J.L. & SOC. JUST. 247, 254–266 (2012). Clinical legal education is garnering more

attention as a vehicle for providing the training required to graduate "practice-ready" lawyers as law schools face economic concerns and increasing expectations from the legal market. To create a school that trains practice-ready lawyers, law schools are increasingly recognizing that they need significant curricular reform. Schools must combine the traditional case method of teaching with experiential learning, where the curriculum focuses not just on doctrine but on training professionals. See also Gregory M. Duhl, *Equipping Our Lawyers: Mitchell's Outcomes-Based Approach to Legal Education*, 38 WM. MITCHELL L. REV. 906 (2012) (discussing William Mitchell Law School's reforms to create an outcome-based legal education system teaching both professional skills and values).

3. Ann J. Iijima, *Lessons Learned: Legal Education and Law Student Dysfunction*, 48 J. LEGAL EDU. 524, 535 (1998).

4. Russell G. Pearce, *Teaching Ethics Seriously*, 29 LOY. U. CHIC. L.J. 719, 727 (1998).

5. Russell G. Pearce, *Professionalism Paradigm Shift: Why Discarding Professional Ideology Will Improve the Conduct and Reputation of the Bar*, 70 Y.U. L. REV. 1229, 1231 (1995); ANTHONY T. KRONMAN, THE LOST LAWYER: FAILING IDEALS OF THE LEGAL PROFESSION (1993), at 113; WILLIAM P. LaPIANA, LOGIC AND EXPERIENCE: THE ORIGIN OF MODERN AMERICAN LEGAL EDUCATION (1994), at x, 254.

6. Deborah L. Rhode, *Legal Education: Professional Interests and Public Values*, 34 IND. L. REV. 40 (2000).

7. *Id.*

8. *Id.*

9. *Id.* at 453.

10. Barry, *Are We Practice Ready Yet?*, 247, 249.

11. *Id.*

12. *Id.* (citing Eric Schnapper, *The Myth of Legal Ethics*, A.B.A.J., 202, 205 (Feb. 1978).

13. Rhode, *Legal Education*, 23, 40 (2000).

14. *Id.*

15. *Id.*

16. *Id.*

17. *Id.*

18. *Id.* at 41–42, noting that professors are wary about "turning podiums into pulpits or inviting 'touchy feely' digressions from 'real law'"; *see also* Iijima, *Lessons Learned*, 524, 535.

19. Dan Levine and Kristina Cooke, *In States with Elected High Court Judges, a Harder Line on Capital Punishment*, REUTERS (Sept. 22, 2015), http://www.reuters.com /investigates/special-report/usa-deathpenalty-judges/.

20. Melinda Gann Hall, *Electoral Politics and Strategic Voting in State Supreme Courts*, 54 J. POL. 421, 443 (1992).

21. *Harris v. Alabama*, 513 U.S. 504, 520 (1995) (Stevens, J., dissenting).

22. Randy Ludlow, *Justice French Defends "Backstop" Comment at GOP Rally*, COLUMBUS DISPATCH (Oct. 27, 2014), http://www.dispatch.com/content/stories/local/2014/10 /27/justice-french-defends-comments.html; Ian Millhiser, *Ohio Supreme Court Justice: Vote for Me Because "I Am a Republican" Who Will Uphold GOP Laws*, THINKPROGRESS

(Oct. 31, 2014), https://thinkprogress.org/ohio-supreme-court-justice-vote-for-me-because-i-am-a-republican-who-will-uphold-gop-laws-293f66df7410/.

23. American Freedom Builders, Fighting for Freedom in America (2015), http://www.americanfreedombuilders.com/about.

24. Peter Applebome, *Arkansas Execution Raises Questions on Governor's Politics*, N.Y. TIMES, Jan. 25, 1992, 8. Clinton never granted capital clemency when he was the governor of Arkansas. He was liberal in granting noncapital clemency in his first term as governor but not in subsequent terms.

25. In his absence, the lieutenant governor would make the decision, and he had already declared that he would uphold the sentence. See Marshall Frady, *Death in Arkansas*, NEW YORKER, 124 (Feb. 22, 1993), http://archives.newyorker.com/?i=1993-02-22#folio=105.

26. Appleborne, *Arkansas Execution*.

27. *Rector v. State*, 659 S.W.2d 168, 169 (Ark. 1983).

28. *Id.* at 175.

29. *Id.*

30. *Id.*

31. *Id.*

32. *Id.*

33. Frady, *Death in Arkansas*, 111.

34. *Id.*

35. *Id.*

36. *Id.* at 115.

37. *Rector v. Lockhart*, 727 F. Supp. 1285, 1286 (E.D. Ark. 1990).

38. *Rector v. State*, 638 S.W.2d 672 (Ark. 1972).

39. Stephen Bright, *The Politics of Crime and the Death Penalty: Not "Soft on Crime," But Hard on the Bill of Rights*, 39 ST. LOUIS L.J. 479, 485 (1995).

40. Frady, *Arkansas Execution*.

41. *Rector v. Lockhart*, 727 F. Supp. 1285, 1287–1288.

42. *Id.* at 1285; *Rector v. Lockhart*, 783 F. Supp. 398 (E.D. Ark. 1992).

43. *Rector v. State*, 659 S.W.2d at 175.

44. *Id.*

45. Frady, *Death in Arkansas*, 117.

46. *Rector v. Bryant*, 501 U.S. 1239 (1991).

47. *Id.* at 1241 (Marshall, J., dissenting). Somewhat diminishing this argument, Marshall also said that "adhering to my view that the death penalty is in all circumstances cruel and unusual punishment prohibited by the Eighth and Fourteenth Amendments, *Gregg v. Georgia*, 428 U.S. 153, 231, 96 S.Ct. 2909, 2973, 49 L.Ed.2d 859 (1976) (Marshall, J., dissenting), I would grant the petition and vacate the death sentence even if I did not view the issue in this case as being independently worthy of this Court's plenary review." *Id.* at 1242.

48. Frady, *Death in Arkansas*.

49. *Id.*

50. *Id.*

51. *Id.*

52. *Id.* at 124.

53. *Id.* at 131.

54. Amnesty International, *"A Macabre Assembly Line of Death": Death Penalty Developments in 1997* (Apr. 1998), http://www.amnesty.org/en/library/info/AMR51/020/1998/e.

55. *Id.*

56. Frady, *Death in Arkansas*, 105.

57. *Id.*

58. *Id.*

59. *See, e.g., In re* Hawthorne, 2005 Cal. LEXIS (Cal. 2005) (post-conviction adjudication of retardation as a bar to execution).

60. *See* Margaret Colgate Love, *Of Pardons, Politics and Collar Buttons: Reflections on the President's Duty to Be Merciful*, 27 FORDHAM URB. L.J. 1483, 1491 (2000) (citing information from Office of the Pardon Attorney, *Presidential Clemency Actions by Fiscal Year, July 1, 1900 to June 20, 1945* [Mar. 24, 1999] and Presidential Clemency Actions by Administration, 1945 to Present [Feb. 1, 2000]).

61. *Id.* at 1492.

62. *Id.* at 1497.

63. Margaret Colgate Love, *Taking a Serious Look at "Second Look" Sentencing Reforms*, 21 FED. SENT'G REP. 149, 149–152 (2009).

64. 28 C.F.R. § 1.2.

65. *Id.*

66. Love, *Of Pardons*, 1498.

67. *Id.*; *Clinton Pardons Preston King, Figure in Race-Bias Case*, CN.COM (Feb. 21, 2000), http://archives.cn.com/2000/US/02/21/king.pardon/.

68. Clemency Action, 4, at 68, http://abcnews.go.com/Politics/story?id=121550 and https://scholarlycommons.law.northwestern.edu/cgi/viewcontent.cgi?article=7371&context=jclc

69. David Johnston & Don Van Natta Jr., *The Clinton Pardons: The Lobbying; Clinton's Brother Pursued Clemency Bids for Friends*, N.Y. TIMES (Feb. 23, 2001), http://www.nytimes.com/2001/02/23/us/clinton-pardons-lobbying-clinton-s-brother-pursued-clemency-bids-for-friends.html?pagewanted=all&src=pm.

70. *Id.*

71. Presidential Pardon, 34, at 454. Scott Bomboy, *Explaining President Obama's Outgoing Pardon Powers*, CONSTITUTION DAILY (Nov. 16, 2016), https://constitutioncenter.org/blog/explaining-president-obamas-outgoing-pardon-powers; Mario Almonte, *The Race Is On for Presidential Pardons from Outgoing President George Bush*, HUFFPOST (Dec. 26, 2008), https://www.huffingtonpost.com/mario-almonte/the-race-is-on-for-presid_b_146345.html.

72. Johnston & Van Natta, *Clinton Pardons*.

73. *Id.*

74. *Id.*

CHAPTER FIVE

1. Ellen Joan Pollock, *Enron's Lawyers Faulted Deals but Failed to Blow the Whistle*, WALL ST. J. (May 22, 2002), http://www.wsj.com/articles/SB1022015509705465440.

2. *Id.*

3. *Id.*

4. *Id.*

5. *Id.*

6. *Id.*

7. Paul M. Healy & Krishna G. Palepu, *The Fall of Enron*, J ECON. PERSP., Spring 2003, at 11.

8. *Id.*

9. *Enron's Lawyers: Eyes Wide Shut?*, FORBES (Jan. 28, 2002), http://www.forbes.com /2002/01/28/0128veenron.html#.

10. Pollock, *Enron's Lawyers Faulted Deals.*

11. *Id.*

12. *Id.*

13. *Id.*

14. *Id.*

15. *Id.*

16. *Id.*

17. *Id.*

18. *Id.*

19. *Id.*

20. *Enron's Lawyers: Eyes Wide Shut?*

21. *Id.*

22. Naftali Bendavid, *Enron's Law Firm Begins to Draw Fire*, CHI. TRIB. (Mar. 14, 2002), http://articles.chicagotribune.com/2002-03-14/news/0203140277_1_enron -vinson-elkins-lawyers.

23. *Id.*

24. *Id.*

25. *Id.*

26. *Id.*

27. *Enron's Lawyers: Eyes Wide Shut?*

28. *Id.*

29. *Id.*

30. *Id.*

31. *Id. See also* comments by Boston University Professor Susan Koniak: "They have a duty to make sure a client's managers aren't breaking their duties to the corporation." *Id.*

32. Pollock, *Enron's Lawyers Faulted Deals.*

33. William C. Kashatus, *New Book Reveals History Behind Kids for Cash Scheme*, CITIZENS' VOICE (Nov. 4, 2012), http://citizensvoice.com/arts-living/new-book-reveals -history-behind-kids-for-cash-scheme-1.1397168.

34. *Id.* at 14.

35. *Id.* at 17–25.

36. *Id.* at 24 (quoting Greg Skrepnak as stating, "Things have been like this for so long, that I don't think many people see a lot of wrong in what they've done." Skrepnak was a Luzerne County commissioner who pleaded guilty to taking multiple payoffs from a developer; he was a former All-American football player at the University of Michigan).

37. *Id.* at 24 (quoting local historian William C. Kashatus).

38. *Id.* at 29–31.

39. In 1993 he sued Wilkes University on behalf of a woman who claimed her husband died from exposure to toxins in the university's lab, but four years later the woman pleaded guilty to murdering her husband with rat poison. *Id.*

40. *Id.* at 32.

41. *Id.* at 34.

42. In 1994, a transcript of Ronald Belletiere's trial surfaced. A witness testified that Conahan had called him to warn him against buying drugs from the man under investigation, Belletiere later called the witness at the direction of Conahan to see if they could do business. Conahan was never indicted in the matter despite the federal prosecutor referring to him as the "unindicted co-conspirator." *Id.* at 34.

43. Dave Janoski, *Prosecutor: D'Elia's Downfall Kickstarted Kids-for-Cash Probe*, TIMES-TRIB. (SCRANTON, PA.) (Feb. 9, 2011), http://thetimes-tribune.com/news/prosecutor-d-elia-s-downfall-kickstarted-kids-for-cash-probe-1.1107444.

44. *Id.*

45. *Id.* at 36. The district attorney and school superintendent supported the policy; only a few defense lawyers objected.

46. When Ciavarella received a tape for juvenile judges on balance and restorative justice, the opposite of zero tolerance, he threw it in the trash. *Id.* at 41.

47. *Id.* at 36–37.

48. *In re* A.M., 766 A.2d 1262 (Pa. Super. 2001).

49. WILLIAM ECENBARGER, KIDS FOR CASH: TWO JUDGES, THOUSANDS OF CHILDREN, AND A $2.6 MILLION KICKBACK SCHEME (2012), at 42.

50. *Id.*

51. *Id.*

52. *Id.* at 44.

53. *Id.*

54. *Id.*

55. INTERBRANCH COMMISSION ON JUVENILE JUSTICE, PUBLIC HEARING, at 17–18, http://www.pacourts.us/assets/files/setting-2038/file-1844.pdf?cb=20dd2e.

56. *Id.* at 18.

57. *Id.*

58. In a useless document, Powell agreed to a $15,000-per-month lease over ten years or $1.8 million for the condo, but he paid thirty-nine months' rent or $585,000 in just the first nine months of 2004. ECENBARGER, KIDS FOR CASH, at 63.

59. Powell later told federal investigators that he allowed Mericle to run the money through him due to a fear that the judges would bankrupt him. *Id.* at 66.

60. *Id.*

61. *Id.* at 49.

62. *Id.*

63. *Id.*

64. *Id.* at 64. By contrast, in New York today, fact-finding hearings take place over the course of several days and are scheduled for at least ninety minutes at a time. This doesn't even include the dispositional hearing or pretrial hearings. With an eight-hour workday, a judge would hear at most six fact-finding hearings.

65. *Id.* at 65.

66. INTERBRANCH COMMISSION, at 39.

67. *Id.*

68. ECENBARGER, KIDS FOR CASH, at 76–77.

69. *Id.* at 93–94.

70. INTERBRANCH COMMISSION, at 6.

71. Lindsey Davis et al., *Pennsylvania Judge Convicted in Alleged "Kids for Cash" Scheme*, ABC NEWS (Feb. 21, 2011), http://abcnews.go.com/US/mark-ciavarella-pa-juvenile -court-judge-convicted-alleged/story?id=12965182&singlePage=true#.UOSG0m88CSo.

72. ECENBARGER, KIDS FOR CASH, at 91–94.

73. *Id.* at 93.

74. *Id.* at 63–64.

75. Warren Richey, *"Kids for Cash" Judge Sentenced to 28 Years for Racketeering Scheme*, CHRISTIAN SCI. MONITOR (Aug. 11, 2011), http://www.csmonitor.com/layout/set/print /USA/Justice/2011/0811/Kids-for-cash-judge-sentenced-to-28-years-for-racketeering -scheme.

76. *Id.*

77. *Id.*

78. *Id.*

79. Davis et al., *Pennsylvania Judge Convicted.*

80. *Id.*

81. *Id.*

82. *Id.*

83. *Id.* at 87–88.

84. PA Rules of Professional Conduct 8.3(b).

85. *Id.* at 3.8(b).

86. INTERBRANCH COMMISSION, at 31.

87. *Id.*

88. *Id.*

89. *Id.*

90. *Id.*

91. *Id.*

92. *Id.*

93. *Id.*

94. *Id.* at 95.

95. *Id.*

96. *Id.*

97. *Id.* at 36.

98. ECENBARGER, KIDS FOR CASH, at 50.

99. *Id.* at 112–113.

100. *Id.* at 28.

101. INTERBRANCH COMMISSION.

102. *Id.*

103. *Id.*

104. *Id.*

105. *Id.* at 29.

106. INTERBRANCH COMMISSION, at 28.

107. *Id.*

108. *Id.*

109. *Id.*

110. *Id.*

111. *Id.*

112. *Id.*

113. *Id.*

114. *Id.*

115. *Id.*

116. *Id.*

117. *Id.*

118. *In re Jessica Van Reeth; H.T., a Minor Through Her Mother, L.T.; on Behalf of Themselves and Similarly Situated Youth*, Juvenile Law Center, April 2008, https://jlc.org/sites/default/files/case_files/Application%20for%20Extraordinary%20Jurisdiction.pdf

119. Order Granting Motions for Appropriate Relief, No. 97 CRS 47314-15, 6–7 (N.C. Sup. Ct. 2012), http://www.law.msu.edu/racial-justice/Golphin-et-al-RJA-Order.pdf.

120. *Id.*

121. *Id.* at 156.

122. States News Service, *Federal Officials Announce Filing of Federal Fraud and Tax Charges Against Two Luzerne County Common Pleas Court Judges In An On-Going Public Corruption Probe* (Jan. 26, 2009), http://www.justice.gov/usao/pam/Corruption/Ciavarella_Conahan/Ciavarella_Conahan_01_26_09.htm.

123. *Id.*

124. Peter Hall, *Supreme Court Suspends Embattled Judges*, 239 LEGAL INTELLIGENCER 1 (Jan. 29, 2009).

125. Dave Janoski, *Ciavarella, Conahan Withdraw Guilty Pleas*, CITIZENS' VOICE (Aug. 24, 2009), http://citizensvoice.com/news/ciavarella-conahan-withdraw-guilty-pleas-1.208291.

126. Patrick Sweet, *Conahan Had Plenty of Support*, CITIZENS' VOICE (Sept. 25, 2011), http://citizensvoice.com/news/conahan-had-plenty-of-support-1.1208570.

127. *Id.*

128. Terrie Morgan-Besecker, *Corruption County*, TIMES-LEADER (WILKES-BARRE, PA.) (June 20, 2015), http://www.timesleader.com/archive/268480/stories-corruption-county113704.

129. Dave Janoski, *All Apologies: Contrition as Corrupt Conahan Is Sentenced to 17½ Years*, CITIZENS' VOICE (Sept. 24, 2011), http://citizensvoice.com/news/all-apologies-contrition-as-corrupt-conahan-is-sentenced-to-17-years-1.1208207.

130. *Id.*

131. INTERBRANCH COMMISSION, at 6.

132. David Janoski, *Federal Judge Approves Mericle Settlement for "Kids for Cash,"* CITIZENS' VOICE (Dec. 15, 2012), http://citizensvoice.com/news/federal-judge-approves-mericle-settlement-for-kids-for-cash-1.1416602.

133. *Id.*

134. *Id.* at 9.

135. *Id.* at 10.

136. *Id.*

137. *Id.*

138. *Id.* at 11.

139. *Id.* at 12.

CHAPTER SIX

1. *See* Abram Chayes & Antonia H. Chayes, *Corporate Counsel and the Elite Law Firm*, 37 STAN. L. REV. 277–280 (1985); Mary C. Daly, *The Cultural, Ethical, and Legal Challenges in Lawyering for a Global Organization: The Role of the General Counsel*, 46 EMORY L.J. 1057, 1059 (1997).

2. Robert Eli Rosen, *The Inside Counsel Movement, Professional Judgment, and Organizational Representation*, 64 IND. L.J. 479, 484 (1989).

3. David B. Wilkins, *Team of Rivals? Toward a New Model of the Corporate Attorney-Client Relationship*, 78 FORDHAM L. REV. 2067 (2010); Ben W. Heineman, Jr., *The Rise of the General Counsel*, HARV. BUS. REV. (Sept. 27, 2012), https://hbr.org/2012/09/the-rise-of-the-general-counsel.

4. Wilkins, *Team of Rivals?*

5. *Id.*

6. Deborah A. DeMott, *The Discrete Roles of General Counsel*, 74 FORDHAM L. REV. 955, 960 (2005).

7. *See generally* Robert W. Gordon, *A New Role for Lawyers? The Corporate Counselor After Enron*, 35 CONN. L. REV. 1185 (2003); Sung Hui Kim, *The Banality of Fraud: Re-Situating the Inside Counsel as Gatekeeper*, 74 FORDHAM L. REV. 983 (2005); Sung Hui Kim, *Gatekeepers Inside and Out*, 21 GEO. J. LEGAL ETHICS 411 (2008); Donald C. Langevoort, *Where Were the Lawyers? A Behavioral Inquiry Into Lawyers' Responsibility for Clients' Fraud*, 46 VAND. L. REV. 75 (1993).

8. *See* Gordon, *New Role for Lawyers?* Robert W. Gordon, *A New Role for Lawyers? The Corporate Counselor After Enron*, 35 CONN. L. REV. 1185 (2003) at 2079–2080; Sung Hui Kim, *The Banality of Fraud: Re-Situating the Inside Counsel as Gatekeeper*, 74 FORDHAM L. REV. 983 (2005)

9. Susanna M. Kim, *Dual Identities and Dueling Obligations: Preserving Independence in Corporate Representation*, 68 TENN. L. REV. 179, 200 (2001).

10. Carl D. Liggio, *The Changing Role of Corporate Counsel*, 46 EMORY L.J. 1201, 1208 (1997).

11. See CAROLE BASRI & IRVING KAGAN, CORPORATE LEGAL DEPARTMENTS, § 2–4 (3d ed. 2004).

12. Sarah Helene Duggin, *The Pivotal Role of the General Counsel in Promoting Corporate Integrity and Professional Responsibility*, 52 ST. LOUIS L.J. 989, 1012 (2007).

13. *See id.* at 1011 (quoting Chayes & Chayes, *Corporate Counsel*, 284–289).

14. *Id.*

15. DeMott, *Discrete Roles*, 970 (describing different corporate legal departments and noting that nearly all corporate legal departments are centralized).

16. *Id.*

17. *Id.* (noting that the general counsel must create some special system of oversight in a decentralized department so that he or she doesn't become too remote from the different that arise throughout the company); *see also* Robert L. Nelson and Laura Beth Nielsen, *Cops, Counsel, and Entrepreneurs: Constructing the Role of Inside Counsel in Large Corporations*, LAW SOC. REV. 34 (2000), at 471.

18. Robert L. Nelson & David M. Trubek, *Arenas of Professionalism: The Professional Ideologies of Lawyers in Context*, in LAWYERS' IDEALS/LAWYERS' PRACTICES 177, 208 (Robert L. Nelson et al., eds., 1992) ("corporate counsel occupy an ambiguous position both within the legal profession and within their employing organization").

19. Kenneth N. Gilpin, *Former Rite Aid Executives Charged with Defrauding Investigators*, N.Y. TIMES (June 21, 2002), http://www.nytimes.com/2002/06/21/business/former -rite-aid-executives-charged-with-defrauding-investors.html; Eriq Gardner, *The Ties That Bind*, CORP. COUNS., Oct. 2003, at 17–18.

20. *Id.*

21. Richard M. Strassberg et al., *Lawyers on Trial*, N.Y.L.J., July 18, 2005, at 9 (reporting the conviction of former general counsel of Inso Corporation on a perjury charge stemming from the preparation of documents to facilitate a scheme to create the appearance of greater sales).

22. Strassberg et al., *Lawyers on Trial*, at 126–128.

23. BASRI & KAGAN, CORPORATE LEGAL DEPARTMENTS, §§ 2–11.

24. For discussion of this phenomenon and its consequences in the context of securities disclosure, see RESTORING TRUST IN AMERICA'S BUSINESS INSTITUTIONS 214–218 (Margaret M. Blair & William W. Bratton, eds., 2005).

25. *See* BASRI & KAGAN, CORPORATE LEGAL DEPARTMENTS, § 2–3.

26. *Id.*

27. *Id.*

28. *Id.*

29. *Id.*

30. *Id.* at 4.

31. Ellen Nakashima, *Between the Lines of HP's Spy Scandal*, WASH. POST (Sept. 28, 2006), http://www.washingtonpost.com/wp-dyn/content/article/2006/09

/27/AR2006092701304.html; Valleywag, *Patricia C. Dunn of HP Testifies*, YouTube (Sept. 29, 2006), https://www.youtube.com/watch?v=QdmznxwjjnU.

32. Associated Press, *HP's Top Lawyer Ressigns Ahead of Hearing*, NBC News (Sept. 28, 2006), http://www.nbcnews.com/id/15043041/ns/business-us_business/t /hps-top-lawyer-resigns-ahead-hearing/#.WkZ9W2eWzIU.

33. *Id.*

34. James B. Stewart, *The Kona Files*, New Yorker, Feb. 19, 2007, at 123. Dunn and Baskins corroborate Hurd's account of this event, but Keyworth disputes it.

35. *Id.*

36. *Id.*

37. *See generally* Gerald B. Lefcourt, *Fighting Fire with Fire: Private Attorneys Using the Same Investigative Techniques as Government Attorneys: The Ethical and Legal Considerations for Attorneys Conducting Investigations*, 36 Hofstra L. Rev. 397 (2007).

38. *Id.*

39. *Hewlett-Packard Pretextors Fined* (May 28, 2008), http://www.piava.wordpress .com/2008/05/28. This item includes a link to a Federal Trade Commission press release regarding the settlement.

40. Damon Darlin, *Hewlett-Packard Spied on Writers in Leaks*, N.Y. Times (Sept. 8, 2006), http://www.nytimes.com/2006/09/08/technology/08hp.html. *See also Ousted Hewlett-Packard Chairwoman: I Consulted Others in Leak Probe, Never Doubted Legality*, Fox News.com (Sept. 27, 2006), http://www.foxnews.com/story/0,2933,216200,00.html.

41. *Id.*

42. Patrick M. Arenz, *The Truth Behind Pretexting: In-House Investigations and Professional Responsibility Concerns*, Robins Kaplan (Apr. 30, 2007), http://www.robinskaplan.com /resources/articles/the-truth-behind-pretexting-in-house-investigations-and-professional -responsibility-concerns.

43. Sue Reisinger, *Saw No Evil*, Corp. Couns., Jan. 2007, at 68.

44. Stacy Cowley, *Wells Fargo Review Finds 1.4 Million More Suspect Accounts*, N.Y. Times (Aug. 31, 2017), https://www.nytimes.com/2017/08/31/business/dealbook /wells-fargo-accounts.html?_r=0.

45. *Id.*

46. *Id.*

47. *Id.*

48. Wells Fargo Bank, 2016 C.F.P.B. 0015, 4 (2016), http://files.consumerfinance .gov/f/documents/092016_cfpb_WFBconsentorder.pdf. *See also* Cowley, *Wells Fargo Review*. Senator Elizabeth Warren defines cross-selling as "pushing existing customers to open more accounts." *Unauthorized Wells Fargo Accounts: Hearing Before the S. Comm. on Banking, Hous., & Urban Affairs*, 114th Cong., C-SPAN (Sept. 20, 2016), at 1:29:00, https://www.c-span.org/video/?415547-1/ceo-john-stumpftestifiesunauthorized-wells -fargo-accounts.

49. *Unauthorized Wells Fargo Accounts: Hearing Before the S. Comm. on Banking, Hous., & Urban Affairs*, at 1:29:20; Scott Reckard, *Wells Fargo's Pressure-Cooker Sales Culture Comes at a Cost*, L.A. Times (Dec. 21, 2013), http://www.latimes.com/business/la-fi-wells-fargo -sale-pressure-20131222-story.html.

50. Reckard, *Wells Fargo's Pressure-Cooker Sales Culture.*

51. *Unauthorized Wells Fargo Accounts: Hearing Before the S. Comm. on Banking, Hous., & Urban Affairs,* at 1:29:24.

52. *Id.*

53. *Id.* at 1:29:20.

54. *Id.*

55. *Wells Fargo Team Member Handbook,* WELLSFARGO.COM 112 (July 2016), https://teamworks.wellsfargo.com/handbook/HB_Online.pdf.

56. Emily Glazer, *How Wells Fargo's High-Pressure Sales Culture Spiraled Out of Control,* WALL ST. J. (Sept. 16, 2016), http://www.wsj.com/articles/how-wells-fargos-high-pressure-sales-culture-spiraled-out-of-control-1474053044.

57. *Wells Fargo Salaries,* GLASSDOOR.COM (Oct. 20, 2016), https://www.glassdoor.com/Salary/Wells-Fargo-Salaries-E8876.htm.

58. Glazer, *How Wells Fargo's High-Pressure Sales Culture Spiraled.*

59. *See* Reckard, *Wells Fargo's Pressure-Cooker Sales Culture.*

60. *See* Glazer, *How Wells Fargo's High-Pressure Sales Culture Spiraled.*

61. *Unauthorized Wells Fargo Accounts: Hearing Before the H. Fin. Serv. Comm.,* 114th Cong., C-SPAN (Sept. 29, 2016), at 2:25:45, https://www.c-span.org/video/?415981-1/ceo-john-stumpf-testifies-unauthorized-wells-fargo-accounts.

62. Glazer, *How Wells Fargo's High-Pressure Sales Culture Spiraled.*

63. *Id.*

64. *Id.*

65. *Unauthorized Wells Fargo Accounts: Hearing Before the H. Fin. Serv. Comm.,* at 2:27:15.

66. Reckard, *Wells Fargo's Pressure-Cooker Sales Culture.*

67. *Unauthorized Wells Fargo Accounts: Hearing Before the S. Comm. on Banking, Hous., & Urban Affairs,* at 2:21:10. Former CEO John Stumpf testified that he was unaware how many Wells Fargo employees were fired for failing to meet sales goals. *Id.*

68. Reckard, *Wells Fargo's Pressure-Cooker Sales Culture.*

69. David Lazarus, *Did Wells Fargo Target Seniors with Its Bogus-Account Scheme?,* L.A. TIMES (Sept. 27, 2016), http://www.latimes.com/business/lazarus/la-fi-lazarus-wells-fargo-accounts-20160927-snap-story.html.

70. Glazer, *How Wells Fargo's High-Pressure Sales Culture Spiraled.*

71. Wells Fargo & Co., No. 11-094-B-HC1, 3 (2011) (Bd. of Governors of the Fed. Reserve Sys.), https://www.federalreserve.gov/newsevents/press/enforcement/enf20110720a1.pdf (emphasis added).

72. Reckard, *Wells Fargo's Pressure-Cooker Sales Culture*; Elizabeth C. Tippett, *How Wells Fargo Encouraged Employees to Commit Fraud,* THE CONVERSATION, https://theconversation.com/how-wells-fargo-encouraged-employees-to-commit-fraud-66615 (last visited Feb. 9, 2018).

73. *Id.* https://theconversation.com/how-wells-fargo-encouraged-employees-to-commit-fraud-66615

74. *Unauthorized Wells Fargo Accounts: Hearing Before the S. Comm. on Banking, Hous., & Urban Affairs,* at 24:00.

75. *Unauthorized Wells Fargo Accounts: Hearing Before the H. Fin. Serv. Comm.*, at 41:04 (describing a lawsuit filed in Montana in which plaintiffs [former Wells Fargo employees] allege that fake accounts were opened by bankers as early as 2007).

76. *Unauthorized Wells Fargo Accounts: Hearing Before the H. Fin. Serv. Comm.*, at 2:10:00; Reckard, *Wells Fargo's Pressure-Cooker Sales Culture.*

77. *Unauthorized Wells Fargo Accounts: Hearing Before the H. Fin. Serv. Comm.*, at 2:10:00.

78. Letter from a Wells Fargo Employee to John Stumpf, chair and CEO, Wells Fargo & Co. (Sept. 13, 2007), https://www.documentcloud.org/documents/3143757 -Wells-Fargo-Stumpf-Letter.html.

79. *Unauthorized Wells Fargo Accounts: Hearing Before the H. Fin. Serv. Comm.*, at 25:50.

80. Glazer, *How Wells Fargo's High-Pressure Sales Culture Spiraled.*

81. *Unauthorized Wells Fargo Accounts: Hearing Before the H. Fin. Serv. Comm.*, at 4:02:00.

82. *Unauthorized Wells Fargo Accounts: Hearing Before the S. Comm. on Banking, Hous., & Urban Affairs*, at 19:35.

83. *Id.*

84. *Id.*

85. *Id.*

86. *Id.*

87. Yuka Hayashi, *Wells Fargo to Eliminate Retail Business Sales Goals on Oct. 1*, WALL ST. J. (Sept. 27, 2016), https://www.wsj.com/articles/wells-fargo-to-eliminate-retail -business-sales-goals-on-oct-1-1475018165.

88. Jeff Spross, *What on Earth Does Wells Fargo's CEO Do All Day?*, THE WEEK (Sept. 21, 2016), http://theweek.com/articles/649900/what-earth-does-wells-fargos -ceo-all-day.

89. *Unauthorized Wells Fargo Accounts: Hearing Before the H. Fin. Serv. Comm.*, at 1:18:18.

90. *Unauthorized Wells Fargo Accounts: Hearing Before the S. Comm. on Banking, Hous., & Urban Affairs*, at 1:32:35.

91. *Unauthorized Wells Fargo Accounts: Hearing Before the H. Fin. Serv. Comm.*, at 36:30.

92. *Id.*

93. Stacy Cowley, *Wells Fargo to Claw Back $41 Million of Chief's Pay over Scandal*, N.Y. TIMES (Sept. 27, 2016), http://www.nytimes.com/2016/09/28/business/dealbook/wells -fargo-john-stumpf-compensation.html.

94. Matt Levine, *Wells Fargo Opened a Couple Million Fake Accounts*, BLOOMBERG (Sept. 9, 2016), https://www.bloomberg.com/view/articles/2016-09-09/wells-fargo -opened-a-couple-million-fake-accounts.

95. Michael Hiltzik, *How Wells Fargo Exploited a Binding Arbitration Clause to Deflect Customers' Fraud Allegations*, L.A. TIMES (Sept. 26, 2016), http://www.latimes.com /business/hiltzik/la-fi-hiltzik-wells-arbitration-20160926-snap-story.html.

96. *Id.*

97. *Do Checking Accounts Affect Your Credit Score?*, ECREDABLE.COM (2016), http://www .ecredable.com/resources/education-center/credit/do-checking-accounts-affect-your -credit-score; *Unauthorized Wells Fargo Accounts: Hearing Before the S. Comm. on Banking, Hous., & Urban Affairs*, at 1:23:28.

CHAPTER SEVEN

1. Robert J. Emmerling & Richard E. Boyatzis, *Emotional and Social Intelligence Competencies: Cross Cultural Implications*, 19 CROSS CULTURAL MGMT., no. 1 (2012), at 4, http://www.emeraldinsight.com/doi/pdfplus/10.1108/13527601211195592.

2. *See also* DANIEL GOLEMAN ET AL., PRIMAL LEADERSHIP 38 (2002).

3. Daniel Goleman, *What Makes a Leader?*, HARV. BUS. REV. 7 (2004).

4. *Id.*

5. *Id.*

6. Daniel Goleman, *Leadership That Gets Results*, HARV. BUS. REV., Mar.–Apr. 2000, at 39. Emotional intelligence also is viewed as one element of various leadership models. *See generally* Martin M. Chemers, *Integrating Models of Leadership and Intelligence: Efficacy and Effectiveness*, in MULTIPLE INTELLIGENCES AND LEADERSHIP (Ronald E. Riggio, Susan Elaine Murphy, and Francis J. Pirozzolo, ed., 2002), at 139 (discussing contemporary intelligence theories used in effective approaches to leadership). For influential early work characterizing emotional intelligence competencies, *see generally* John D. Mayer & Peter Salovey, *The Intelligence of Emotional Intelligence*, 17 INTELLIGENCE 433 (1993); Peter Salovey & John D. Mayer, *Emotional Intelligence*, 9 IMAGINATION, COGNITION & PERSONALITY 185 (1990).

7. Chris Dulewicz et al., *The Relevance of Emotional Intelligence for Leadership Performance*, 30 J. GEN. MGMT. 71 (2005); Victor Dulewicz & Malcolm Higgs, *Emotional Intelligence, A Review and Evaluation Study*, 15 J. MANAGERIAL PSYCHOL. 341 (2000).

8. *See* DANIEL GOLEMAN, EMOTIONAL INTELLIGENCE 42–44 (1995).

9. Goleman, *What Makes a Leader?*, at 6.

10. *Id.*

11. *Id.*

12. *Id.* at 8.

13. *Id.* at 9.

14. *Id.*

15. *Id.*

16. Amy C. Edmondson, *Teaming: How Organizations Learn, Innovate, and Compete in the Knowledge Economy*, HARV. BUS. REV. 64 (2012).

17. *Id.*

18. *Id.* at 65.

19. DORIS KEARNS GOODWIN, A TEAM OF RIVALS (2005).

20. John M. Darley & Paget H. Gross, *A Hypothesis-Confirming Bias in Labelling Effects*, in STEREOTYPES AND PREJUDICE: ESSENTIAL READINGS 212 (Charles Stangor, 2000).

21. *See* Jane Risen & Thomas Gilovich, *Informal Logical Fallacies*, in CRITICAL THINKING IN PSYCHOLOGY 110–130 (Robert J. Sternberg, Henry L. Roediger III, & Diane F. Halpern, 2007).

22. Charles Lord, Lee Ross, & Mark Lepper, *Biased Assimilation and Attitude Polarization: The Effects of Prior Theories on Subsequently Considered Evidence*, 37 J. PERSONALITY & SOC. PSYCH. 2098–2109 (1979).

23. Douglass Krull et al., *The Fundamental Attribution Error: Correspondence Bias in Individualist and Collectivist Cultures*, 25 PERSONALITY & SOC. PSYCH. BUL., (October 1999), at 1208–1219.

24. *Id.*

25. H. R. Markus & S. Kitayama, *Culture and the Self: Implications for Cognition, Emotion, and Motivation*, 98 PSYCHOL. REV., no. 2 (1991), at 224–253.

26. *See* Shannon Lloyd & Charmine Hartel, *Intercultural Competencies for Culturally Diverse Workteams*, 25 J. MGMT. PSYCHOL., no. 8 (2010), at 846.

27. Anthony Thompson, *Stopping the Usual Suspects: Race and the Fourth Amendment*, N.Y.U. LAW REV. (1999).

28. Patricia Pérez-Arce, *The Influence of Culture on Cognition*, ARCH. CLIN. NEUROPSYCH., Oct. 1999, at 581; Hult News, *13 Benefits and Challenges of Cultural Diversity in the Workplace in 2017*, HULT INT'L. BUS. SCH., http://www.hult.edu/news/benefits-challenges-cultural -diversity-workplace/; *see also* MARK MENDENHALL ET AL., GLOBAL RESEARCH PRACTICE AND DEVELOPMENT (2d ed., 2013).

29. Stanford GSB Staff, *Diversity and Work Group Performance*, STANFORD GRAD. SCH. BUS. (Nov. 1, 1999), https://www.gsb.stanford.edu/insights/diversity-work-group -performance; https://en.wikibooks.org/wiki/Managing_Groups_and_Teams/Working _in_International_Teams; Juliet Bourke, *Working in Multicultural Teams: A Case Study*, DELOITTE, https://www2.deloitte.com/au/en/pages/human-capital/articles/working -multicultural-teams.html (last visited Feb. 9, 2018).

30. *See* Lloyd & Hartel, *Intercultural Competencies*, at 848. *See also* D. Kagan, *The Social Implications of Higher Level Thinking Skills*, 10 J. ACCT. EDUC. (Autumn 1992), at 285–295.

31. Renato Tagiuri, *Person Perception*, in 3 HANDBOOK OF SOCIAL PSYCHOLOGY 395, 422 (Gardner Linzet & Elliot Aronson, eds., 2d ed. 1969).

32. *See, e.g.,* Kirwan Institute for the Study of Race and Ethnicity, *Implicit Bias Review 2013*, http://www.kirwaninstitute.osu.edu/reports/2013/03_2013_SOTS -Implicit_Bias.pdf.

33. *Id.* at 6.

34. *Id.*; Brian Lowery & Sandra Graham, *Priming Unconscious Racial Stereotypes About Adolescent Offenders* (Stanford Grad. Sch. Bus., Working Paper No. 1857, 2004), https://www.gsb.stanford.edu/faculty-research/working-papers/priming-unconscious -racial-stereotypes-about-adolescent-offenders; Kirwan Institute, *Implicit Bias Review 2013*.

35. B. D. Ruben & D. J. Kealy, *Behavioral Assessment of Communication Competency and the Prediction of Cross-Cultural Adaptation*, 3 INT'L. J. INTERCULTURAL REL. (1979), at 15–47.

36. W. B. Gudykunst, *Toward a Theory of Effective Interpersonal and Intergroup Communication*, in INTERCULTURAL COMMUNICATION COMPETENCE (R. L. Wiseman & J. Koester, eds., 1993); W. B. GUDYKUNST & Y. Y. KIM, COMMUNICATING WITH STRANGERS: AN APPROACH TO INTERCULTURAL COMMUNICATION (1997); A. Y. Lewin & C. U. Stephens, *CEO Attitudes as Determinants of Organizational Design: An Integrated Model*, 15 ORGANIZATIONAL STUD., no. 2 (1994), at 183–212.

37. S. Ronen, *Training the International Assignee*, in TRAINING AND DEVELOPMENT IN ORGANIZATIONS (I. L. Goldstein, ed., 1989).

38. *See* Lloyd & Hartel, INTERCULTURAL COMPETENCIES, at 850.

39. Vanessa Urch Druskat & Steven B. Wolff, *Building the Emotional Intelligence of Groups*, 79 HARV. BUS. REV., no. 2 (2001), at 80.

40. ROB CROSS AND ROBERT THOMAS, DRIVING RESULTS THROUGH SOCIAL NETWORKS: HOW TOP ORGANIZATIONS LEVERAGE NETWORKS FOR PERFORMANCE AND GROWTH (2009).

CHAPTER EIGHT

1. The Myers & Briggs Foundation, *MBTI® Basics*, http://www.myersbriggs.org /my-mbti-personality-type/mbti-basics/ (last visited July 21, 2016). *See also* Center for Applications of Psychological Type, *About the MBTI® Instrument*, https://www.capt.org /mbti-assessment/mbti-overview.htm (last visited July 21, 2016).

2. *Id.*

3. *Id. See also* NANCY A. SCHAUBHUT ET AL., MBTI® FORM M MANUAL SUPPLEMENT (2009), https://www.cpp.com/pdfs/MBTI_FormM_Supp.pdf.

4. Project Implicit, *Take a Test*, HARV. U., https://implicit.harvard.edu/implicit /takeatest.html (last visited Dec. 20, 2017).

5. *Understanding Implicit Bias*, KIRWAN INST., http://kirwaninstitute.osu.edu /research/understanding-implicit-bias/ (last visited Dec. 20, 2017).

6. Bonita London et al., *Studying Institutional Engagement: Utilizing Social Psychology Research Methodologies to Study Law Student Engagement*, 30 HARV. J. GENDER & L., no. 2 (2007), at 389–408, http://www.law.harvard.edu/students/orgs/jlg/vol302/389-408 _London.pdf (showing how students of color and women reported, at statistically significant higher rates, feeling invisible, isolated, and alienated, and reported lower frequencies of volunteering in class and three times the experiences of social exclusion). *See also* Elizabeth Bell & Kim Golombisky, *Voices and Silences in Our Classrooms: Strategies for Mapping Trails Among Sex/Gender, Race, and Class*, 27 WOMEN'S STUDIES IN COMMUNICATION, no. 3 (2004), http://communication.usf.edu/faculty/bell/voicesandsilences.pdf (arguing that voice and silence are better understood as performative strategies announcing cultural expectations for the feminine, for race, for ethnicity, for labor, and for hegemonic masculinity); Lani Guinier et al., *Becoming Gentlemen: Women's Experiences at One Ivy League Law School* 143 PENN. L. REV., no. 1 (1994), at 1, 3–4, http://scholarship.law .upenn.edu/cgi/viewcontent.cgi?article=3541&context=penn_law_review (stating that many women are alienated by the way the Socratic method is used in large-classroom instruction, which is the dominant pedagogy for almost all first-year instruction. Women self-report much lower rates of class participation than do men for all three years of law school), Sari Bashi & Maryana Iskander, *Why Legal Education Is Failing Women* 18 YALE J.L. & FEMINISM, no. 2 (2006), http://digitalcommons.law.yale.edu/yjlf/vol18/iss2/3 (proving that despite similar entering credentials, female students at Yale Law School are underrepresented among participants in class discussions and among students who form professionally beneficial relationships with faculty members).

7. ROSS PIGEAU & CAROL MCCANN, THE HUMAN IN COMMAND 163 (2000); Robert R. Leonhard et al., *A Concept for Command and Control*, 19 JOHNS HOPKINS APL TECH. DIG., no. 2 (2010), http://www.jhuapl.edu/techdigest/TD/td2902/Leonhard.pdf.

8. Karl E. Weick, Sensemaking in Organizations (1995).

9. Ryan Leavitt, *How Top Companies Make the ROI Case for Employee Training*, LearnCore (Dec. 8, 2014), https://learncore.com/top-companies-make-roi-case-employee-training/; Northeast Community College Center for Enterprise, https://northeast.edu/CFE /News/pdfs/May-2016.pdf; Sarah Perez, *The ROI of Talent Development*, 2014, http:// www.kenan-flagler.unc.edu/~/media/Files/documents/executive-development/unc -white-paper-the-ROI-of-talent-development.pdf.

10. Vivian Hunt, Dennis Layton, & Sara Prince, *Diversity Matters*, McKinsey & Co. (Nov. 24, 2014), http://boardagender.org/files/MyKinsey-DIVERSITY_MATTERS _2014_-_print_version_-_McKinsey_Report.pdf.

11. *The Bottom Line: Connecting Corporate Performance and Gender Diversity*, Catalyst (Jan. 15, 2004), http://www.catalyst.org/knowledge/bottom-line-connecting-corporate -performance-and-gender-diversity.

12. *Id.*

CONCLUSION

1. *American Express CEO Kenneth Chenault: Valuing EQ over IQ*, Wharton U. Pa. (Nov. 8, 2013), http://knowledge.wharton.upenn.edu/article/american-express-ceo -kenneth-chenault-valuing-eq-iq/.

2. *Kenneth I. Chenault Quotes*, AZ Quotes, http://www.azquotes.com/author/48627 -Kenneth_I_Chenault (last visited Dec. 20, 2017).

3. Jen Fifield, *State Legislatures Have Fewer Farmers, Lawyers; but Higher Education Level*, Stateline (Dec. 10, 2015), http://www.pewtrusts.org/en/research-and-analysis /blogs/stateline/2015/12/10/state-legislatures-have-fewer-farmers-lawyers-but-higher -education-level.

4. Reuben Siegman, *Millenials, Social Media, and Social Justice*, Wash. U. Pol. Rev. (June 9, 2016), http://www.wupr.org/2016/06/09/millenials-social-media-and-social -justice/.

5. *Id.*

6. Sarah Landrum, *Why Millennials Care About Social Impact Investing*, Forbes (Nov. 4, 2016), http://www.forbes.com/sites/sarahlandrum/2016/11/04/why-millennials -care-about-social-impact-investing/#68e659ef65.

Index

Ohio Supreme Court, 82–83
O'Neill, William, 84
on-the-job experience, 6, 34, 174
open-mindedness, 142
optionality, 27, 31, 132, 137–
    138, 160, 166–167, 173
organizational copilot and rudder, 115
outside counsel, 96–99, 116–
    117, 120–121, 123
oversight: decentralization and, 205n17;
    and Hurricane Katrina, 47, 51;
    intersectional leaders and, 74; of
    law schools, 18; and office culture,
    60; positions of authority and,
    95–96; Sarbanes-Oxley requiring,
    140; Wells Fargo and, 129

PA Child Care, 102–104, 107
Paternoster, Raymond, 59
patterns of misbehavior, 67,
    74, 119, 125, 128–131
pedagogy, 156–157
Pennsylvania Supreme Court,
    103, 104, 109, 110
people of color, 194n39; and class
    discussions, 157, 162; in Harris
    County, 58–60; and power,
    16–17; reduced services to,
    142–143; students, 25, 152,
    211n6. See also race/ethnicity
peremptory challenges in jury selection,
    25, 61–63, 65–69, 71, 193nn23
Perricone, Sal, 48–51, 192n128
personal ambition: and Clinton clemency
    decisions, 85, 88–89; elevating one's
    own, 11, 28, 85–89; and leadership,
    91–92, 175; subordinating
    one's own, 21, 137, 160, 178
personality tests, 150–151
plea agreements, 109
political leaders, lawyers as, 6
"populist" sentiments, 169
positional authority, 21, 95–96

Powell, Robert, 59, 102–104,
    107, 110, 201nn58
practical skills theory, 19
"practice-ready" lawyers, 197n2
"pretexting," 122–124
preventive component of
    compliance, 118
prosecutorial authority, 57
public defender's office, 8, 105–
    106, 110, 112, 142, 177
public service and duty, 81
purpose-driven leadership, 35
push back, obligation to, 38, 99–100, 132

race/ethnicity: benefits of diversity, 162;
    conversations/discussions on, 152,
    157, 211n6; death penalty and, 59,
    63–68, 194n39; and jury makeup,
    61; and jury selection, 37, 39, 58–60,
    62–63, 67–72, 194nn27; in legal
    education, 16–17, 152, 155, 157,
    211n6; and power, 16–17; promoting
    diversity, 24–25, 141; proxies for, 69;
    Race IAT, 151; racial slurs/codes,
    58, 60; racism in the workplace, 58–
    60; RJA (Racial Justice Act), 63–69,
    72, 194n43. See also people of color
rape statute exercise, 153–154
Raptors, 98
rational-legal leadership, 185n15
reactive leadership models, 169
Reagan, Ronald, 89
Rector, Ricky Ray, 85–89
recusal, 84
reflective conversations, 164
regulatory component of
    compliance, 118
Reno, Janet, 171
Research and Writing class, 154
responsibilities to client, 120
Rhode, Deborah, 80
Rich, Denise, 90
Rich, Marc, 90